Cursed?

Also by Jess McCann

You Lost Him at Hello

Was It Something I Said?

Cursed?

Why you still don't have the relationship you want and the 5 cures that can transform your love life.

By Jess McCann

Cursed? By Jess McCann

© 2019 Jess McCann. All Rights Reserved.

978-1-7343707-2-0

Copyedited by Summer Hunt

All rights reserved. No part of this book may be reproduced by any physical or electronic process, or in the form of a recording, nor may it be transmitted or otherwise copied for public or private use other than for brief quotations embodied in articles and reviews, without prior written permission of the publisher.

This is a work of non-fiction, however, to protect all clients, names and all identifying details have been altered. For narrative purposes some stories have been time compressed and dialogue created to better execute the advice.

The material in this book is not a substitute for medical advice or treatment. The author's intent is to offer information to help you in your quest to find a loving relationship. The author or publisher assumes no responsibility for your use of the information and its efficacy.

Permissions

From the book *The Power of Now*.

Copyright © 2004 by Eckhart Tolle. Reprinted with permission of New World Library, Novato, CA. www.newworldlibrary.com

For Jordan

A Memo from the Author

Since most of my coaching career has been advising women in heterosexual relationships, the examples I use in this book parrot that experience. However, the information and recommendations are not exclusively for women, or a certain type of relationship. I hope that many different types of people, regardless of gender or sexual orientation, can enjoy this book and learn from it.

TABLE OF CONTENTS:

PART I: THE CURSE 1

Chapter One: Why Is Love So Hard For You? 7

Chapter Two: Cursed Thinking 29

Chapter Three: Love or Wanting? 37

PART II: THE FIVE FACES OF THE CURSE 43

Chapter Four: The Worrier/Lamenter Mind 47

Chapter Five: The Inferior Mind 79

Chapter Six: The Wanter Mind 97

Chapter Seven: The Superior Mind 115

Chapter Eight: The Contestant Mind 141

PART III: THE CURES 161

Chapter Nine: Be Present 163

Chapter Ten: Be Grateful 187

Chapter Eleven: Be Accepting 211

Chapter Twelve: Be Forgiving 237

Chapter Thirteen: Be Loving 264

A Letter From the Author 281

Acknowledgements 282

PART I: THE CURSE

IMPORTANT INTRODUCTION

Ashlee is one of those women who can walk into a room and make every head turn. She is a tall, slender brunette with blue eyes and a wide smile. But good looks aren't Ashlee's only attractive attribute; she is also smart, well-traveled, and outgoing.

But Ashlee has never had a satisfying romantic relationship. She's had numerous boyfriends—in fact, she's rarely single for long—but their interest in her lasts only a few months. She eventually receives a break-up text or is ghosted without any warning. Ashlee cannot understand why she is unable to hold someone's interest and is beginning to worry something is wrong with her.

Felicity is a sweet, shy, 28-year-old editorial assistant whose fiancé abruptly left her two years ago. She knows he was probably not right for her, but even now Felicity still hopes he will regret his decision and come back. She is hardly ever approached when she is out and can't bring herself to join any dating apps. On most nights she sits at home, reading a good book and feeling sad.

Karen has a type-A personality and is married with two children. She met her husband 10 years ago and fell in love at first sight. Their passionate love affair lasted until their first child was born. Now her husband seems disinterested in her, and Karen is becoming increasingly resentful about their marriage. She doesn't understand how the love they once shared has soured to this point. She is currently contemplating a divorce.

Reina is a savvy businesswoman. She loves the thrill of being an entrepreneur, and men often ask for her advice on their own business affairs. But Reina is selective, so she does not date much. She has been involved with a guy named Danny for the last ten months, and although she really likes him, he is unwilling to commit. Reina assumed she would have her own family by the time she turned 35, but with her birthday just around the corner, she's frustrated and perplexed that she is far from that goal. Reina feels like time is running out.

These four women are composites of clients I've worked with over the years. I chose to highlight their stories for a very specific reason: Their romantic situations illustrate common problems and patterns seen by many females today; in fact, you might even see yourself in one of their narratives. However, for all that they have in common with other women, I chose them as examples *because* their stories differ so greatly from each other—from their ages and backgrounds to their work lives and personalities. Most importantly, their relationship troubles appear to run the gamut: from feeling hopeless about finding love, to giving up on it when it's difficult and disappointing. Everything about these four women and their love lives seems unique, yet at the core they all share the same problem: *They don't have the love they want and they aren't sure why.* They might suspect it's because they are picky, or guess it's a lack of self-confidence, but that's not the real story. They might say it's falling for the wrong guys, but there's more to it than that. Beneath the surface lies the one obstacle preventing them from love. It is a hindrance to them, and millions of other men and women, mostly because it's misunderstood and therefore never brought to light and improved on. Because it's never identified as the true source of their problem, it only worsens as the years go on. I call this obstacle, this hindrance, this pervasive problem that prevents so many from ever having the real experience of unconditional love, the *Curse*.

Introduction

As a dating and relationship coach, I've worked with hundreds of people, mostly women, throughout the course of my career. Some of these people had problems that were simple and easy to fix. They sought my help after reading my first book, *You Lost Him at Hello*, and simply needed a refresher course on relationship building. A few lessons on appropriate date conversation or how to handle texting, and they were back on track and heading into a commitment. Others, however, needed much more guidance.

They initially requested help for the same small difficulties: Frustrated by a man's lack of contact or sudden loss of interest, they wanted to know what they needed to do—or stop doing—to get better results. It seemed that no matter what rules they followed, what precautions they took, or how many different guys they dated, their relationships never reached a happy place. Other women seemed to have no luck with the opposite sex at all, rarely feeling interested in anyone or resorting to pining for someone at a distance.

In either case, dating and relationships brought these females anxiety, confusion, turmoil, and disappointment. Even if one of these clients ultimately got the commitment she desired, she never received the love she was hoping to have. It was as if these women were fated to be bad at love. Their love lives had a distinct pattern, and following a set of relationship rules or learning a bevy of dating tactics was not improving anything.

I'll admit, at first I was confounded as to why these clients had such trouble, especially being such smart, beautiful, capable people. I was just as disappointed and frustrated when another promising relationship fizzled or unexpectedly fell apart. Then suddenly I saw it. The origin of their problem revealed itself to me and with the understanding of what it was came the understanding of how to help. The *Curse* and all it's troublesome patterns was finally out in the open after showing itself in the most surprising place: my own relationship.

Cursed?

You likely picked up this book because you yourself may feel hopeless when it comes to love. Perhaps none of your relationships have worked out the way you've wanted, and you can't quite figure out why. Maybe you are currently in a relationship or marriage that you thought would make you happy, but instead you find yourself dissatisfied and aching for something more. Your family and friends may not understand your struggle, but the fact remains that you have always had a difficult time finding and keeping love.

Much like Ashlee, Felicity, Karen, and Reina, it's likely that you, too, are suffering from the *Curse*. I know it may seem strange that a person who cannot attract men initially would share the same problem as someone whose long-term relationships stall just short of the altar. Or that a woman who can't get past a third date has the same obstacle in common with one who has been in several relationships or even married. But after years of research and coaching countless clients, I have found one thing to be true: No matter what the problem or pattern, no matter how old or young you are, or *whether you're a man or a woman*, if you are constantly frustrated and discontented with the lack of love in your life, it is likely that the *Curse* is at the root of it all.

As you read this book, you will learn what the *Curse* is and discover it affects people in different ways, making it so difficult to identify. People who have diverse personalities and are involved in different types of relationships can still share the same problem; the only difference is when it appears and how it causes trouble for each individual. For some, the *Curse* is ever present and therefore inhibits them from meeting people or getting past a first or second date; for others, it can show up like clockwork a few months or even a year down the road. If you seem to encounter relationship issues at the same point in time, it is not a wild coincidence. Everyone's *Curse* has different triggers. They are so strong and so rooted within us that we can often predict when things are about to go awry, despite not knowing the real reason why.

But the *Curse* can do much more than just keep you single; its toxic effect is multi-symptomatic. It can fool you into falling in love with

Introduction

someone who is wrong for you, and it is the reason why some people repeatedly attract the same bad relationships over and over again. It can trick you into blaming yourself for all the problems in your love life, or convince you that you are completely innocent of fault despite evidence of the contrary. The *Curse* is notorious for pushing real love away and only attracting people who have no love to give. The saddest consequence by far, however, is that it can keep you lonely and unfulfilled, depressed, and aching for more even if you find the right person and get married.

But don't despair! In the pages to follow, we will define the *Curse* and reveal its five main manifestations. You will see how it affects people differently and causes them to unknowingly make choices that sabotage love. You will learn where it stems from and how you may have fallen prey to it yourself. And finally, you will discover the tools needed to break free of this affliction so you can finally find love and live *lovingly* ever after.

If you are ready to break the pattern of bad luck in your relationships, and are willing to do what it takes to have lasting love, get comfortable, let down your guard and turn the page!

Chapter One

Why Is Love So Hard For You?

A young woman came to me one day, frantic to speak with me. The guy she had been hanging out with had not texted her in four days, and she was baffled as to why he suddenly stopped all communication. This was not the first time she had been ghosted. In fact, this was quickly becoming a pattern. She sat there, with her head in her hands, and through sobs told me that her life was terrible. Yet again, she failed at a chance for love, and she felt certain it meant something was wrong with her. With tears in her eyes, she looked at me and said something I've heard before from countless other women:

"I think I'm just cursed."

Confused as to why she couldn't get the guy or the relationship she wanted, this bright, beautiful female believed that there was absolutely nothing she could do to change things for herself. She told me that although she maintained a confident exterior, deep inside she was insecure and believed that she was somehow less than other women. Why else would she still be single? Something about who she was had to be innately unattractive or not good enough, and eventually all the men she was interested in came to see it—at least, that's what she had come to believe.

I asked the young woman how often she thought there was something wrong with her.

She replied, "All the time."

"Tell me more about that," I said.

"It's an internal dialogue that keeps playing in my head. It's always there, unless I have a day where I'm too busy to think about it, but even then it's a feeling I carry around ... that I'm never going to be as good as other women, and I'm doomed to living life alone."

"Do those feelings subside if you start dating someone? Do you feel better and become more hopeful?" I asked.

She replied, "Maybe for a brief period of time, but it doesn't last. When I'm dating someone, I usually worry about how much he likes me, or I'm afraid he will meet someone better and dump me. I live in constant fear that one day he will disappear and I'll have to start all over again. I feel like I'm always waiting for guys to realize that I'm not what they want."

"So, your thoughts really don't change depending on your situation," I said. "In a relationship or not, you still feel scared and unsure of yourself."

The woman got quiet for a moment as she searched for the answer. "Yes, that's right," she said. "I keep hoping that when I find someone, those thoughts will change. But in truth, it just magnifies them. I wish I could feel differently, but I don't know how or if it's even possible."

I asked the young woman to come back the next week and see me, but I wanted her to pay close attention to the thoughts she had every day until then. I asked her to write them down and bring them to our next meeting. She agreed.

The following week, she came to my office with a piece of paper. She had done her assignment and recorded her thinking throughout the week. I asked her to read her homework aloud, and this is what she came up with:

I'm worried that no one will ever want me.

I'm scared that the next guy I date will dump me.
I feel like I'm not normal and other people are better than me.
I'm angry that all my friends have boyfriends but I don't have anyone myself.
I feel like I can't really trust anyone because they will probably leave me.
I wish I had more confidence in myself.
I feel like I always do or say the wrong things.
I wish I knew how to act around guys so they would like me and want to be with me.
I am afraid I will always be alone.
I'm afraid I won't be able to have kids because I'll get too old and my window will pass.
I wish I knew my future so that I could stop worrying about this.
I feel hopeless that my life will always be this way and nothing will ever change.

The woman put the paper down.

"What do you think?" she asked. "I'm all over the place, aren't I?"

"Actually, I don't think that at all," I told her. "I think you are only in one place. There is a common theme here. Do you see it?"

The woman seemed confused, but took a guess. "Most of my thoughts are negative?" she asked.

"There is negativity, but that is just the *tone* of your thoughts, not the common theme of the thoughts themselves," I said. "What is at the center of each of those thoughts you have?"

The woman continued to stare at her paper, searching for what I meant. For a few minutes, she seemed at a loss. Then, as if by surprise, the answer appeared to her. "Me," she stated. "I'm at the center."

I nodded.

"Is that bad?" she asked. "I know I'm insecure and that doesn't help with my confidence."

"I don't think confidence is your problem. Your lack of confidence is just a symptom of what's really going on with you," I said. "Let me ask you this: What do you think it looks like to a guy if he's on a date with a girl who is constantly thinking about herself the way you are?"

She thought for a minute. "I'm not sure what it looks like. I really never thought about it in those terms," she said.

"That's okay, but think about it now. If you were a guy, out with a woman who was furiously thinking about her life, where it was going, and what people thought of her, what would that look like to him?" I asked.

"I suppose if I had to guess I could look nervous or distracted? I might not be as friendly or engaging because my mind is elsewhere," she said.

"I would think so," I agreed. "What about taking this a step further: What do you think you look like *in a relationship* where you are constantly thinking about yourself and what will happen to you?" I asked.

"I probably seem anxious," the woman said. "I know I overreact to small things because I'm so concerned about what's going to happen to me if things don't work out. I might seem clingy at times because I don't want to get dumped. I know I can text a little too much and ask for reassurance too often. On the other hand, my fear of losing someone also makes me play hard to get, so I may seem cold and standoffish because I'm trying to keep guys attracted to me," she admitted.

"If you are always thinking about what you want or what's going to happen to you and acting from that motivation, the guy you are involved with probably feels like he's in a relationship with a highly moody person, don't you think? One minute you are needy and clingy, but the next you are cold and withdrawn. Tell me this: Have you ever been in a relationship with a man who is constantly thinking about himself and what he wants, never thinking about you or your needs?"

The woman didn't have to ponder that question. "Yes, I have—it was awful!" she said. "I don't know why, but I guess I've always thought it was okay for me to behave this way. That a guy acting this way would mean he's a jerk, but a woman acting this way is normal or expected."

"And what way is that?" I asked.

The woman paused. "Too focused on myself... I didn't think it was a problem until having this conversation, but I'm much more concerned with myself than I am with any guy."

"It's interesting how much you want to be with someone and how badly you want love, and yet even when you are with that person, you are still thinking about *you* and *your life* instead of him," I said.

"Yes," she agreed. "It is interesting..."

In case you are wondering who is narrating this story, my name is Jess McCann. I'm a dating and relationship coach as well as an author of self-help books. I started my career in this line of work back in 2007, not long after I had my first awakening about relationships which led to teaching single women how to apply sales strategies to their dating life in my book, *"You Lost Him at Hello."* The second awakening, which brought a deeper and more profound level of love to my life and to the lives of my clients, is what this book, *"Cursed?"* is all about.

Over the last decade, I've noticed a lot of change in the relationship arena. Getting married and having a family is still a big priority for most people, and we now have more ways to connect with each other than we've had in the past, but cultivating real love is seemingly more elusive than ever. People go on dozens of first dates that never turn into seconds. Some carry on virtual courtships for weeks, only to have the other person suddenly go dark on them. If a match is made and there's equal interest on both sides, sex is often expected but commitment is not, so the only certainty is confusion or disappointment. One of the most interesting, yet troubling trends I've noticed, however, is that while the female population is historically at its peak—with women being more beautiful, successful, and capable than ever before—there is a growing subset who have a pattern of relationships ending (or never getting off the ground) and only the vague explanation that something was "just missing" from the relationship. Like the young woman who sobbed in my office, too many women today are displaying a pattern of unproductive attempts at love, and I am frequently the last-ditch effort, as they try to identify why despite being on their A-game in all other areas of life, the same unwanted outcome keeps happening over and over again.

Most new clients begin a session with me the same way. "I think the problem is me. I'm doing something wrong, but I don't know what it is." I came to call the problem "the Curse" after so many women contacted me, half-joking that the only explanation for their pattern of unsuccessful relationships was being cursed with bad luck. Why else would every guy lose interest after three months? What other reason could there be for every boyfriend going on to marry the next woman he dated? Whether a guy disappeared, or a boyfriend wanted space, many women would speculate that yet again, they were victims of doomed circumstance.

In truth, they weren't far off the mark. In my opinion, there *is* a curse causing the repeated demise of their relationships, but it has nothing to do with misfortune or voodoo. What I came to witness in my coaching practice was that many people were unintentionally sabotaging their relationships. To a degree, they knew this but couldn't put a finger on how it was actually happening. As I listened closely to their backstories, followed them on each date, and in and out of every relationship, the *Curse* became clear. It was not what they were *doing*, but how they were *thinking* that created their unsuccessful patterns. The *Curse* is a mindset —one that has long been present in our society, but has recently grown and intensified due to technology and social media. It is a mindset that is extremely detrimental to relationships. I should know. For a long time I had the *Curse* myself.

What is the mindset? How could a person both want love and simultaneously work against having it? Although behaving in a way that contradicts your primary life goal might seem maniacal, we humans do it all the time. We do it because we have different facets of our brain at play and they don't always cooperate with each other nor are we conscious enough to notice them. It's why we might vow to start getting more exercise but then find a reason every day to avoid the treadmill. Or we might pride ourselves on being the most helpful person in our community but then we get behind the wheel of our car and road rage takes over. It's also why we choose to date the bad boy with little future potential, even though a really good guy is standing right in front of us, ready to commit. It's actually very easy, and in some ways inherent, to behave in a way that counteracts what we aspire for. Regardless of what we say we want, the unconscious part of our mind can have conflicting thoughts and ideas, and unfortunately, the unconscious mind is usually our commander-in-chief.

So what could be happening in your unconscious mind that is thwarting your chances at love? If you have a strong pattern of dissatisfaction, drama, or lacking in your relationship(s), or the theme of your dating history could be "same story, insert different guy," it's possible that your unconscious mind has become conditioned to excessively ruminate about yourself and your life, much like the client in my opening story. That might not appear to be a significant problem in regards to a relationship at first, but consider this: If you are constantly fixated on *yourself*, what *you* want or don't want, what will make *you* happy or unhappy, after so many years you can and will condition yourself to only see life from your perspective. That can lead to several big problems when attempting to build a relationship with another person; the first being a skewed perception of who that person is. Assessing if someone is a good person and ready for a relationship is essential in choosing a partner, right? But too much ruminating on ourselves can interfere with that assessment. This is why you or someone you know might have held on to a rocky, unhealthy, or even a non-relationship with a person who everyone else saw as non-committal, untrustworthy, or just not interested. If we are too driven by the wants of our unconscious mind, and more specifically *who it wants*, we often end up ignoring any facts that conflict with those desires.

But even if the men (or women) you've dated have been nice and normal, self-focused thinking can stop a relationship in its tracks. Eventually you will default to prioritizing your own thoughts and emotions over anyone else's, **and you won't even be aware that you are doing it.** Think back to the last time your boyfriend or spouse was mad at you. How much of the argument was him pointing out something that you'd done that you were completely oblivious of? Even more telling, how much time did you spend defending yourself, claiming you did no such thing?

The bottom line is this: an easy way to ruin a new romantic opportunity is to make judgments and act on assumptions based solely on your point of view. A fast way to destroy rapport with someone is to repeatedly overlook or misread his feelings and favor your own. If we agree that the key to a happy, committed relationship is putting the other person first, then wouldn't constantly obsessing about ourselves and our wants, be the cause of its demise? Love might be what you consciously desire, but if your unconscious thinking has become accustomed to focusing on yourself, you will unintentionally subvert any chance at love that comes your way.

As you will read more about in the pages to come, unconscious thinking that is centered on ourselves not only affects how we perceive and react to our romantic situations, it also stifles our ability to truly connect with other people. For many of the women I've coached, this is where the big breakdown would happen in their love lives. They felt lost when it came to understanding or relating to their person of interest, and they struggled to form a solid and trusting bond. Unable to form a connection, they relied heavily on attraction as a means of enticement. While attraction alone may get you a date, or even into a relationship, it cannot sustain or deepen into love. The end result would frequently be the sudden dissolution of the relationship, with the other person citing that "something was just missing." In my opinion, that "something" that was missing was true connection.

Before I go any further into explaining the *Curse*, I want to stop and prepare you for what you are about to read. The first half of this book may cause a guarded reaction within you because you are going to learn the particulars of the unconscious thought habits you might have that create your relationship patterns. Point is —it's going to involve some heavy self-reflecting and for certain people that might be painful. It is vital that you lay down all your defenses at this point and accept your humanity of being imperfect. If you allow shame and criticism to dominate your thinking as you take in the material, or view the information as yet another example of how you aren't worthy of a partner, you will not benefit or grow from this book. So I implore you, when you come across concepts that strike a sore spot within, do not jump to self-blame or self-defense, as you will be engaging in one of the very thought patterns this book is attempting to help you end once and for all. I also want to point out that the unconscious, self-focused mindset we are going to discuss is not exclusively a woman problem. It is a human problem; so men also suffer from this condition of the mind. For that reason, you may see examples in the chapters to come that bring more understanding to someone you've dated in the past. That will hopefully be helpful to you, but as best you can, attempt to take the information to heart for yourself more than anyone else. You are the one who is here reading this and that means you're the one who can actually benefit from the material. Regardless of how toxic your ex was, or how selfish your partner can be, we can only change our relationship destiny when we take ownership of our own habits first.

Now, I want to give you a tool to help you digest what you are about to learn. It's a quote that I hope you carry with you as you read. "The wound is the place where light enters you." This passage by 13th century poet Rumi epitomizes what I experienced on my own journey for love and what I believe is necessary for anyone seeking answers as to why their relationships aren't working, or why their dating life is lifeless. The phrase means that emotional pain can lead you to self-awareness. When you feel an unpleasant reaction to what you are reading, when you feel yourself responding to what you are learning with a sense of embarrassment, self blame, self-loathing, or even anger towards me, recognize that this is the wound that Rumi is speaking of, and know that if you don't run from those feelings and instead see them as a guide to what you need to know about yourself, the light will not only enter you, but transform you completely. What we react strongly to always gives us insight about ourselves. I hope you will use Rumi's quote as a tool to help open yourself to this information as you continue to read.

Are You Self-Absorbed?

You may be thinking that so far what you've read has made sense, but you still aren't convinced that the *Curse* is the cause of your dating and relationship problems. You might not even be sure what the *Curse* is at this point, and I would not blame you. Thus far, all we have figured out is that there's a prevalent mindset in our culture in which most people's day-to-day thoughts are centered around themselves and it could be hindering your chances at love. You might hear the term self-centered and immediately feel defensive, convinced that I couldn't be talking about you. After all, doesn't being self-centered mean to talk about yourself in a positive and boastful way? Sure, you might post selfies on social media, but you're more likely to put a guy's needs before your own to the point where you've often felt you were suffocating your own spirit and being treated like a doormat.

While you would be correct in your definition, overly positive self-affirmation is only one way that self-centeredness can be exhibited. Self-centered thinking does not always involve talking about oneself, nor is it always positive. Being self-centered—or perhaps it's more accurate to say self-absorbed—by definition means **to be preoccupied by one's own thoughts, emotions, interests, and life.** Therefore, you don't need to believe you are great in order to be self-absorbed. You can have a very low self-perception, be highly insecure, and still fit the self-absorbed mold. The hard fact is whether you spend all your time reveling in how wonderful you are or worrying about how inadequate you are, at the end of the day, you are still thinking about *you*.

The *Curse* is more than being too absorbed in yourself, however. It is being self-absorbed *fueled by the need for self-relevance.* In other words, when you have a "*Cursed* mindset", you're not just constantly thinking about yourself, your interests, and your life but also how those things make you feel about yourself and your level of worth. You don't simply think, *"I have a meeting at 4pm and then a date at 7pm. I have a meeting at 4pm and a date at 7pm..."* Which would be an example of thinking about yourself and your life. You think, *"I have a meeting at 4pm and I cannot be late or so-and-so will shame me and I'll be so embarrassed again. I hope I can get home in time and get ready for my date at 7pm because last week I didn't have enough time and I didn't feel my best. I'm sure it's why that guy didn't ask me out again. I have to have time to blow out my hair or the whole night will be ruined again! I can't believe how many dates I have to go on to find someone. What's wrong with me?"* When you have a *Cursed* mindset, your self-centered thoughts are always flavored by how you feel about yourself and your value.

I mentioned earlier that this mindset has been present in society for a long time but recently it's become more pronounced. It's true that social media has recently turned everyone's focus further inward, luring us into an environment where we are made to feel as if we are at the center of the world, but the good old mass media (television, magazines, etc.) has long played a role in how we perceive ourselves. Its messages are constantly and insidiously judging our worth. We are too fat, too thin, too sexual, not sexual enough, too emotional, too successful, or not successful enough. The media has been telling us for decades that we need to strive for more so that we can have more *in order to become more*. This constant evaluation of ourselves has seeped into the cultural psyche of females, which leads many of us to continually question, *"are we enough yet?"*

Many experts have tried to help women placate the anxiety of "being enough" with books and mantras meant to instill us with a sense of "enoughness". There are articles, vlogs, podcasts, and apps dedicated to specifically help us feel like we are perfect the way we are. While some of the recommendations can be helpful, they largely ignore the real problem — that we should not even be asking ourselves if we are enough in the first place. The question itself *is* the problem because it beckons us to self-obsess.

So if you have read other books shedding light on the struggle for self-worth or assumed that you need to focus on feeling "more worthy" to glean better relationship results, I respectfully disagree. Yes, feeling confident and capable and having a high level of self-respect is important, especially in regards to dating and relationships, but I've found that those particular feelings do not increase by spending time thinking about or studying them. The most interesting observation I've made in all my years of coaching is that the more someone focuses on or attempts to enhance their feeling of self-worth, the more unhappy, unproductive, and unloved they feel.

I stumbled upon a blog called *Refine the Mind* years ago that articulated this point quite well. The creator, Jordan Bates, said this in a post titled "The Surprising Paradox of Self-Esteem":

"There is an inverse relationship between self-esteem (self-worth) and thoughts of self. If anyone is puzzling over the definition of inverse relationship, it simply means that as one goes up, the other goes down. As self-esteem increases, thoughts of self decrease."

This would mean that as thoughts of self increase, self-esteem actually decreases—which is exactly what I've witnessed. I have also observed that the more a person focuses on themselves and their feelings of self-worth, the more they develop damaging thought patterns that are the basis for most self-perpetuating relationship problems. These harmful thought patterns typically go unnoticed by the individual, which is the reason they cannot identify why certain complications repeatedly arise in their romantic endeavors. This is the focus of this book: to explore how the unconscious, self-absorbed mindset, attempting to enhance or protect feelings of self-worth, causes a myriad of thought patterns — all of which sabotage love and result in you feeling "cursed".

Unfortunately, women have long tied their sense of worth to being in a relationship because, for centuries, society deemed us "unworthy" if we reached a certain age without a husband. Although we've made tremendous strides as a gender, that culture-wide mentality hasn't died out. And in many ways, it's resurging as a result of technology. Our lives, as well as the lives of everyone else, are on full display. We have a bird's eye view not only of our own social circle, but anyone we've ever known or wanted to know. We can see who's in a relationship, who's gotten engaged, who's getting married, and who's having a first, second, and third baby. This lures us into an ego game called "whose life is better?" Or, in *Cursed* speak, "who is more worthy?" Escaping the thoughts that we may not be as happy, as loved, or as worthy as our peers is now much harder, and unfortunately it drives many of us to unconsciously use our relationships to fulfill the needs of our *Cursed Mind* instead of the needs of our heart. Instead of looking for real love, we look for our relationship to make us feel more whole, more comparable to others, and happier with ourselves. When this is our motivation, even if it's not an entirely conscious one, the result is a relationship that is fragile, tumultuous, or unable to move to the next level and grow into something meaningful.

The Facets of the Mind

Awakening to the fact that you might have a *Cursed* mindset and are allowing your unconscious thoughts on your self-worth control, or at the very least interfere with your love life, might be hard at first. Naturally, no one likes to think of themselves as being self-absorbed, but try not to let that or the word *Cursed* bother you because you are more than just your mindset, which is what we are discussing here. In my opinion, the core of who you are lies in your heart and spirit; it is not your mind or your thoughts, which might be a new concept for you to grasp. Most people assume that your thoughts make you who you are—but as you will hopefully learn as you read, that is also a trick of the *Cursed Mind*. It wants you to believe that your mind is who you are because then it can stay in control. But you are far greater and much more complex than just *thinking*. Thinking, after all, is intangible, often chaotic and wildly erroneous at times. How could thinking ever really be the core of you? If the three-pound organ in your head was *you* that would mean when you are attracted to someone, you are only attracted to their brain. Or when you fall in love, you are in love with their brain. If you have ever been in love then you know that can't be true because we fall in love with the whole person, not just how they think. In fact, you could argue that you can fall in love *despite* how someone thinks! The core of a person is so much more than the conditioned thought habits they engage in. My point is this: *You* are so much more than your mind.

I also want to add that having a *Cursed*, or self-absorbed mind searching for value doesn't make you a bad person. If you have already conjured ideas that I'm characterizing you as a narcissistic, uncaring, and completely egotistical individual, then you are not going to want to finish this book! Let me reassure you again that the term self-absorbed is referring to your unconscious thought process, not you. We will talk more about the real you—we will call that person your *Core Self*—and how you originally developed this state of mind in a moment, but I first want to make it clear that possessing a *Cursed* mindset does not mean you are suffering from a personality disorder, like narcissism. As you read, you will start to see many people you know who also think like this, and I doubt you'd think they all needed psychiatric help.

In my study, there are five dominant ways that a *Cursed* mindset can present itself in the context of relationships. I call them *"The Five Faces of the Curse."* We will cover all *Faces* in great detail because it is very likely you will see parts of yourself in many if not all of them. If you want to work to change your relationship patterns, you have to understand all the different forms of the self-absorbed mind so you know when you encounter it, and some are not so easily recognized.

It may be a surprise, for example, to learn that most people pleasers have a *Cursed Mind.* Quite frequently, those who seem to be the most concerned about making other people happy have a self-focused motivation behind it. This is because most pleasers aim to please in order to win approval, which is a worth-seeking motivation. If you try your hardest to please people, ask yourself what your real reason is for doing so. Are you pleasing out of the goodness of your heart? Or are you trying to control or preserve someone else's perception of who you are? Do you get upset when your pleasing doesn't yield the return you wanted? There is a difference between giving of yourself to show love and pleasing people to gain their approval (or avoid their disapproval). If you have a habit of pleasing men in the hopes to win them over or avoid having them leave you, you have just found the primary source of all your problems.

Perhaps you are the opposite of a pleaser, extremely self-confident, and often unfazed by what other people think but are alone, unhappy, and bored with men. This is another form of the *Cursed Mind* presenting in a different *Face* from the previous one. You may find that you don't have interest in many guys, but the few you do find intriguing never seem to like you back. This is not the universe being ironic. You will learn how even positive thoughts about yourself can become detrimental to finding love. A *Cursed Mind* can distort a healthy self-esteem and turn a person into love's worst enemy, inciting habits like extreme pickiness, superficiality, and a tendency to judge—all traits that are inspired by a desire to have high value but will keep love at bay.

The majority of people will find themselves somewhere in the middle. You might be confident in some situations and insecure in others. You may be selfless and giving at times but also have an angry or selfish streak. It is not unusual to exhibit many different or contrasting character traits. This is because most people with a *Cursed Mind* vacillate from one Face to another depending on certain situations or triggers, which is why you will likely see parts of yourself in several of the *Faces*. In fact, only the most deeply self-focused individuals, those who are functioning solely through their worth-searching mind 100% of the time, exhibit only one Face of the *Curse*. If you find that you are that type of person, one who has only identified with one specific Face, it could take more work to break free and begin to change. The good news, however, is that people who are fully entrenched in a self-absorbed mindset feel the most joy and experience the deepest sense of love when it is finally gone.

How Did You Become Cursed?

Cursed?

It might relieve you to know that you were not born *Cursed*. No one is. It's something that happens over time and usually begins in adolescence. As a young child, you don't have thoughts or concerns about yourself or your value as a person. You are hardly aware of yourself at all. Back then, you were likely just happy to be alive. Life itself was fascinating, and you spent most of your time exploring the world and everything in it. If at any time something upset you, then you might have cried about it, but within moments you were back on your feet playing again. Pain was not something you held on to or analyzed. Once an unpleasant experience was over, you moved on. You weren't concerned with what others thought of you, and you certainly never bothered to think about how you measured up to them. That meant all actions you took came from a genuinely joyful place. You probably smiled at strangers. You likely looked people in the eye. You might have even openly and honestly expressed how you felt. You certainly never woke up with yesterday's problems, and you didn't go to sleep worried about tomorrow's either. We all enter the world this way: with a completely loving heart and no interest in ourselves beyond our basic needs. This is the person I call your *Core Self*. It's the person you were from day one on this earth, the real you that people fall in love with.

Unfortunately, as you grow up, a change happens within that greatly affects your being. The people you are closest to significantly influence your unbiased perspective on life. As Louise Hay, author of *You Can Heal Your Life*, put it: "We learn how to feel about ourselves and about life by the reactions of the adults around us." Your parents, teachers, and peers cast judgment on you, either consciously or unconsciously, and without hesitation you begin to believe them. How could you not? They say, "You are so this! You are not that! You can't do this! You should do that!" You develop an identity based on who others think you are, and that identity usually gives you a sense of self-worth or a sense that you lack it.

Along with all the words people used to describe you, a few pivotal events during adolescence embolden your beliefs about who you are.

Maybe something negative happened, like someone not wanting to be your friend at school or a parent frequently ignoring or criticizing you. This may confirm the thoughts you have about yourself. Maybe the negative experience was humiliating or traumatizing beyond typical adolescent strife. A parent didn't demonstrate love appropriately; you were taken advantage of by a family member or bullied by a schoolmate. At that point, you may decide your worth is menial, and the identity of being less than others stuck with you for good.

Or perhaps you grew up with extremely positive experiences that made you feel good and special. Your parents or teachers held you in high esteem and doted on you constantly. You started to feel entitled, believing you were a cut above your peers, or began to constantly crave more and more attention from others. You may, at times, have felt disappointed and disliked because not everyone seemed to love you and treat you as the special person you were. At that point, the identity of being better than others (or at least the desire to be) began to form.

Whether your adolescence was positive, negative, or somewhere in between or the people around you intentionally or unintentionally judged you, this was when your focus began to shift. You became less in tune to the world and the people around you and more concentrated on yourself, on how others perceived you, and most importantly how you felt about yourself. Your *Core Self*—the person that was born into this world curious, authentic, and full of love—began to wane, and the *Cursed Mind* began to surface, one that was fully focused on and absorbed in itself and its worth.

As you aged, it is likely that our digital cultural and the habits breeding from that pushed your focus inward even more —habits like rating people, places and things, judging what's good or bad, and soliciting attention for yourself and your beliefs. Not realizing that social media is a breeding ground for self-obsession, many of your daily interactions offline started to mimic those habits online. Without much notice, you might have developed a habit of comparing yourself and your life to others, making you feel good or bad, ahead or behind them. By then, the *Cursed Mind* and its tendencies would have moved to the forefront—leading you to feel insecure and worried, perhaps a bit angry and jealous, but most of all lonely and isolated. Through the years, you may have searched for ways to feel whole and good again or avoid feeling low and dejected; having someone to love you may have seemed like the fastest way to accomplish that goal. At times you might have succeeded, and having that person and their attention made you feel better. But the satisfaction never lasted, and neither did the relationship. This is the *Curse*: Your mind spends all of its energy attempting to enhance your feelings of self-worth or protect you from feeling worthless while destroying the purity and goodness of what it's focused on having—real love.

The *Cursed Mind* is certain that love will cure you of the thoughts and feelings about yourself and finally provide you with the happiness that's been missing in your life. But in truth, only by curing yourself of the *Cursed Mind* and living as your *Core Self* can you ever have real love and feel happy! Many people will struggle their whole lives repeating an infinite cycle of finding someone, almost attaining true love, and then having it all fall apart because they don't understand this.

But I can help.

I can show you how to see your own *Cursed Mind* so that you don't continue making the same unconscious mistakes in your relationships, and I'll teach you how to break free of it so that you can find and keep love for the rest of your life. How can I be so confident? Because not only have I helped save other people from the quiet sabotaging effects of the *Curse,* someone also helped save me.

My Story

I mentioned before that I discovered the *Curse* through my own relationship. It happened when I was around 30 years old. Until then, I had lived most of my life with a *Cursed Mind.* When I was an adolescent, I was negatively self-absorbed, constantly worried about what people thought of me, and quite certain I was less than other girls. I was also extremely anxious and worried about the future constantly. Throughout high school and college, I was in a handful of relationships, all of which were unloving and unhealthy, making me feel worse about myself. I thought the reason I was repeatedly cheated on and broken up with was because something about me just wasn't good enough. Here are some of the thoughts I frequently had in the back of my mind during that time.

I'm not as pretty as other girls.
Why don't I have more friends?
I feel so lonely.
Why aren't people nicer to me?
How can I show everyone I'm good enough?
If only I wasn't so awkward and skinny my life would be better and more people would like me.

After college, as you might have read in my other books, I started my first job in sales. I quickly rose through the ranks, becoming a top producer, and ultimately opened my own sales office. I began applying the relationship-building tactics I employed in my work to my dating life and saw miraculous results. Suddenly, guys that never noticed me before were giving me the attention I always wanted. For the first time, I didn't feel that I was inferior to other women, and I believed my self-worth was high. I wrote my first book wanting to help others who had struggled in relationships like I did. By the time it hit the bookstores, I had met and started dating the man who would become my husband. And although he proposed after only 18 months together, I hadn't achieved "happily ever after." Yes, I had figured out how to date effectively and found the person I wanted to marry, but because I was still *Cursed,* I didn't really know how to be in a healthy, committed long-term relationship.

My thoughts about myself were no longer negative, but since I was still possessed by my worth-searching mind, my self-absorbed thinking had simply switched from negative to positive. Now instead of believing I was less than everyone else and looking for ways to avoid rejection, I thought I was great and constantly looked for how I could enhance positive feelings about myself. Naturally, this took a toll on my new relationship. I remember one day before we were married, my husband and I had a fight. I don't recall what it was about, but I do remember him saying, "You always want more from me. Nothing I do satisfies you for more than a day. Do you think you just deserve the best in life because you are *you*?" I remember answering, "No, I don't think that!" However, some little voice inside me whispered, *"Yes! Yes, you do!"*

It was that pivotal moment that woke me up to what was going on inside my head. What a disparity there was between what I said to my husband that day and what that inner voice said to me. Why did I think I just deserved the things that I wanted? Why was I in a perpetual state of wanting my husband to shower me with attention and adoration to the point he was exhausted and then irritated with me? At 30 years old, I was on the cusp of getting married, and yet, I suddenly felt as bad about myself as I did when I was a teenager. I thought I had found confidence and self-worth, but what I had found was a different Face of the *Cursed Mind*.

I spent the next year going through a sort of identity crisis. I wasn't sure who I was anymore. One thing I did realize was that I spent a lot of time thinking about myself, my happiness, and what I needed to feel whole and complete. I noticed that it was a never-ending search that I often sucked my husband into as well. Then, by pure luck, someone finally made sense of everything I was dealing with. It was as if an angel rescued me from the torment in my head—and that angel was a man by the name of Eckhart Tolle.

Eckhart Tolle is an author of many best-selling books; most notably, *The Power of Now* and *A New Earth*. He had a similar story to mine, one about incessant talking in his head and the toxicity that his thoughts brought into his being. He had his first break in his own awareness of his mind when he was a student at the University of London. He was an intellectual, but was plagued by anxiety and depression. Every morning he would take the subway to the library and one day a woman sat next to him who was talking very loudly and angrily to herself. He thought she was insane as she was so absorbed in her thoughts that she was unaware of the other people around her. Her monologue went something like, "She said that to me…and I said how dare you! And then I told her I didn't trust her anymore and she had betrayed me." The woman got off at the same stop as Tolle and walked in the same direction. Just as he was surmising that she was mentally ill, she entered into one of the University buildings. He was shocked. How could a person like that be affiliated with the school he himself attended? But shortly after, he had the revelation that there was very little difference between himself and the woman. Tolle's mind was always thinking and he often conversed with himself, too, he just didn't do it out loud like the woman had. He kept his thoughts in, while she let them out. Her thoughts were mostly angry, his were mostly anxious. If she was crazy, then wasn't he crazy, too?

After that incident Tolle devoted himself to understanding the common dysfunction of the human mind and how to transcend egoic thinking in order to live a more joyful and fulfilling life. He became a teacher of this, and then an author and speaker. I read everything that he had written in order to understand what was happening inside myself. Finally, I found the answer I was looking for. I realized why I had said, *"No! I don't think that"* when my husband accused me of demanding the best for myself, while another part of me insisted, *"Yes! Yes, you do!"* My *Core Self* was fighting my *Cursed Self.* What Tolle called my "ego," is what I ultimately came to see as the *Cursed Mind* and I had to break free of it.

As I gained awareness of this part of myself, I started noticing how self-absorbed and ego-filled I had been throughout my entire life and how it had affected my circumstances. Even more enlightening was how very clear it became that any time my husband was upset with me, it was typically because I had done or said something that came from one of the five types of self-absorbed thinking. It took some time to cure myself of my *Cursed Mind*, as thought habits that are decades old don't just disappear in a day, but I was determined to live a better life and preserve my relationship. I read Tolle's books over and over again. I highlighted quotes that resonated with me. I began meditating and journaling. As I grew in awareness of my *Cursed Mind,* I was able to catch myself from giving into its thought patterns. I saw that who I was had nothing to do with how I had been thinking. My self-absorbed thoughts were just habits; they weren't *me*. Within a year, I stopped being anxious (which my parents didn't think would ever be possible!) Fights with my husband became less heated and then almost non-existent. Our communication got better and our love for each other grew to a new level. Most notably to me, the desire to prove myself and show that I was just as worthy as other people completely vanished from my being.

    I am not a spiritual teacher and I haven't morphed into a Buddhist monk. There are still days where my *Cursed Mind* makes an appearance, like when I haven't slept in days and I'm really exhausted, but it doesn't dominate me like it did when I was younger. I am aware of it now, and therefore, it has lost its power over me. I can rather confidently say that my *Core Self* is what I bring to all of my relationships. At 42 years old, I have been married for 10 years, have two wonderful children—and life is good!

    I hope that this book will be the resource you need to finally stop suffering from the perpetual misery of your own *Cursed Mind* and all the negative relationship patterns it has created in your life. Once you are able to see the *Cursed Mind* clearly, I will give you the five practices I used—what I call "The Cures"—that will assist you in bringing your *Core Self* to the forefront of your being. When she is back in control, a new pattern will emerge for you, and it will be positive, productive, and full of love. You will see. When you shed all the ideas of who you need to be and seek love selflessly, you will then attract it effortlessly.

Chapter Two

Cursed Thinking

About now, you may be thinking that you are not so different from everyone else. That yes, you do think an awful lot about yourself, but so do other people. How can a person possibly survive, let alone succeed in life, if they don't think about themselves? And you are right: You do have to think about yourself at certain times. You cannot go through life completely unconcerned about yourself. You would not go to work or school. You would not eat right or exercise. You might put yourself in harm's way or fail to stand up for yourself in times of injustice. In terms of working and protecting yourself as a human being, you do have to think and care about yourself. You also need to use your mind for analytical thinking, which means being creative, strategizing, and working to solve problems. What you *don't* have to do, and what you must work to break, is the *Cursed* thinking you do every day that revolves around *yourself, your wants and fears,* and how they pertain to your worth. There is a big difference between being conscious of your physiological health and well-being, or being creative or analytical at work, and obsessively analyzing or worrying about your own value as a person, especially against the backdrop of your relationships.

When you're consumed by the *Cursed Mind,* your brain hardly ever shuts off. This is the number-one symptom of having a self-absorbed mindset and the most conspicuous way to know that you indeed have this problem. As you go through each day, you are, without fail, accompanied by constant background chatter in your head, almost as if you are having a conversation with yourself, about yourself. Some of the most frequent thoughts of the *Cursed Mind* sound like this: *"Will I ever get married, or will I be an old single woman forever? If I just knew the future, I could relax about being single and stop being so anxious. What's the use, I'm never going to find anyone! I'm going to die alone! What's wrong with me? If only I had done XYZ with my ex-boyfriend, I'd be engaged by now. Why does everyone else have it so easy in relationships? Maybe I should text so-and-so and just date him. If only I was prettier/thinner/smarter/had more confidence I would not be having this issue."*

If any of this sounds like you, I would expect that you have similar thoughts even when you are in a relationship: *"Why did my boyfriend say that to me? Is he losing interest and going to dump me? I wish I knew if he was telling me the truth about his feelings. Maybe he's just using me until someone better comes along. Why is he playing games! Maybe I should just break up with him first. No, then I'd be alone and have to start over again and that's so much worse!"* You can be certain it's a *Cursed* voice you are hearing in these examples because it's marked with worry, stress, judgment, comparing, and wishing something were different. These are the mental constructs of the *Cursed Mind,* which you will learn about in the upcoming chapters. In all the above examples, you can see that the thoughts are self-focused but notice how they are also rooted in protecting or enhancing your self-worth. You may not have realized it before, but if you stop yourself in the middle of *Cursed* chatter and ask yourself, *"Why am I thinking about this? Why do I care?"* the answer is usually grounded in self-preservation or self-enhancement. Most of the time we are so caught up in the content of our "mind conversations" that we don't realize the theme is always the same. We are forever looking for ways to strengthen whatever idea we have about ourselves in any situation.

You might think that your brain is simply more active than most people's, but I assure you that this is not just "how you are." It's how your mind has been conditioned to think over time. Life events and the opinions of others have shaped your thought process, and you are now stuck in a cycle of self-absorbed thought habits, which you've mistakenly assumed is just you. You have likely listened to and followed these thought habits, acting upon what they are saying and hoping that doing so would help solve whatever problem you were currently having with a guy or get you whatever it is you want from him. However, it's the constant thinking that is the problem. The voice of the *Cursed Mind* has been leading you astray.

The most important concept to grasp before reading any further is that *you* are not your conditioned mind. The *Cursed Mind* may be doing a lot of thinking *as you,* but it is not you. Your *Core Self* is the person listening. It may sound strange, almost as if two people are cohabitating inside of you. And to some extent, that is what's happening. Your *Cursed Self,* your worth-searching, self-absorbed mind, can be babbling away, and your *Core Self,* the heart and soul of who you are, is listening (and sometimes, cringing).

You know what I mean, don't you? You might be catching up with someone, chatting and joking, and then suddenly you hear yourself say something that didn't feel right. Or maybe you walk away and then realize it. *"Why on earth did I say that,"* you ponder. That's your *Core Self* hearing your *Cursed Mind.*

Obviously, I'm not the first to introduce the concept of this voice in your head perpetrating as you. Many people, dating back centuries, have not only acknowledged it but extensively studied it and the immense trouble it can cause. I call the voice the *Cursed Mind* because it's the architect of certain self-sabotaging patterns that lead some people to feel "Cursed", but it has many other names. Sigmund Freud first referred to it as the ego, which is how I learned to identify it through the works of

Eckhart Tolle. Tolle also refers to it as ego or the unconscious mind. Some religions entitle it as "temptation" or "the devil," within us, but nearly all faiths have some word or terminology for the self-absorbed mind chatter that dominates people and compels them to be self-serving. I mention this so that after you finish this book, you can continue to learn about the voice of the mind through other teachings if you wish to do so.

It doesn't matter what name you use for it—the ego, temptation, the *Cursed Mind*—the point is that assuming the thoughts and feelings that stem from these dysfunctional habits of the mind are actually your *Core Self* is the reason you haven't yet succeeded in love. You've been taking advice from the wrong place within you. You've been following the wrong voice. This is why when trouble hits on the romantic front you might confidently react in a certain way, but then soon regret that reaction. Or you might become confused and ask yourself questions like, *"Am I being irrational, or is he being unreasonable? Should I be mad, or am I overreacting?"* Why are you always confused, unsure, or justifying something you've said or done? Because you are dealing with two different *you's* and they are usually in disagreement with each other. You question how you think and feel because your *Cursed Mind* is likely the first to react (and it reacts rather loudly), but your *Core Self* is still present and attempts to get you to reassess that self-focused reaction.

It's almost impossible to see the truth of a situation, to be objective about it, or react appropriately to it, when you are unaware and under the rule of your *Cursed Mind*. This is why understanding its habits and then completely ridding yourself of it is the only real way to find and keep a loving relationship. When you act from your *Core Self,* the self-doubt is removed and you are able to handle the ups and downs, the questions and setbacks, without any fear or uncertainty. You gain a much clearer understanding for how to proceed in all of your relationships. Best of all, without *Cursed* thinking distracting you and pretending to be you, the pathway to love becomes so much easier and enjoyable.

Your Vibe

As you'll learn as you read about the *Five Faces, Cursed* thoughts are full of fear, doubt, and regret, and those emotions not only interfere with your decision-making in dating, but they also make you much less attractive to a potential partner, even if you never verbalize them. This is because *your thoughts* create *your energy* and *overall vibe.* As you already may know, attraction is not just physical; it is also mental and emotional. How many times has a guy gotten more attractive to you because he's confident, relaxed, and self-assured? His vibe enhances your attraction to him. Likewise, your vibe can add to, or detract from, your physical appeal. If your mind is filled with unpleasant ideas about yourself and your life, it will affect the vibe that you radiate. Therefore, if you are notoriously worried, fearful, remorseful, or unaccepting, your energy will likely feel desperate, clingy, depressing, or to use a popular male-coined term, "crazy" to the guys you come in contact with. It won't matter if you try and hide how you feel when you're on a date or hanging out with someone because the energy you create by constant self-absorbed thinking sticks with you. It lingers and never fully goes away until you become consciously aware of it and begin to stop it. So, even if you think, *"I'm happy when I am with the guy I like, and I only think this way when he's not around,"* it won't matter.

Guys that you are interested in dating aren't aware that your mind is stuck in a self-absorbed thought pattern, but they absolutely feel the effect of it. You might not know what your energy feels like, but you've likely felt *Cursed* energy from other people. Do you have a friend who is very draining to be around or who seems to suck the life right out of you? Maybe you know someone who makes you feel stressed out just by talking or texting with them on the phone? Have you ever been in a relationship with someone who always seems to be in competition with you, or known someone whose mere presence puts you on pins and needles? This is how the *Cursed Mind* is seen from an outsider's perspective. When you are around someone who is functioning through their self-absorbed mind searching for value, you can sense a strong vibe from them, which is why they can make you feel defensive, annoyed, drained, angry or depressed without much of a reason.

The energy that you emanate is what a guy first feels when he meets you and what some will point to as the reason they have lost interest. "There wasn't any chemistry," a guy might say, or again, "something was missing" and that often means the *Cursed Mind* has done its dirty work and created an undesirable vibe. In order to improve your level of attraction and make more of a connection in your relationships, you must change that energy. To do that, you have to go to the power source—your thoughts—and recalibrate.

The Good News

Although having a *Cursed Mind* doesn't sound like good news, it should be a relief to some extent. Why? Because it is the reason, despite all the trying you have been doing, nothing has worked out the way you've planned in regards to your relationships. It's why the rules you've followed or the strategies you've implemented have failed to produce good results. When the *Cursed Mind* is navigating your romantic life, the tools and techniques that work effortlessly for some other people will stall and straggle like a car in desperate need of a tune-up.

For example, maybe you've attempted to implement some of the techniques you've learned from my book *Was It Something I Said?* like waiting 24 hours to text someone back or ending your date at the height of impulse, only to have the strategy backfire or not work at all. When you use a relationship-building tool for the wrong purposes (read: *Cursed* purposes), men can either see that you are trying to manipulate them and the situation, or they sense a deep sense of lack in you that you are attempting to have them fill, which instantly turns them off and renders the techniques useless. Second, when your *Cursed Mind* decides it wants someone, it disregards or ignores any information that could be counterproductive to achieving its goal—information that might have told your *Core Self* that pursuing a relationship with someone was going to be difficult, harmful or a complete waste of time.

Let's say you meet a cute and charismatic guy that you are highly interested in. During your first date, you learn certain things about him, some of which are questionable. He checked his phone several times, told you his last relationship ended only a few weeks ago, and interrupted your conversation frequently to say hello to the women he knew at the bar (which strongly suggested he hangs out there a lot.) If your *Core Self* were in control, you would have felt it in your heart that this guy doesn't seem to have finding a committed relationship as his top priority, and that might have been your last date. But your *Cursed Mind*, filled with the need for validation and temptation for what it wants, says, *"He's so attractive! All these other girls like him, so he really is a catch. Maybe you can get him to fall for you! He asked you on the date after all. It would be so great if this worked out and you didn't have to go on another Bumble date!"* Because your *Cursed Mind* is navigating the ship, you ignore the facts and decide you want to see where the relationship could go. You end your date at the height of impulse, as you've read in my other books, only to wait a week to hear from the guy again. You decide to wait 24 hours to respond because you know it's best to make him wait a little as you waited for him, but when you finally text back, he never replies and ghosts you completely. Then you suffer through the aftermath of thoughts about what happened, all of which are centered on you having done something wrong or being something wrong.

Can you see in this example how your *Cursed* thinking got in the way of your *Core Self* evaluating the potential of this guy and why the strategies didn't work? If you can't see it yet, don't worry; you will as you read on.

In the chapters to come, we will break down the five *Faces* of the *Curse* and what recurring thoughts accompany each one so that you know without a doubt when the *Cursed Mind* is talking for you. It's important to note again that you will likely identify with every one of the *Faces* because they are all presentations of the one unconscious, egoic mind. Some may be more dominant than others, but all are still proverbial branches of the same tree. Learning to identify your own

Cursed Mind is crucial as the awareness of it is what begins the process of liberating yourself from it—hence stopping your recurring bad patterns.

When you read about any of the *Faces* and see yourself in the examples, do your best to avoid saying, *"That is me! I do that!"* and feel as if you cannot change, or beat yourself up for not knowing better. Instead, think to yourself, *"That is a function of my unconscious, conditioned mind"* and, in that moment, separate yourself and your being, from those thoughts. Look at any thought pattern you identify with as a habit you have but never noticed before. Once you see it, decide to work on quitting the habit. Who you are is unchangeable, but how you think is absolutely capable of transformation. And if you start to feel frustrated, discouraged, or defensive, just remember, the wound is where the light enters you.

Those who have elevated above *Cursed* thinking are the ones experiencing long-term, meaningful relationships. You can join them and achieve the same, but it will require you to dismantle your old thought process and rebuild it to be more in line with who you truly are at your core. You can be one of the success stories. It will take work and practice, but I promise that if you put in the effort you will see the results, and you will see them faster than you ever thought possible.

Chapter Three

Love or Wanting?

The woman returned to my office a week after our breakthrough conversation. She had a burning question that she needed answered.

"I've been thinking a lot about what you said," she began. "I have some things in my head that don't add up, and I'm confused."

"Sure, let's talk it out. What have you been thinking about?" I asked.

"I do understand that my thinking might be causing me to act in a way that is unattractive. When I'm around people who are nervous or obsessive about things, I find myself feeling a bit drained, and if it's a guy who's acting that way, I'm completely unattracted to him. What I don't understand is the part of the conversation that you and I had about me being so focused on myself. I mean, aren't you supposed to be the most important person in your life? Aren't you supposed to look out for yourself and put yourself before a man?" She searched my face for answers even as she was asking the question.

"I can see why you might ask this," I replied. "Many women are brought up with the 'you can take care of yourself' mentality and are taught to guard themselves against getting hurt by men. However, this mentality has been taken to the extreme and, quite frankly, is anti-love."

"How is that?" the woman asked.

I answered this question with another question of my own. "What is the definition of love?"

She pondered this for a moment. "The definition? I don't know the literal definition. If you wanted me to describe how it feels, I think I could do that."

"Alright let's hear it," I said. "What does love feel like to you?"

Her demeanor changed as she spoke. "It's a rush," she explained. "It's a feeling of wanting to be with someone all the time. It's feeling like they complete you, and not wanting to be with anyone else. When I'm in love, I'm tingly all over and just excited at the thought of the other person texting me."

"While that's a very common description, I'd say that is more infatuation or what most would call the feeling of 'falling in love,' which is feeling an extravagant urge to be with someone, but that feeling is typically short lived," I said. "It does not sustain the way love does."

"Then, what is love?" she asked.

"Love, in the simplest terms, is the benevolent concern for the good of another person," I explained. "It is devoid of anything selfish. When you find this romantically with someone, it is the gift of your devotion. You would put the other person's life before yours. Because when you love someone, you think of them before you think of yourself. Their life and happiness simply mean more to you than your own, and that makes you happy and fulfilled. That's love."

She thought it over before speaking. "So, if I'm the most important person in my life, I'm not open to love because I'm putting myself first. Is what you are saying?" the woman asked.

I nodded. "Exactly. If you are the most important person in your life, and you are entering your relationships putting yourself first, then how are you creating a place for love to happen? Should the guy put himself first, too? How would two people both putting themselves first ever connect or fall in love with each other? Do you think both of you should put you first because you're the woman?"

Love or Wanting?

The woman understood, but she was still confused. "I see what you are saying, but how can I put a man who I don't even know first?" she asked. "If I'm just beginning to see someone, I'm supposed to put their concerns over mine? I understand how this would work when I'm actually in the relationship. And I think I would put my husband first once he was my husband. I just don't understand how it works when you are just starting to date someone, though."

"A great question," I replied. "Thinking about the other person and acting from a place of love does not mean putting your needs and concerns aside for a complete stranger. Love doesn't mean compromising yourself. When you have lived your life with a self-absorbed mindset for so long, it would seem that being struck by an extraordinary feeling for someone else, what you may think to be love, would be the only way you would ever *want* to put someone else first. But that is the biggest myth that people tell themselves, and it is what keeps them lonely throughout their lives. The reality is that love is not something to reserve for one special man you have been waiting for. It's a way of life and a state of mind you carry with you always. Love is something you can give to everyone you encounter, regardless of how well you know them, without compromising anything. And for you to find romantic love and have it thrive, you have to get to the place where you do this."

"So, I should give love to everyone?" the woman asked.

"Yes. And I know that feels so opposite of everything you have thought about dating, getting men to chase you and how to keep them interested, but you can be a loving person and still be strategic about building a relationship. You can give love to someone and still have boundaries. Think about it like this: When you are absorbed in yourself, you are essentially blind to the world around you and the people in it. You see only what you need or want and disregard the rest. That is the opposite of love. When you learn how to act from your *Core Self,* however, you see everything and everyone. You are loving to all people because you know that love is not scarce, it's abundant and it's already within you. You are able to connect with people in a way you couldn't before, and then you find opportunities for love at every corner, whether you are in a relationship or not. You are putting so much love out into the world that it naturally comes back to you. And if you encounter someone you like but who is not capable of loving you, you know without a doubt that he is not the person you are meant to be with."

Love

It is important to know the true meaning of the word because thinking it is something else has most people chasing something else. As you will see in more detail throughout this book, your *Cursed Mind* will have you mistakenly pursuing the wrong relationships because it doesn't understand what love actually is, nor does it care to obtain it.

Love is a virtue representing all of human kindness. It is the unselfish and genuine concern for the good of another. People mistakenly assume they are in love when they get a gnawing in their gut or a rush of butterflies in their stomach, but that is the feeling of "wanting," not love. When you are truly in love, you cannot want or ache for more. That initial feeling of wanting quickly develops into something even greater—a sense of contentment and comfort. Love doesn't feel like you are standing on the edge of a 400-foot cliff. Love that is true and lasting feels like a warm, cozy room with a fireplace. It is safe, peaceful, and naturally happy.

When most people find romantic love, they put the other person first because they want to make them happy. But for people who are driven by their self-absorbed mind, that unselfish desire only lasts for so long. For some, it lasts until they know they have the other person or until they enter into a commitment. For others, it can be much shorter, and that selfless concern for someone else abruptly ends after being intimate or going on a few dates. This happens because the *Cursed Mind* has gotten what it wanted, what it thought it needed to feel good about itself, and has now returned to looking for something else in order to feel fulfilled. The ability to really develop love is lost on anyone who is functioning through their *Cursed Mind*, because a self-absorbed mind eventually turns its thoughts back to itself and what it wants, interrupting the outpouring of thoughts, concern, and love for the other person.

Unfortunately, many people today have forgotten what real love looks and feels like. They are driven only by what they want and how they can get it for themselves. This self-focused motivation propels their daily actions and goals in not just their relationships but everything else in their lives, too. While it's necessary to have goals and things you want to accomplish, becoming so obsessed by your own desires can turn you into an unhappy (and therefore unlikable) person. Excessive wanting of a relationship, or within a relationship, is dangerous because that feeling is what drives you to ignore red flags, excuse bad behavior, and hold onto someone who is wrong for you. You tell yourself it's because you are in love, but the truth is you are simply "in wanting" and have become unknowingly addicted to that bittersweet feeling that comes with desiring and obtaining whatever you've set your sights on. We will talk more about this specific aspect of the *Curse* in Chapter Six, The Wanter Mind.

On the opposite end of the spectrum, having a *Cursed Mind* also means concentrating more on being loved than giving it, which unknowingly causes you to search for the perfect person to satisfy that desire. If you tend to be attracted to people who are not good for you or not that interested in you, it's likely because you have not truly been looking for love and connection. Instead, you might have been trying to win over people who you find attractive or who your mind thinks will advance its feelings of worth (read: *"If he likes me, I must be good enough!"*). To yearn for someone to love you will keep you in an unhappy, self-absorbed, and generally painful mental space because the only thing you have control over is the love you give, not the love you receive.

You might be thinking, *"But I'm so empty. I'm so lonely. I'm so sad. I'm so frustrated. I won't be any of those things if someone loves me. And I'm trying to give love, but it keeps getting rejected."* On the surface it may seem that way, but when your motivation for love stems from the self-absorbed mind wrestling with its value, you either target the wrong people or emotionally drain the right ones. To put it another way, when you date or love with your *Cursed Mind*, any guy you become involved with will feel the inclination of you wanting him to give you some sort of fulfillment that you think you can't achieve on your own. Then, it is only a matter of time before he loses interest in you and moves on.

To be able to recognize love, invite it in, and sustainably nurture it, you have to become cognizant of the mindset that has you unconsciously repelling it. Everyone has the ability to change their self-focused mentality and rid themselves of the *Cursed Mind*. Just like you have full reign over your arms, legs, tongue, or toes, you also control your mind and can stop the very thing that has kept you from a happy, committed relationship. The key is to first fully understand the *Cursed Mind* and how it dominates you in different ways. Then, using certain techniques, retrain it to the way it naturally wants to think—the way it thought before outside influences shifted your focus. It's not about thinking positively or "willing things to happen"; doing those two things still inevitably keep the focus on you. It's about bringing your *Core Self* to the center of your being again because she is the one who acts purely from love, and that is the only way to ensure that your patterns change going forward.

PART II: THE FIVE FACES OF THE CURSE

It would be foolish of me to say breaking your *Curse* is as simple as taking the focus off yourself and turning it onto others or urging you to act from love rather than from self-interest. If it were that straightforward, there would be no need for this book. Unfortunately, when you've lived with a certain mindset for years, changing it isn't that easy. Attempting to switch focus will feel forced and fake when your mind has been habituated to think only about you for so long. In fact, you will often find yourself backsliding and unconsciously thinking the way you always have for a little while.

It's important to not get frustrated and give up just because it's tough. Telling yourself you can't change or shouldn't have to will only have you repeating the same past disappointments. Understand that transformation of this magnitude will take a little time. All the work you need to do in order to shed your *Curse* might seem overwhelming, but instead of looking at how far you have to go, get excited about who you will become: You are about to evolve into the best version of yourself.

Until now, you've likely confused your *Cursed Mind* for who you are. Therefore, we are going to first identify the five ways your *Cursed Mind* incarnates. Without knowing your *Cursed Mind* and the patterns it creates, you will confuse it for your *Core Self* time and time again.

Cursed?

Seeing yourself in the following stories and examples and learning how you might have unconsciously affected your past relationships may cause some sadness or frustration within you as you read. I'm sorry if that happens, but this is the only way I know how to help you. If I knew an easier way, I would have chosen it. The bright side is that with each of the five *Faces* of the *Curse*, there are also five Cures. The answer to solving this problem is coming; you just have to stick around long enough to get to it.

As you read this next section, it is very important to not hold on too tightly to who you think you are up until this point in your life. Any identity or label you put on yourself will only encumber you in this process, because it is very likely *Cursed* in some way. What do I mean by that? If you have unequivocally decided something about yourself, it can hurt your personal growth. If you have ever said the words, "That's just how I am," "I've always been that way," "I'm just an anxious person," or "I'm naturally competitive," you are holding on to a label that very well could inhibit your self-improvement, and therefore, your relationship outcomes.

In order to better yourself, you have to be open to questioning things about yourself and letting go of some of the stories your *Cursed Mind* has been telling your *Core Self* through the years. If you feel yourself resisting or justifying your own behavior as you read, know that your conditioned mind is just being challenged, and that is to be expected. Try not to fight any resistant feelings, and be open to the possibility of true transformation of yourself. Be mindful when resistance, frustration, or anger surfaces in your body. To really cure yourself of the *Curse,* try not to question the words you are reading, but instead question your own reaction to them. Is your *Core Self* reading and absorbing new information to help you, or is your *Cursed Mind* resisting anything that makes it feel wrong (and therefore less worthy)?

If you learn to recognize your unconscious mind habits and practice each of the Cures, the result will be your *Core Self* emerging, ready to fall in love and primed to receive it. Many of my clients have already

PART II

experienced life-changing results by ridding themselves of *Cursed* thinking and putting the Cures to practice. One client came to me on the heels of a bad breakup, and within three months of understanding her unconscious thought habits, she was already in the most loving, committed relationship she had ever had in her life. It is my greatest hope that you achieve the same.

By the time you are finished with this book, you should not only find yourself less stressed, anxious, sad, and frustrated about your romantic life but also more joyful, optimistic, and in control. Best of all, when love does enter your life, you will not have to worry about how to behave or fear that you will be rejected again. Instead, you will naturally embrace and experience love on a level you had never before imagined.

Are you ready?

Chapter Four

The Worrier/Lamenter Mind

When Ashlee came to see me, I was surprised that she was having any sort of trouble with men. She was not only breathtakingly beautiful, but she also had a warm personality and keen sense of humor. Ashlee was, on paper, the kind of woman men desired: fit, pretty, sweet, and fun. Unfortunately, those attributes didn't help her in her quest for love. Men avidly pursued her in the first few months, but shortly after the chase would end, they were practically running from her. Her most recent relationship had lasted three months and ended abruptly with her boyfriend texting her that he didn't see the two of them working out in the long run.

Ashlee wanted to find love and have a family, but as she entered her thirties, she began to worry that dream would never come true.

We sat on the couch one day as I listened to her talk about someone she'd recently started dating. As she spoke about their latest date, I heard her repeat something she'd said about her previous boyfriend: She wondered why this guy had not yet brought up the relationship talk. She was clearly frustrated, and after only three weeks of dating, she was getting anxious to find out where they stood and where the relationship was going.

This was a breakthrough. I had finally found the cause of Ashlee's pattern of guys coming on strong but then but quickly disappearing. She never spoke of the connection she had with any of them and rarely shared any deep, personal details. The only thing she wanted to discuss with me was how much I thought they liked her and how soon they would commit. To Ashlee, what mattered most was securing a relationship with whomever she was dating. The future of their relationship was always in the front of her mind. She could not enjoy the present moment and the process of getting to know someone, and it was the reason men continued to break things off. Ashlee's pattern was a result of her *Cursed Mind* being immersed in the future.

The Curse of the Worrier Mind

The most common symptom of the *Curse* is that it causes you to spend most of your time living in your own head, thinking and obsessing about yourself and your life. Sometimes that obsessive thinking is in the context of your future. When the *Cursed Mind* shifts into future thinking, it is rapidly speculating, worrying, and stressing about what will happen tomorrow, the next day, the following year, and so on. You may already know that you spend a great deal of time worrying, and have even accepted that part of yourself; but what you may not have noticed is all your worries are self-focused, future fears — things you are afraid might happen to you and could possibly endanger your feelings of contentment and self-worth down the line.

The *Cursed Mind* in future mode constantly thinks about *when things will happen for you*. When will you meet someone? When will he commit? When will you get engaged? The reason it continually considers these questions is because it has decided that your happiness and value as a person are contingent on the answers. When it ties both of those things to the future of any relationship, it causes you to spend all of your time obsessing about its fate and trying to control its outcome. Every date must turn into a relationship, and every relationship must turn into a marriage, or else you will feel like you've failed and weren't good enough to make it happen. You may have a timetable of what milestones you must achieve by a certain date, and you might even work backward to see how soon you must meet someone to realize this goal. If you have already passed the age where you think you should have been married, it's likely that you feel defeated and now must settle for a less-fulfilling backup option.

The big problem with having a *Cursed Mind* that is stuck in a pattern of future thinking is that you end up rarely content with the present moment. This can hurt your chance for a relationship with someone because being happy, accepting, and "in the moment" is absolutely crucial for establishing a connection and keeping it strong. If your mind is preoccupied with the worry of a hypothetical future outcome, however, that connection can't happen. If you are single, future thinking will make it difficult to find any joy with your current situation, even if your life is otherwise very good. Although it may seem that an opportunity for love would give you more hope and happiness because you would be moving closer to achieving your goal, the reality is that when your mind is programmed to obsess about the future, being with someone romantically often causes more stress and worry, not less.

In this chapter, we will first explore how the habit to "future think" can cause you to sabotage new opportunities for love and how this mindset not only blocks connection with someone but can also destroy the rapport and affection you have with him once you are in a relationship.

How Future Thinking Creates Self-Sabotage

When Ashlee began dating her last boyfriend, Jeff, her naturally fun and flirty attitude reeled him in. They had several great dates and began falling for each other. But after the first few weeks, the *Curse* began to surface in Ashlee. She decided she liked Jeff, and so she could no longer just *be* with him and appreciate their time together. Her mind shifted to the future, and she began obsessing about their relationship status. *"Where is this going? Is he going to want a relationship or not? I can't waste my time if this isn't going somewhere. I'm getting too old and I need someone who will commit quickly. OMG, what if this doesn't work out!"*

From that point on, every word Ashlee spoke and every action she took was motivated by some self-absorbed, future worry. When she was with Jeff, her mind was frequently elsewhere, scrutinizing everything he'd said and trying to decipher if it was a clue to the fate of their relationship. If he didn't text in a timely manner or wasn't affectionate enough, she panicked and questioned if things were going well. Sometimes she would drop hints about getting married or make jokes about her biological clock ticking to see what he would say because her self-absorbed mind wanted assurance of the future.

From Jeff's perspective, Ashlee seemed like two different people. One was fun and happy, but the other seemed overly stressed and easily upset. Being around her made him feel tense. He started feeling like Ashlee was watching his every move and always searching for his agenda. After a couple of months, his attraction to her began to wear off, and by the three-month mark, Jeff had completely checked out of the relationship.

When you begin liking someone, the possibility of the future you want actually happening causes your Worrier Mind to jump to attention. The voice in your head anxiously whispers, *"This is my chance for happiness! This is my shot at the life I want! I can't screw it up. If I do, I'll never be able to handle the disappointment. If I have to start all over with someone new, I'll just die!"* This is why you hate dating and find the whole process stressful. People may suggest that you should stop putting so much pressure on yourself and try to have more fun, but you can't even begin to understand how to do that. Your future focused mind makes it impossible to enjoy anything unpredictable and dating has no certainty. Much like reading spoilers for *The Bachelor* to find out who gets the final rose, your mind begs to know what will happen in your relationship, too. This was the root cause of Ashlee's pattern. Even though she craved a relationship, once she got into one, she never felt happy or relaxed. The uncertainty of where it was going haunted her at every stage. Her mind was always fast-forwarding to the end because that was what it was conditioned to do. Unfortunately, that caused her to rush the relationship and live in fear of it not working out instead of enjoying it in the moment.

Like Ashlee, many women subvert their opportunity for a relationship as a result of their self-absorbed future thinking. Even if they are meeting lots of men, or already have a partner, they fret and panic about what will happen next and when it will happen, which inevitably puts unspoken but very palpable pressure on themselves and any guy they might be dating. Quite often, they don't have to say a word, yet most anyone can sense their aim to secure the future they want for themselves. This is how the *Curse* of the Worrier creates self-sabotage; a woman aches for commitment not because she loves the guy or thinks he is the one, but because she is trying to placate her *Cursed Mind*, itching to know *what will happen to her*. For a Worrier, love is rarely her primary focus or motivation, and anyone she is involved with can feel that.

Future thinking is a dangerous habit to indulge in while dating because it will prompt you to take action that is incongruent with the circumstances of your relationship. In a moment we will discuss the most common mistakes and patterns brought on by the Worrier Mind and the consequences that follow, but first, let's talk about the energy it produces and how that energy affects people's perception of you.

The Worriers Vibe

The energy that your body gives off as your mind longs for the future is one of the many ill effects of this Face of the *Curse*. At the onset of someone's interest, you might feel as happy as a schoolgirl, completely present in the moment, and emanate a vibe that is stress-free and fun. However, when your mind starts to future think, worried that it won't achieve its long-awaited goal, that vibe changes. Consequently, when a man is hit with that energy, it can turn him off, regardless of how physically attractive he finds you. You know what energy I'm speaking about. Most people refer to it as anxiousness.

As someone who worries, your body suffers the regular consequence of anxiety, which can make you feel stressed, nauseated, and lead to panic attacks. If you have tried to let go of your anxiety before and failed, it may very well be because you used a popular, but insubstantial strategy; the most common being the attempt to prepare yourself for the worst-case scenario. *"If this relationship doesn't work out, I'll call my back-up guy"* Or, *"If I don't get married by the time I'm 30, I'll move to Australia, get plastic surgery, and start all over,"* for example. This doesn't work because you are still engaging the Worrier Mind and perpetuating the habit of thinking about yourself and your future. You also end up exhausting all your mental energy on situations that likely aren't going to happen. Do that a few times a day, everyday, and you can see why you're always mentally drained by the end of it. And let's be honest, how much has planning for the worst really reduced any of your fears?

Anxiety is palpable, so you aren't the only one that feels the affect of it. Other people feel it, too. It can cause trouble before you even meet someone. Like Cara, who is 27 and single. She contacted me because she was tired of going out and never getting approached. She went to lots of different events and happy hours, and continually put herself in male-friendly environments, yet she often ended up talking only to the person she'd come with. Her girlfriends met men effortlessly, even while they were simply out grocery shopping. Why did they have such good luck and she didn't?

When I sat down with Cara, I asked her what she thought about when she was out prospecting for men. She told me that most of the time, she thought about how much she wanted to meet someone and wondered when it was going to happen. After only a few minutes of being somewhere, she began worrying that the night was going to be another bust, and she would never meet anyone she liked. Her mind spun out of control with thoughts of being alone forever and never feeling anything for anyone again.

What Cara didn't realize was that even though she physically put herself in places where someone could approach her, mentally she was miles away, in the projection of a bleak future. Because she wasn't paying acute attention to everyone around her, her eyes were either cast down in heavy thought or darting around the room in search of her future boyfriend. Guys who noticed her perceived her as unapproachable because of her body language. They were looking for a sign that she was friendly and available: eye contact, a smile, or even just a positive or easy-going vibe. Cara was not able to communicate any of those things because her *Cursed Mind* kept her from enjoying herself in the moment. She missed opportunities to meet people because her mind was always in the future, making her anxious and affecting other people's perception of her.

The *Cursed Mind* firmly believes that a secure relationship is your way out of the misery called anxiety. *"If I was at least dating someone, I would feel better,"* it seems to say. Or, *"If I knew I was his girlfriend, I'd relax,"* and *"Once we get engaged, I'll calm down."* What you may not realize is that the anxiety and suffering you feel isn't coming from being single. It's not coming from *any situation* you are currently in—it's only coming from your self-absorbed future thinking.

Why does future thinking give you anxiety? Because having your body exist in today but your mind anchored in tomorrow (or any other time that isn't now) splits your being, which feels terrible. It's akin to living in Virginia but wishing every day that you lived in the Land of Oz or some other impossible travel destination. Your body is here but your mind longs to be somewhere else, and won't stop trying to get there. How could living this way make you feel anything other than miserable? The physical misery of wanting so badly to be in the future *is* anxiety. And because you are feeling miserable, your Worrier Mind holds on even more so to the hope that tomorrow (or any time in the future) will be better and feel better.

The problem is, the future never really comes. When it does, it's not the future anymore. It's the present. The present is where everything in life happens, and in a romantic relationship, the present moment is the most important moment. But this Face of the *Curse Mind* doesn't care about the present; it only cares about the future. This goes back to the core essence of the *Cursed Mind* and its belief that it is not yet whole and complete. It looks to the future for the opportunity to have the self-fulfillment it believes it does not currently have. If you decided you were worthy and had all you needed right now, your Worrier Mind would have no purpose and cease to exist. And so, in an effort to stay in control of you and continue its survival, it continues to think that the future is better than today, and stresses about the likelihood of obtaining that future, which creates an anxious energy.

In my experience there is only one way to end anxiety and change the vibe that comes with it and that is by abandoning the thought habits that produce it. If you learn how to cure yourself of self-absorbed future thinking, the natural energy of your *Core Self* can shine through, allowing people to see who you really are without the uneasy and tense cloak of anxiety weighing you down. If you are ready to meet someone, but having difficulty generating conversations, getting guys to approach you, and creating meaningful connections, it may be time to commit to ceasing your future thinking once and for all.

Think about how many opportunities you miss every day because you are caught up thinking about tomorrow? Think about how many men you pass as you go out to lunch, work out at the gym, or even walk to your car. Are you looking at people and smiling as they walk by, or are you lost in thought and wearing a blank look on your face? Or worse, is your head buried in your phone? If your problem is meeting guys and being approached, it's likely that simply not being present is keeping you secluded from the world. In essence, you've created a dark tunnel in which you travel to and from one destination to the next. You might have thought you were just cursed with misfortune, but the reason you have not been successful with meeting new people is due to your own thinking. Fortunately, that also means you have the power to change your luck. Remember this: When you keep yourself focused on the future, you keep yourself absent from the present. And being present is of the utmost necessity when it comes to finding love.

Acting from the Future

Let's slow down now and take a careful look at how this Face of the *Curse* starts out as thoughts in your head but quickly turns into real, troubling action. Obsessing about the future causes extreme impatience with life in the present day, and impatience in dating can lead to major mistakes. For example, say you exchange numbers with a guy you had a good conversation with, but you still worry that he may not contact you. As the hours roll by, your future-focused mind cannot stop thinking and eventually triggers full-blown anxiety. Your *Cursed Mind* in Worrier mode says, *"Why isn't he contacting me already? Maybe he thinks I'm not that interested! Should I reach out and text him instead? What if he was perfect, and now our chance for a relationship is over? What if no one ever likes me again? I need to do something or I'll never get married."* Even though only a short amount of time has passed, your mind has made you antsy and you are unable to wait for the guy to make his move. The intense feeling that your opportunity for love is slipping away starts to motivate you. And this is where all the problems begin.

Your impatience causes you to take action—maybe you send him a text, or you add him on social media so he won't forget about you. Regardless of what action it is that you take, it is motivated by obsessive fears of a future you are trying to obtain (getting into a relationship with him) or attempting to avoid (ending up alone). This is an example of how this Face of the *Cursed Mind* results in self-sabotage. Your need to have the future of this relationship play out *right now* prevents you from playing it cool, timing things well, and allowing it to progress naturally. The guy, who was attracted to you and enjoying the thrill of having his interest piqued, might see your text or add and feel a little less interested in pursuing you because you are now pursuing him. If and when he responds, you will likely continue to behave according to what you are afraid *might* happen in this relationship instead of what is *actually* happening. When you act based on a projection of a sad, lonely future, your interactions with any guy will inevitably come off as desperate and anxious, and the vibe he feels from you will be needy or overeager. Ultimately, being absorbed in yourself and your future ends up distorting the true picture of your relationship in the present day. You misread signs and signals from someone and then take impulsive action based on fear instead of reality.

Another way future thinking sabotages love is by interfering with your chance to connect with someone when you do get a date with him. When you first meet someone, he's not only assessing his attraction to you, he is also considering the rapport, or what some people call "the spark," between the two of you. Self-absorbed thinking disables your ability to create that connection, which is why a guy might seem highly interested in you when he asks you out but seemingly loses interest after you spend a few hours together.

Let's say that the guy who asked for your number in the previous scenario texts you and actually sets up a date. You meet him and are excited to get to know him, but as you are talking, your *Cursed Mind* starts racing with future thoughts like these: *"Will he ask me out again? Will he want a serious relationship? He said he is going out of town next week. Should I text him while he's away so he will want to see me when he returns? I think he could be the one. I wonder how many children he wants?"* Although the night has only just begun, you have fast-forwarded through the date and are now thinking about what's going to happen next. Because you are not focused on the present, the simple act of being engaged in what is going on *right now*, you do not make a connection. You miss half of what he says, in fact. You don't catch that serious comment he makes or laugh at his subtle but funny quip. Your *Core Self* was not present due to your future thinking and analyzing the possibility of this date resulting in a relationship for you.

When your mind feverishly wanders with uncontrollable *Cursed* thoughts, you make mistakes without even knowing it, and you block the connection between you and the other person. The guy is trying to get to know you in the present, while you are busy thinking about your potential future. He didn't realize that you were future thinking, of course, but he certainly did notice the connection he was hoping for wasn't there. If he's highly attracted to you, he might keep in contact with you for a little while, but without feeling a connection, the relationship won't grow beyond a certain point. Any attempt you make to get him more interested (e.g., being slow to respond to his texts, or using a little "sense of urgency") won't work because first and foremost a guy must feel there is compatibility, understanding, and rapport building between you. If that base isn't there, there's nothing you can do to entice him further.

Beyond failing to connect with a guy, *Cursed* thinking on a date can also cause you to miss clues that can give insight into his character and personality, which is vital information for choosing a good partner. You are so busy thinking about you that you don't learn much about him. For some men, not having a strong connection with a woman might be acceptable as long as they are getting one of their other needs met (e.g., regularly having sex), so they will continue on with a subpar relationship. Thus, another consequence of not being present while dating someone is that you can land yourself in a relationship that isn't right for you. Quite often it's not until it's too late—after the ring is on their finger, the wedding is paid for, or the kids are born—that some women with this *Curse* discover that they didn't choose their partner wisely.

When it comes to finding the right person, nothing is more important than carefully and thoughtfully getting to know someone in the present so that the future you want is the one you get. Some worriers think that any relationship is better than no relationship, but that is only because the *Cursed Mind* fears that remaining single means you are unlovable. When you believe that to be true and allow it to drive you in your selection process, the outcome is always poor and disappointing. This is why breaking the habit to future think will be a must for finding and connecting with the right person.

What-If Scenarios

Sadly, many women live their entire lives in a state of waiting for the future to play out. The thought in their head is always, *"When this happens, I will be happy,"* whether it's finding a boyfriend, getting engaged, being married, or anything else. This thought, which is rather unconscious within them, causes them to be completely dissatisfied with their present situation. While they silently stress or openly fret about an impending outcome to materialize, the *Cursed Mind* tries to cope with the time between then and now. There is a big gap that needs to be filled between the present and the future with lots of potential problems and circumstances that could pop up during the wait time and potentially derail the plan. In attempt to prepare for anything that could arise, the *Cursed Mind* fills that large gap of time with "What-if" scenarios.

What-if scenarios are a Worrier's best friend (because they are always together) and worst nightmare (because they create an enormous amount of anxiety.) The future-focused mind creates the atmosphere for them to happen and then engages in these hypothetical occurrences as a way to get ready for them (in case they happen.) If the mind can foresee a potential problem before it occurs, then it believes it has a better chance for controlling it or, at the very least, mentally readying itself for the blow of disappointment. What you might never stop to realize is that all your time, energy, and emotions are spent on an imaginary problem—something that may or may not ever happen.

Ashlee, for instance, let what-if scenarios dominate her thoughts whenever she wasn't with Jeff. Earlier this year, when her birthday was nearing, she became extremely anxious when thinking about what he would do to celebrate this occasion with her. *"Why hasn't he mentioned my birthday yet? Is he just going to let it pass? OMG, he's probably forgotten! Should I break up with him now so I'm not hurt when he doesn't do anything for me? Or what if he remembers last minute and asks me out on my birthday at 5 p.m.? Should I go or should I tell him I have plans? Maybe I should make plans now, and then he'll learn the hard way to plan ahead better."* I told Ashlee she was spending too much time mulling over what *could* happen on her birthday, which was all rooted in the fear that she would be disappointed and her *Cursed Mind* feeling like a fool. I reinforced that Jeff was a very nice guy who would do something for her, although we couldn't know what yet and that was okay. I asked her to be conscious of how her mind was creating anxiety in her and urged her to disengage from the what-if scenarios. When her birthday arrived, Jeff took her out to a nice dinner and gave her a dozen roses. Later, when I asked her if she enjoyed her day she replied: "It was fine. He asked what I was doing for the holidays. Do you think that means he doesn't want to spend it with me? Should I make plans with my family and not invite him? Why would he ask me that and then not invite me to his house? Do you think he's losing interest?"

Being so consumed by these imaginary situations never prepares you like you think it will. The only certainty that comes with what-if scenarios is anxiety and mental exhaustion. If you do secure a commitment and get married, thinking this way will not only wear on you but drain your partner, too. The *Cursed Mind* does not stop once you reach the goal you have set for yourself because it is programmed to look for what else it needs to feel worthy, regardless of your life situation. If you have this Face of the *Curse,* you will continue to look to the future for fulfillment because that is what your mind has been conditioned to do for years. You will simply find new things to worry about, even if you are married and have a family. Whether you stress silently or vents your concerns openly, the result is living with a tense and anxious version of you. *"What if we can't have kids? What if they have health problems? What if you lose your job? What if we can't afford our life? What if, what if, what if, what if?!"* The partner or spouse of the Worrier is often at a loss for how to deal with this. How can anyone really deal with a problem that isn't a problem yet? Worriers think they are being proactive, but what they are really doing is attempting to control each and every aspect of life, which can make living with them exasperating.

If this sounds like you, stop and consider how your habit to future think will affect the man in your life. Once you finally do get married, how will living with you and your worries of tomorrow disturb your relationship with your husband? What will it do to the love between you? Being in a relationship with a person who constantly contemplates worst-case scenarios and tries to control everything that could happen to her sucks all the joy and spontaneity out of life. It takes what could be fun and adventuresome and makes it taxing and depleting. It overlooks what could be enjoyed right now by speculating what could or should happen next. And for what? How can you really know if the future you *think* you should have is really the one that is best for you? Especially now that you know the *Cursed Mind* has been the one plotting your course.

Mary Jane became an example of how future thinking can worry you into and out of a relationship. She was a very anxious person who never stopped thinking about getting married and having kids. She scared most guys away within just a few weeks of dating, so it took her many years to finally find The One. At 40, she finally got married. With medical assistance, she was able to have a child. Seemingly, she got what she wanted, and the future she perpetually stressed about having was finally hers. However, her *Curse* was not cured, so she worried about other aspects of life, albeit on a much smaller scale. She worried every day about not getting her child to bed on time and about discipling him the right or wrong way. She worried about the strange mole on his leg, what she should wear to her husband's Christmas party, how much weight she had gained, and everything else under the sun. Her husband tried to be supportive, but over the course of two years, her worrying had gotten to him, and he asked for a divorce. "No part of our life was easygoing and happy because she was always concerned about something bad happening," he said. "It was no way to live. It was depressing for me."

Because Mary Jane never rid herself of her *Curse* and the habit to future think, she continued to do it her whole life. From the outside, it seemed she was only planning for the worst, but looking more deeply into her thoughts, most things she worried about did not have consequences as severe as she feared. All these so-called problems were self-focused worries rooted in avoiding the pain of not feeling good about herself. She spent more time thinking about that than she did thinking about her relationship with her husband. Her need to feel good and cautiously protect her sense of worth in the future ended up destroying the very love she worked so hard to get.

What About Planning?

Perhaps you believe there is no way to stop thinking about your future, especially because you're reaching an age where most other people are married with children and you don't even have a prospect on the horizon. You don't want to date someone who isn't ready to settle down, and besides that, you are a planner by nature. While forethought is certainly not a bad thing, and you absolutely should ask a guy early on about his thoughts on marriage, you must realize that the *Cursed Mind* has you doing much more than just planning for the future. It lives for it, believing that happiness lies somewhere far away from you right now, while simultaneously fearing that you will never reach that place. *Fear* is the driving force behind every thought and interaction you have if you are *Cursed* with future thinking. Fear of the future creates anxiety; which creates an energy that ultimately counteracts your goal. Any guy will feel how anxious, uncertain, and eager you are. This is why when you ask simple date questions like, "What are you looking for in a relationship?" or "Do you want to have a family?" which my other books recommend doing early on, your delivery does not come off well. There is a palpable difference in asking those questions because you're thinking about yourself and what the answer means for your future, and asking because you want to get to know the guy. When you are *Cursed*, you are afraid of how he will answer, and you may even ignore his response. When your *Core Self* asks the question, you no longer feel that fear, thus your delivery is more confident and you're more accepting of his reply.

The same thing can be said when you first enter into a committed relationship. If you immediately create a Wedding Board on Pinterest or secretly pray that your new relationship will be the one that will deliver you from singlehood, you can actually hinder the progress you are hoping for. When you know the other person has good relationship qualities—as I talk about in *Was It Something I Said*—and he has mutually stated his hopes for a family, you then have to sit back and savor the relationship for what it is for the time being. You have to date *presently*. There will be a point when you both must discuss the next step as a couple, but the key is to wait until that time actually comes. Let the relationship ripen to that stage, and then speak about where it is headed. If you don't know exactly when the time is right, because you always feel like you are ready to talk about it, it's because you have been led by the *Cursed Mind* for so long that you now believe that every interaction must have purpose that works toward the goal for your future. But here is why that inevitably works against you: When you are constantly trying to move things along with your thoughts, words, and behavior—whether that means becoming exclusive, getting married, or anything else you want—your interactions with a man won't be relaxed, easy, or loving. Instead, the guy will sense you want more from him without you having to say a word. That feeling of "wanting more" can manifest as pressure, neediness, or desperation, but mostly it just comes off in one extremely adverse sensation: feeling used.

There is no motivation that is more anti-love than using someone. When you desire a relationship for self-focused reasons, you are using the other person to satisfy your own wants. Not wanting to be single anymore, fearing you'll end up alone, wanting security or a certain lifestyle, or simply craving to be loved are all self-focused motivations that will inevitably make a man feel he's being used. When you are driven by any of these reasons, you are not genuinely looking for love, and men who could offer you a loving relationship will feel that from you.

The need to control the future comes from the self-absorbed mind wanting to know it will be okay. It lives in fear of not being okay and suffering some ill-fated consequence. Not being okay in the future *is* its greatest worry. But the reality is that *all you will ever be able to know is that you are okay right now.* You will never know how you are tomorrow because tomorrow never really comes! When it does, you aren't "in tomorrow." You are still "in today." Therefore, making *now* the priority in your life, and accepting that you will only ever need to deal with *this moment*, is how you cure this Face of the *Curse*.

The Curse of the Lamenter Mind

Maybe you are someone who spends more time stressing over things that have already occurred. Perhaps you spend a great deal of time living in your head, but you're more likely to think about yesterday than tomorrow. If you find yourself frequently replaying conversations and events like a broken record and have trouble letting go of mistakes and disappointments, you may have the mind of a Lamenter who spends much of her time living in the self-absorbed past.

Having a past focused mind means that you mentally hang on to hurtful or disturbing events and the emotional pain that followed as if it occurred just yesterday. It doesn't matter if something happened last week or 20 years ago; the memory (or the emotion you felt) remains fresh in your head because this Face of the *Cursed Mind* unconsciously believes that all situations in your life are an indication of who you are as a person. Therefore, deep down you believe that most past events happened to you because of who you are, and if someone else were in your shoes, a different outcome might have occurred.

Bailey, for instance, was a client whose mind was conditioned to think about the past. Her parents never gave her the emotional support needed growing up because they were very self-absorbed themselves. As Bailey grew into adulthood, she constantly lamented about how terrible her upbringing was, and any time she got a boyfriend, her past thinking caused problems. Her last boyfriend, Jarod, was a good guy who cared for her, but he was constantly accused of not being emotionally supportive. If he spent a few extra minutes texting his friends, or forgot to immediately ask how a work issue was going at the office, Bailey would blow up at him for being "just like her Dad." Bailey wasn't aware of it, but her past thinking corrupted how she viewed her present day relationships and it was the main reason she had a pattern of losing boyfriends at the year mark.

Many women subvert their opportunity for a relationship as a result of past focused thinking. If you keep enough stories of failure or pain in your head, you begin to believe that *all* men are bad or out to hurt you, and you start to expect that the next person you love will do the same. You might never see a new relationship with fresh eyes because this Face of the *Cursed Mind* taints every experience in the present with the past.

While other people may have no memory of childhood or might easily move on from something considered traumatic, someone with a past focused mind carries the effects of the past with them every day. If you grew up feeling unloved by a parent, your mind will convince you it was because you are somehow unlovable or unworthy of their love. You haven't consciously considered the alternative: That the person who was supposed to love you was deeply flawed and *Cursed*, too. You may unknowingly subscribe to the idea that how your parents loved you is how you should be loved by anyone else. Only by seeing the illusion in this and that how someone loves you is indicative of their capability—and not your value—can you change any of your relationships going forward.

As I mentioned earlier, the past first plants the seed of the *Curse* and that means how the *Cursed Mind* operates is in large part due to your history, whether you are aware of that or not. In a way, having a *Cursed Mind* means you are a Lamenter to some degree, although it might not be the primary *Face* of your own *Curse Mind*. There is an easy way to know if you are a predominately a past thinker, however, because if you are, you inevitably hold grudges. You might hold grudges against people, or grudges against life itself. The underlying *Cursed* thought that fuels a grudge is, *"That shouldn't have happened to me! Now I can't be happy because that happened."* If you often think back on your past and find yourself feeling those sentiments, your mind is likely conditioned to "past think."

You might hope that the right romantic relationship will remedy the pain you carry from a rocky or traumatic past, but only recognizing your habit of self-absorbed thinking can do that. Until you understand and decide to cure your habit of past thinking, you will continue to lug all your old emotions and judgments with you as you move through life, adding more as you go, which will keep you perpetually sad, angry, and bitter. As I said with the *Curse* of the Worrier, so is true with the Lamenter: It is not that being single is keeping you lonely and depressed; it is your habit to past think that is doing that.

How Past Thinking Creates Self-Sabotage

Eventually, past thinking over time leads to one very dangerous place: resentment. You may become hardened and bitter after years of keeping a running tally of the many ways men have slighted or disappointed you. This can create a wall that is hard to penetrate, prompting people to say, "You always have your guard up" or "You never let me in." In addition, the resentment you feel radiates from your body without having to say or do much at all. Eckhart Tolle sums this up well: "While you think about and feel your grievance (i.e., resentment), its negative emotional energy can distort your perception of an event that is happening in the present or influence the way in which you speak or behave toward someone in the present." Therefore, instead of starting a new relationship with curiosity, hope, and openness, the resentment causes you to begin with caution, apprehension, and a guarded heart. This makes it difficult, if not impossible, for you to have a chance at love with anyone.

Jean, who was nearing 30, kept overlaying her past relationships onto her present ones. If a guy took too long to text her back, she would immediately disregard him as a prospect because one of her old boyfriends who had cheated on her was also slow to respond. If an app date asked to meet her somewhere closer to his neighborhood instead of her own, she assumed he didn't respect her enough and was lazy like another guy she had dated. Jean presumed she knew exactly who a man was because she evaluated everyone through the eyes of her past and continued to carry the resentment into all her romantic opportunities. For women who are conditioned by this Face of the *Cursed Mind*, seeing their present situation through the lens of the past is how they sabotage most opportunities for love before they even get started.

While it is useful to learn from old experiences in order to avoid making the same mistake twice, there is a stark difference between using the past as a learning tool and living in fear that the past will repeat itself.

For instance, Nora, who was abandoned by her father, said to me, "I don't let go of my past because those who don't know history are doomed to repeat it." She believed the guys in her life might walk out on her at any moment, just as her dad did, so she entered each new relationship with suspicion and became overly emotional without warning. Because she was waiting for the guy to disappoint her (because they always had before), any sign of discord put her into a tailspin. The problem was that some of the men she dated were actually good guys with honorable intentions, but because Nora treated them as if they were criminals with a nefarious agenda, they felt insulted and backed away. As someone with a past focused mind, she worried she could be hurt yet again, so she never allowed anyone to get close to her. Ironically, because she lived in fear that each relationship would leave her heartbroken, they always did.

There is a healthy way to apply what you have learned from a previous relationship to a current one, and that is to be observant and ask good questions when you are beginning to get to know someone. If you have been in several tumultuous relationships with people who abuse alcohol, for example, you likely know the signs to look out for, as well what questions to ask a guy before you get too deeply involved. If he tells you he drinks 4–5 times a week, has blacked out recently, or has a couple of DUIs, you can be fairly certain that a relationship with him will parrot one from your past. Yes, he is a different person; however, with so many fish in the sea, it is best if you keep on searching for someone who doesn't present the same potential problem as your last boyfriend or husband. The real task will be turning down such a guy, even if you know it's the smart thing to do, because the *Cursed Mind* engrossed in the past loves what is familiar. Reminders of the past bring a certain level of comfort and attraction, even if it is so obvious to others that the person or situation is bad. Walking away from someone will get a lot easier once you break the *Curse* because you will be able to recognize your attraction to a man as real and genuine or just a past habit. We will discuss how to do that in Part III.

If you have a Lamenter's Mind, you might fear getting hurt, but still believe a loving relationship will help you come to terms with your past and give you back the happiness that was taken from you long ago. The problem is that the past is over and cannot be changed, so no man can assist you in in rectifying your feelings. Because the *Cursed Mind* doesn't know this, it continues to look for someone outside itself to heal the pain from the past and is often disappointed when that person fails to help. Then that relationship becomes yet another example of how men historically aren't trustworthy, reliable, or genuine and the pattern continues.

The Lamenter's Vibe

The past truly has no meaning on who you are today. It is only significant to the self-absorbed mind because the past can give it a story about your identity. The past is what the mind uses to decide how worthy you are based on events that have happened in your life until now. Where in the past were you slighted? Where were you hurt? Where were you wronged? Ah there is the story! The Lamenter Mind uses the story and creates a bigger, overall story about you. The overall story is usually, "How I'm always taken advantage of", or "How no one respects me." It could also be, "How I'm unlucky in life and love." Whatever the story is, it's usually a sad one that makes you feel bitter, angry or dejected. The people you come in contact with don't know what story you carry around but they feel the vibe of the story. Your vibe can be dismal and draining, if the story is depressing. Or your vibe could feel combative or agitated if the story is about you constantly being mistreated. Some Lamenters come to a point where they don't have to even think about their past story any longer. Over the years the negative energy from the story finally attaches itself to their body and it is there wherever they go, whatever they do, without thinking about it at all. Any event that occurs that is similar to their overall story – someone breaks up with them, or disappoints them in some way – is then added to their ongoing saga and grows their negative energy, making it bigger and stronger. Eckhart Tolle calls this the Pain-Body and if this sounds like you, I'd urge you to read more about it in his books.

Pauline, for instance, was a successful lawyer who was very smart and attractive. Lots of men noticed her and asked her on dates. Pauline had trouble getting a follow-up dates, however. One day she asked me to follow her to meet someone she matched with on Hinge so I could figure out what she was doing that might prevent a second date. As I watched and listened, it was noticeable that Pauline's energy was very heavy and serious. She didn't laugh much on the date and she brought up how guys had betrayed and hurt her more than once. (This was a first meeting, mind you!) On this date, she asked the guy if he had ever been dishonest with a woman and made a joke about how he probably wouldn't admit it if he had. When the date was over, Pauline said she thought the meet-up went really well and asked what I thought. She only remembered making the joke and became defensive when I told her that the past was taking a toll on her natural energy and she would have to work to let go of it in order for her dating pattern to change. Pauline thought her energy was light and jovial, but I didn't observe it to be that way and since the guy from that night never followed up with her, it's likely he agreed with me.

Being aware of your past story and how it has shaped your thinking is step one in breaking the Lamenter's *Curse* and the vibe that accompanies it. No one has a childhood or relationship history that is devoid of disappointment or hurt, but those who learn to see their unhappy memories separate from their value and are able to let go of what happened, do not suffer the burden of the heavy, pessimistic energy of the Lamenter. Do not concern yourself now with how you will let go of your past. We will get to that part. For now, just keep learning the ways it can interfere with your present day situation so that you can be aware of the problem.

Acting From the Past

Let's slow down now and discuss how past thinking can lead to making mistakes early on in a relationship. Constantly reliving the past means that whenever something happens to you, you spend much of your time reviewing and analyzing it. You go over things you said or that were said to you so frequently that it often keeps you up at night. If a guy texts you, you can't just appreciate it and carry on from there. Your lamenting mind instead ponders, *"Why did he text me so late? What does that mean? Why didn't he use punctuation? Is he a player? Last week he said he was busy on Friday and now it's Friday and he's texting me?"* It is easy to claim that you like studying men and merely enjoy speculating their motives and feelings; however, if that was the truth, your body would not feel the angst and unrest that it does when you engage in this type of thinking. The reason you constantly evaluate the things that happen in your relationships is because you are assessing your worth through the interactions you have with men. When they do something that you feel might be potentially threatening to your worth, like cancelling a date or forgetting something important that you told them, your self-absorbed mind becomes obsessed with thinking about it. You are always looking for the hidden meaning in a guy's message, trying to deduce not only his level of interest but also how secure (good or not good) you should feel about yourself.

Although on occasion it is fun to replay a date in your head, it's important to understand the ramifications of obsessive past thinking, or what most people call over analyzing. When you think too much about something that's happened in the past, and especially if you are trying to glean something about yourself from it, your perception becomes distorted. In other words, events replayed in your mind will look different than how they actually occurred. You then run the risk of acting from a skewed reality, based on what you think happened instead of what actually happened.

For example, you may replay a first date over and over again, hoping to come to the resolution that you made a good impression. You may regret something you said out of nervousness and grapple with your date's reaction. The more you think about it, the more certain you become that your date took your comment the wrong way and now he might not be interested in you anymore. After thinking about the conversation dozens of times, you convince yourself that what you said was, in fact, taken the wrong way, and you must explain yourself immediately. You then do something you should not do, such as initiate a text and over-explain yourself.

Making a move in an attempt to fix a problem that might not have even occurred is what starts most problems for someone who functions under this Face of the *Cursed Mind*. When your course-correcting strategy fails and the guy responds negatively or not at all, you can be immediately remorseful of doing anything in the first place. It's difficult to stop this pattern, however, because the self-absorbed mind continues to search for worth and inevitably jumps to take action when it feels devalued. The trick is to catch your mind when it engages in this thought pattern and quickly remind yourself that over-thinking something usually makes everything worse, not better.

If the opportunity for a relationship has definitively passed and the guy you were so excited about has unquestionably moved on, the Lamenter Mind tends to go through a period of self-loathing, which creates yet another setback. Hours, days, or weeks can be spent searching for the perfect words or actions that would have gotten you a better outcome and kept the guy interested. You think it's because had you done something differently, you would have gotten a happier ending. Had you dressed better, listened closer, asked more questions, asked less questions, or (insert anything you could have done but didn't at the time), the possibility of love would still be there. This is a past-focused thought habit called "should-have" scenarios—the hindsight equivalent of what-ifs. The *Cursed Mind* wants to find words or actions you could have said or done to produce better results, convinced that you are the reason a relationship didn't work out.

One of my clients, Kristen, was very much this way. As soon as she started seeing someone, all she wanted to discuss with me was the mistakes she had made on her dates and what she should have done to get the result she wanted. When she started dating Paul, she vowed to follow the standard dating rules in the hopes it would lead to a relationship with him. What she didn't count on was that her Lamenter Mind brought excessive analyzing with her on their dates, making her seem jumpy, hesitant, and tense.

When we met after her date with Paul, she launched into her usual cycle of should-haves: "He sat next to me on the couch and I tensed up again. I know he felt how nervous I was, and that's why he didn't spend the night. I should have smiled at him and moved in closer! Do you think he would have stayed over if I had done that? He asked me what I was doing this weekend, and I blanked. I said I had so much to do because I wanted to seem busy. I'm sure he would have asked me out if I had said anything else but that! I made it seem like I was too busy for him. I am kicking myself for how the whole night went! Don't you think I could have said something and gotten him to stay over? What should I have said?"

Although it's beneficial to learn good communication techniques and learn from mistakes on dates, believing that saying the perfect thing or making the perfect move would massively change the direction of any relationship is a fallacy not worth ruminating on. If Kristen had not been obsessively thinking and calculating every move in her head and instead focused more on engaging with Paul, things might have gone differently. Her energy would have been lighter and more relaxed, and he may have felt more connected to her. Or, she might have seen a red flag because she was focused on really getting to know him instead of being fixated on how she was being perceived and getting the outcome she wanted.

"Should-have" scenarios are a mind pattern of the *Curse* that you have to be cognizant of when they occur. If you engage in them and allow them to create an emotional reaction in you, you can sink to a new level of despair. Or worse, they can cause you to take impulsive action in attempt to reverse what happened. If you repeatedly find yourself in situations where you want to "correct" how a date or relationship concluded, and your actions to do so never seem to restore your chances for love, you may be letting "Should-have" scenarios get the best of you. Remember, any action that stems from the *Cursed Mind* and not the heart, will inevitably fail you.

Wasting Time

The long-term sabotage of the Lamenter Mind comes not from course correcting but from wasting time or putting energy into a relationship with little hope for lasting love. A client of mine lamented for six months over a man she went out with once from a dating app. She had a really good time and thought he was very attractive but never heard from him after their first and only date. She cried for half a year over him (a guy she barely knew) and swore off dating for good. Her friends could not believe how upset she was over the situation, but that's only because they didn't understand the mind of a Lamenter. She was not crushed because she was in love with the guy; she was crushed because her past-focused mind could not stop thinking about the experience. As with anyone who is *Cursed*, she took his disinterest as indication of her desirability and worth (or lack thereof), and getting over that is much more difficult than accepting that the guy wasn't into her.

As if ruminating over a lost opportunity isn't bad enough, past-focused thinking also keeps you in limbo, waiting for someone who does not have high interest in you and causing you to waste valuable time, neglecting other guys who may have real potential. If you had a handful

The Worrier/Lamenter Mind

of dates or a couple of hookups with someone that went seemingly well, you might keep replaying those events in your head, despite the guy distancing himself or decreasing contact. The habit to past-think keeps you feeling connected to him, all while you are disconnected from the reality of the situation. I call this "mentally dating".

When you continue to "mentally date" someone by constantly thinking about old times with them, and especially if you still have some level of contact with them, you can waste weeks, months, or even years of your life hoping that a relationship will transpire. The past focused mind is notorious for spending a lot of time on someone with very little promise because it loves to think about the unresolved past.

Adrienne, a long-standing client of mine, was a prime example. She had met Wynn, a professional basketball player, while he was on the road. He spotted her in the crowd and asked his manager to bring her to meet him. They spent that night together, and Adrienne was overwhelmed with emotion at being the one girl Wynn had picked from the crowd. He told her he couldn't wait to see her again and texted her often over the next few weeks. They went on a few dates, but Wynn's contact soon began to slow. His texts became more and more infrequent; finally, Adrienne was the only one initiating their messages.

When she came to me, Adrienne was in tears. She wanted to know how she could fix this. How could she get Wynn as interested as he was that very first night?

There was nothing Adrienne could do, however. Wynn had made it clear that he was no longer interested in her by his waning contact, but Adrienne could not accept this. She kept telling me how he had picked her from a sea of women and had told her several times how beautiful he thought she was.

For the next year, she continued to pursue Wynn by texting him, showing up at his games, and finding excuses to run into him. She truly believed that the past stood firm. If he was interested before, that meant something. They had a connection, and she would work every day to get it back. She kept replaying the night they'd met in her head, and she was living and acting from that place in the past instead of from what was happening in the present day.

Whenever the present is bleak, the happy past is what this Face of the *Cursed Mind* falls back on. If a guy was charming and thoughtful when you met him, you hold on to that perception of him even if he begins to change. If he suddenly becomes cold, distant, or mean, you might not know how to process this new information about him. Your *Cursed Mind* tells you to try and get back to the past, not realizing you are now seeing the guy for who he truly is or how he naturally behaves when he's comfortable in a relationship.

In all relationships, you must analyze, make decisions, and work from the present. Holding on to the past and ignoring what's currently happening will only cause you to make poor choices and potentially waste the valuable time you have to look for the right person. Adrienne showed me the numerous flirty text messages she had received from Wynn right after they met, but as I told her, contacting him because he flattered her four months ago was disregarding the fact that time had changed things. And although Adrienne was frozen in the past, Wynn was not.

Many of my single clients have a pattern of hanging on to unpromising relationships. They are wonderful women who can't understand why they are still single after years of dating. When I review their histories, it is clear to me that the biggest contributing factor is their inability to move on when a guy no longer shows high interest in them. I explain that if they can let go of *what was* and instead focus on *what is*, their road to love will miraculously become shorter.

A Victim Mentality

At its peak, this Face of the *Curse* creates a victim mentality. This happens when the Lamenter Mind reaches full capacity of painful past stories and decides you should receive more empathy, support, and leniency from others because of what has happened to you. When your *Cursed* thinking evolves to this state, you often expect the men you are involved with to placate you or go easy on you because of what you've previously endured. *"I've been cheated on before,"* the *Cursed Mind* will say, *"so you have to reassure me of your feelings often"* or *"You know I've had a hard time with trust because of my last boyfriend, so you have to reply to my texts right away."* You might expect your partner to treat you with kid gloves because it's what you deserve after all you have been through. What you never think about is how such conditions and demands affect the other person in your relationship and put pressure or limitations on them, which stifles their growing affection. When your *Curse* is this bad, you might feel entitled to special treatment and often become frustrated and angry when people, especially those you love, don't give it to you.

Making yourself a victim is extremely toxic to love because victims don't give. They don't think they can. Since they believe they are less than everyone else, they don't believe they have anything to give. Victims look at others and think, *"They have everything, and I have nothing. What could I give them? I can't believe they expect something from poor me!"* Of course, they do have something to give, and that is love, but victims don't know how. So, they turn themselves into the takers of the relationship. Everything bad that happens to them they use as proof of how the world is against them and they need more support, attention, and love than anyone else.

A victim mentality is so hard to break because playing the victim is how you get others to focus on you. You make yourself the centerpiece of the relationship when you play this role. If you aren't getting attention this way, how will you get it? The Lamenter Mind loves being the victim because it gives you a sense of identity and relevance. But giving into that feeling will counteract affection and passion in your relationships. Through your thoughts and actions, you are saying to potential partners, *"I want you to save me from my past and make me feel complete."* No man will ever want to sign up for that job. Why would he? What is he getting out of the relationship? And the truth is, he cannot save you from the past anyway—only you can do that.

The Present Holds the Key

The Lamenter wants salvation from her past, which she is certain only a man or a relationship can give her. The Worrier wants to be assured of a fulfilling future, which she also believes only a man or relationship can give her. But this belief, that someone outside yourself can rescue you from the unhappiness in your life and make you feel worthy, is the very thing that is keeping you from love.

There is a constant inner struggle that you may not have noticed until reading this book. The struggle is what produces anxiety and frustration in your body and keeps you unhappy and aching for a relationship. You are hoping that a man and his love can end your struggle, but this problem starts in your mind and ends there as well. Therefore, you are the only one who can solve your problem and bring you what you are really looking for: peace. I know you might have thought that love would bring you that peace, but it is the opposite. **Peace within will bring you love.** So, it is time to change course and learn to be at peace with yourself first so that love can happen.

Where is peace? How can you find it? It's so close and accessible to you that all you need to do is close your eyes and ask for it. It is here in the very moment you are living and breathing in. To be at peace, you only need to be present. Being present is how you break the Worrier/Lamenter mindset, and as you will read more about in Chapter Nine, it is the first Cure of the *Curse*.

REFLECTION

Take the time now to reflect on the chapter you've just read. If necessary, go back and reread it to ensure you have grasped all the information, as there is an overwhelming amount to digest. Then, put the book down for a day and see if you can catch your mind in the future or past.

Chapter Five

The Inferior Mind

Felicity could not get through a coaching session without breaking into tears. It took almost three months to get her to a place where she could talk about her ex without sobbing. The relationship had been over for a while, but it was obvious she was still very heartbroken. She wanted to move on. In fact, her reason for contacting me in the first place was to help her get back on the dating scene, but each time we sat down to discuss how to meet guys or create a good online profile, she started rehashing her relationship with Kevin.

"I can't help but be angry with myself. I know that it's all my fault that he left," she told me one afternoon.

"How was it your fault?" I asked. By her account, Kevin broke up with her out of the blue on a Wednesday afternoon. They had gone to his parents' house that weekend, and Felicity had tried very hard to make the weekend special for him. Later that week, when he came home from work, he told her he was leaving her and their New York apartment to stay with his friend, she was blindsided. Kevin, along with all of his belongings, was gone the next day.

"I just know it was me. I can't say it's something I've done. I always knew deep down that he was going to leave me someday because..." she trailed off.

"Because what?" I urged her.

"Because I'm just not good enough for him," she replied. "He's such a great guy. He's smart, handsome, and funny. He could have any girl he wanted, and I knew it was only a matter of time before he realized he could find someone better."

The Curse of the Inferior Mind

The second Face of the *Curse* is the Inferior Mind. When the mind takes post in the Inferior Face, you are consumed with self-absorbed thoughts that are negative and pessimistic. The conditioned voice in your head tells you that you are cursed with several uncontrollable flaws, which is the underlying reason you haven't yet been able to find or keep love. Your mind might designate what it is about you that is so deficient: You're not pretty enough, not smart enough, not interesting or feminine enough ... or it may have no idea what it is that guys don't like about you but is sure you are lacking something. This perception of a "lesser self" can hold you back in achieving many things in your life but is most noticeably damaging when it comes to romantic relationships.

Because your own mind cannot accept who you are and the flaws that you have, you can't wholeheartedly believe anyone else would accept you either. The effect of this thinking leads to interacting with others under a constant state of self-protection in order to avoid more rejection than what you are already giving yourself. Opening up to anyone or admitting how you really feel seems too scary and risky. What if the person doesn't like what you have to say? What if he decides you're strange and disapproves of you? Ultimately, you stunt the growth and development of most of your relationships because you won't share yourself on a deeper level, and therefore, no one ever feels that close to you.

If you are single, you might refrain from opportunities to meet new people or put yourself online, because the fear of more non-acceptance is far greater than your hope to find happiness. The *Cursed Mind* convinces you that other women will greatly outshine you, so attempting to meet someone seems futile. On the rare occasion when you do put yourself in a male-friendly environment, it's likely that you often feel disappointed. You might frequently be overlooked by a more attractive girlfriend or only approached by men that you have no interest in. The longstanding fear held by the Inferior Mind is that you will forever be alone because you're not good enough for anyone (or anyone that you would like.)

The biggest problem with having a negatively self-absorbed mind is that you think everything that happens (or doesn't happen) in your love life is because your worth is menial. You don't realize that the feeling of "not good enough" is just the byproduct of thinking about yourself so much and in no way a true assessment of yourself. This is why trying to find a relationship to make you feel better never works. You can only cure feeling "not good enough" and the effects of that feeling when you become aware of, and consciously stop, your *Cursed* thinking.

As we will read later in this chapter, this Face of the *Cursed Mind* creates unbalanced relationships because negative self-absorbed thinking leads to the unconscious assumption that your significant other is more important than you are or doesn't love you as much as you love him. That, along with other *Cursed* thoughts, leads to several toxic dating and relationship habits such as seeking validation through sex, taking things personally, and seeing problems that aren't really there. Only by understanding where these patterns come from can you effectively end them and create new and productive habits that can lead to love.

How Inferior Thinking Creates Self-Sabotage

When your mind repeatedly tells you that you are "lesser" or are lacking in some way, it creates a deep-seated need for approval from others, especially from anyone that you are dating. Having someone in your life not only provides you with love and support but also gives your *Cursed Mind* a sense of validation. It thinks, *"I am more worthy than I was before because I now have a boyfriend."* Or, *"I must not be lacking now because someone likes me."* Believing that the person you are dating or in a relationship with makes you more worthy, means that losing that person is absolutely terrifying. Losing the person equals losing that feeling. Although fear of heartbreak might seem normal, when you have an Inferior Mind the apprehension runs deeper than most because not only would you have to deal with the disappointment of another failed relationship, your *Cursed Mind* would use the breakup as proof of your inadequacy, returning you to feeling less than again. Therefore, it's not uncommon to be paralyzed by this fear and never express any feelings you have to your partner other than what qualifies as happy and content, or battle this fear by doing everything you can to please him so he won't leave you.

If you are the former and fear that speaking up about your wants and emotions will rock the relationship boat and cause guys to see you as demanding or pressuring, you may have found yourself trapped in the hookup culture, unable to find a way out. While other girls might subscribe to a liberal, feminist view on sex, if your mind is conditioned to negative self-absorbed thinking, you are having sex because you are either afraid to say no when a guy wants something from you, or you are secretly hoping that having sex will eventually evolve into a relationship without you having to say anything.

Unfortunately, this means that you aren't having sex because you think it's fun and enjoyable; you are using sex as a vehicle to get the guy to like you and commit to you which never works. Because what you are doing is in conflict with how your *Core Self* really feels, your self-respect is taking even more of a beating. Guys that you are involved with won't see you as cool and easygoing as you're hoping. On the contrary, what they see is a willingness to compromise your body to be with them. It is very common for someone with this *Curse* to have sex with a guy for months or years without ever having the talk to determine the relationship, despite really wanting to do so. This is one of the main differences as to why some women can have sex on a first date and have it result in a relationship, versus others who do so and are ghosted. It's not always the physical act that sways the relationship one way or another; it's the motive behind it.

Although you long for a connection with someone, this Face of the *Cursed Mind* can't do the one thing necessary to get it—and that is be vulnerable. You might have a difficult time admitting you like someone, even when it's obvious they like you in return, or sharing certain things about yourself, fearing he won't approve of you. *"If I tell him I am on antidepressants, he won't like me. If I tell him my family is estranged, he won't like me. If I tell him I have an STD, he won't like me."* In its quest to self-protect, the negatively self-absorbed mind won't allow you to open up, and therefore a real connection never happens. Even asking a guy thoughtful questions about himself might be difficult because you likely fear that being too invasive will reflect negatively upon you. Many guys who have dated women with this *Curse* say the same thing: *"She was pretty, smart, and sweet, but I never felt like we really got close."*

In order to really fall in love, you have to be more concentrated on connecting with someone than protecting yourself from possible judgment or potentially losing them. In order to do that, you have to allow your *Core Self* to be on display rather than allowing your *Cursed Self* to convince you to hide who you are or project a prettier picture of who you think you need to be in order to be loved. No man will ever love or connect with your *Cursed Self,* no matter how pretty or perfect she seems.

If you don't know where you stand with a man and you are too scared to ask, the Inferior Mind will urge you to do the one thing it thinks it can to keep him happy: please. It thinks, *"If I can make him happy, he won't leave me,"* or *"If I anticipate all his wants, he will love me."* But being a people pleaser won't preserve your relationship, because your actions aren't truly motivated by the goodness of your heart. Your expectation is that by pleasing the guy, he will repay you with his loyalty, commitment, and acceptance. You are giving with the expectation to get something back, which is not an attribute of love. This is how many women end up over-giving and overextending themselves in their relationships. Giving out of love feels good to the other person, but pleasing for approval feels as if something is missing in you, something that you think the other person has and can give you. In a subtle way, that can feel like use, which feels draining and clingy. Depending on the type of person you are in a relationship with, two outcomes can occur. If the man is a good guy, he will feel fatigued by your over-giving and need of approval (most commonly called neediness) and simply lose interest. Most guys want to be with a woman they know they can depend and lean on in tough times, and if you are needy, the perception is that you cannot stand on your own, so how could he possibly lean on you? The second outcome is much worse: If you are involved with someone who is not a good guy, your need for approval can result in being taken advantage of and used for things such as money, sex, and other favors.

Felicity was a people pleaser who suffered from having the Inferior mindset. Her relationship with Kevin started out promising but sadly crumbled under the power of the Inferior Mind. Kevin saw her out one night with her friends, approached her, and asked for her number. He took her on several dates, always opening her door and paying for her meal. A month into seeing each other, Kevin told her he wasn't seeing anyone else, and Felicity echoed the same sentiment with delight. Kevin was unlike any other man she had been with, and she fell in love with his strong, confident persona. The first three months of their relationship was the happiest time of her life. But by the beginning of their fourth month together, *The Curse*, which had lain dormant for a time, slowly crept back into Felicity's mind, and she began to have old familiar thoughts. *"What if Kevin stops loving me? I really don't deserve him. He's eventually going to regret spending all this time and money on me and then resent me for it. I'm older than his last girlfriend. What if I start to age, and he becomes less attracted to me? He's so much smarter than I am. He is going to get bored because I'm not interesting enough for him."*

Soon her mind was filled with thoughts of her own worth. Her focus shifted from loving Kevin and enjoying their time together onto herself and all her inadequacies. She became consumed with the idea that Kevin would see she was not good enough for him and leave. Her sweet and easygoing nature faded, and soon she was desperately looking for ways to reassure herself of Kevin's love. She needed his approval daily, so she began doing things for him just to hear him praise her. Then she could rest easy for a bit. She never asked for anything, even when it was important to her, out of fear she would be seen as demanding and high maintenance. *"I'll not ask for anything,"* she thought. *"He'll think I'm so easy and flexible that he will never want to leave me."* Kevin, unaware of her thoughts but feeling a strong vibe that she was afraid to express herself and wanted him to give her confidence, found himself becoming more annoyed and impatient with her. Slowly, he started to believe what Felicity did: that she needed him in order to feel good about herself and function well emotionally.

Felicity didn't realize it, but when she turned her thoughts to herself, she unknowingly turned off the love she was giving to Kevin and their relationship. Her focus was *"How can I get him to stay with me, and keep loving me"* instead of *"How is Kevin doing?"* They are two very different focal points resulting in two different impressions. Because Felicity was concentrated on the former, Kevin felt pressured to keep her happy. Not only did he have to manage his work and other personal agendas, he had to manage her emotions and feelings of self-value. When he did do nice things for her or gave her compliments, they were quickly disregarded. The love he had to give was being rejected because Felicity's Inferior Mind made her believe she did not deserve it.

If you think that you are unworthy of someone's love, the remedy to the problem is not to try and do more or be more for him. The answer is to focus on loving him by being a thoughtful partner who is present, supportive, and not consumed with herself. When you are fixated on the fear that you are somehow lacking, you are not concentrated on the love you could be giving. This is how you unconsciously block the pathway to love. Being too self-absorbed blinds you to seeing your partner and understanding his needs. Felicity only saw her relationship as a barometer to gauge her worth, and because of that, it ended.

The bottom line with this Face of the *Curse* is that the self-absorbed mind prioritizes the feeling of self-approval before love. When the mind finds someone from whom it craves approval, it attaches itself and its value to that person, not realizing a large part of why it wants to be with the person is to feel better about itself. When that is your primary motivation, the relationship becomes unbalanced very quickly and the odds of it thriving are low. Love has to be given without fear of what the other person will think, and although you might not know how to do that now, it can absolutely happen once you rid yourself of the Inferior Mind.

The Inferior Vibe
You might readily admit that your overall feelings of insecurity drive men away. Maybe you already know the vibe you effuse is somewhat uncomfortable, awkward, or uneasy. Perhaps you've tried to reconcile your feelings of self-doubt by spending money on books, workshops, or classes in an attempt to learn how to love yourself and thus, be more confident. As I said earlier, there are many relationship experts who tout self-love and high self-worth as being absolutely essential for success in relationships. But trying to cure insecurity with positive self-talk or affirmations does not remedy the problem, in my opinion. Two outcomes typically occur with this commonly suggested solution: First, you may simply exchange negative self-absorbed thinking for positive self-absorbed thinking, as I did. In truth, many positively self-absorbed women start out feeling like they aren't good enough in adolescence and make the switch to the opposite mindset as they get older. It may seem as if they have come a long way and cured their low self-esteem because they become more outwardly confident, but the reality is that they are still highly focused on themselves but have learned to self-obsess in a different way. If you have ever known someone who acts arrogant but is insecure, you are seeing the effects of a *Curse* shift. This is why it's important to learn to clear this mindset completely and not merely redirect it.

The second outcome of attempting to build up your self-worth is that you can inadvertently train your mind to continually look for what needs fixing in you, thus creating a spin-off mentality that you are always a work in progress. Because human beings are not perfect and never will be, you can spend your whole life trying to improve yourself and never reach a level of satisfaction. You might think, *"Once I lose those 15 pounds I'll be perfect,"* or *"Once I get my nose fixed, I'll feel better."* All that truly needs changing is the mentality that you need to be more than what you are right now.

A fitting example of this was a client named Helen that I saw years ago. She sought my help after a breakup, claiming she was *Cursed* because all her relationships ended with guys calling things off with her. Helen said in the beginning guys were good to her, but by the end, they were treating her poorly. Her last boyfriend was charming when they met, but after a few months, he grew very mean-spirited and frequently made fun of her. He would berate Helen in front of their friends by calling her airheaded and slow. When I asked her why she didn't want to break up with someone who made her feel so bad, she replied, "Because deep down I don't feel good about myself, so I feel like he's right to treat me that way."

Helen went on to say that if she lost more weight, got her finances in order, and moved out of her parents' house, then she would feel better about herself and, thus, not let someone treat her so poorly. She felt those things were bringing her down and causing her to accept her boyfriend's degradation. Once she got her life in order, she felt sure that she would attract better men or demand better treatment. So, I asked Helen if there was another time in her life when she was at her desired weight, living on her own, and saving money, and she told me there was. She said that when she was 24, she looked and felt her very best, and her life was in great order. However, when we examined the relationship she was in at that time, it was even worse that her most recent one!

It might seem that Helen simply had a hard time expressing her boundaries, but because her mind was conditioned to think she was inferior to the men she dated, it was impossible to create any boundaries at all, let alone stick by them. She first had to understand how her mind was enabling her insecurity, which led to tolerating poor treatment from others.

Regardless of what you improve upon on the outside, the *Cursed Mind* will always find something that could be better about you. As you will read in the Superior Mind chapter, one of its main functions is to find opportunities to enhance your feelings of worth, and because it has no benchmark to indicate when that task is complete, it keeps doing its job. When you also wrestle with having an Inferior Mind, you won't ever believe that you've reached a point of worthiness. In the meantime, you will continue to put out the vibe that you are still not enough. A truly confident and self-assured vibe can only come from your *Core Self* because that is the *"you"* that doesn't spend time thinking about your worth at all! Your *Core Self* is intrinsically happier and more beautiful when you are concentrating on other people and allowing the love inside you to guide you in your interactions with them.

Acting From Negative Self-Absorbed Thinking

Let's take a look at how this *Face* of the *Curse* sees negative situations in your love life as problems stemming from your low self-worth, prompting you to feel slighted, down, or outright offended; often motivating you to action when no action is necessary. A more common way to describe this habit of the Inferior Mind is taking things personally.

The Inferior Mind can use anything disappointing in life as evidence of how you aren't good enough. That habit can start wreaking havoc on a new romance fairly quickly and cause you to unintentionally sabotage your chance for a relationship. The guy you had lukewarm interest in doesn't text one morning, and your mind immediately goes into a state of self-obsession and blame. *"OMG! He's lost interest! I said something stupid. I should have paid for our drinks. I kissed him too much and didn't leave at the height of impulse. He probably saw the cellulite on my legs and was instantly turned off. Now what am I going to do?"* Because you feel responsible for this terrible turn of events (the guy not texting one morning) you might try to correct it. However, all actions you take from this point are purely motivated by your fear of not being good enough to keep the guy interested. You might not have known him very well or even had much attraction to him, but the fact that he may not like you anymore ignites your negatively self-absorbed mind. You are compelled to win back his interest because the mind believes not having it is proof that you really aren't enough. This is where most women with this *Curse* veer off the road toward love and start barreling down a side street to self-protect. You are no longer concentrated on the guy or your relationship with him. Now your thoughts are totally focused on avoiding more hits to your self-worth. If you don't realize this is what is happening, you will mistake your sudden surge of emotional attachment to the guy for genuine feelings for him. You might text him to see if he will respond or try to bait him with an excuse to see you again. But, of course, anything you do from here will only cause the relationship to descend rapidly because the guy will sense your attempt to hold on to him for the wrong reason.

    Because your negatively self-absorbed mind thinks about you all day long, it's only natural for it to assume you're the cause of anything bad that happens. If someone is rude to you, the *Cursed Mind* assumes it is because that person doesn't like or respect you, not realizing they are simply having a bad day. If a guy doesn't ask for your number, it believes it's because you weren't pretty or interesting enough, not because he was already involved with or getting over someone else. And if someone breaks up with you, your mind firmly concludes that it's because something is wrong with you, not because the guy might have been *Cursed* with his own problems. When your mind takes everything personally, you will get angry or sad about things that have absolutely nothing to do with you, such as your boyfriend not responding timely to a text or your partner being in a bad mood. Your Inferior Mind might yell or pout, *"What did I do to deserve that?"* or *"I must have done something wrong for him to act that way!"* This is because your mind has been conditioned to put you at the center of everyone else's lives, assuming they think about you as much as you think about yourself. This can lead you to overreact to small complications or to try and fix something that isn't really wrong in the first place.

Anytime Kevin's mood was low, Felicity immediately assumed it had something to do with her. He couldn't just be tired, stressed, or grumpy from work. If Kevin was unhappy, she immediately worried it was something she had done and worked to correct it. One week, Kevin had to work overtime and didn't get home until almost midnight each day. His boss was pressuring him to perform, and at the same time, another co-worker quit and Kevin had to temporarily pick up the slack. Most of the time he and Felicity would text throughout the day, but now he was too busy to respond. One morning, she texted Kevin telling him to have a good day but never heard back. She waited all day to hear from him. At 5 p.m., she texted him again, asking where he was but still got no response. Becoming increasingly panicked that his silence meant something, she texted a third and fourth time. Her thoughts ran rampant: Was he mad at her? Was he becoming distant because he secretly met someone else? Was he tired of their relationship? How could he be so busy? It only takes two seconds to write a text!

When Kevin finally wrote back later that evening, she peppered him with questions attempting to find out the answer. She repeatedly asked him if everything was okay between them, and why couldn't he just text her saying he was busy? Was something else going on she needed to know about? She wanted to come over and talk with him about things, but Kevin didn't have the energy and was annoyed she was making the situation about something it wasn't. A bit agitated and sleep deprived, he grunted that everything was fine and to stop acting crazy—which, of course, sent Felicity into an even deeper, darker place. Her *Cursed Mind* prevented her from thinking about Kevin and how he was feeling after a long, stressful week. She only thought about herself and holding on to her relationship with him, which Kevin did not appreciate.

When you break the habit of self-absorbed thinking and realize your worth is not and never has been on trial, you are able to see the reality of a situation, instead of the Inferior Mind convincing you that *you* are the reason for someone acting the way they do. When your significant other is in a bad mood, you can assess their situation more clearly because you don't see yourself as the center for all issues. And because you are connected to them, you are more tuned to their needs and what you can do to help them feel better.

Felicity reacted with fear and insecurity when Kevin's mood changed, but some women with this *Curse* will respond with anger to situations that are confusing or unexpected. When someone behaves in a curious way, the Inferior Mind wants to self-protect and might assume it is being taken advantage of or purposefully disrespected. In an effort to defend its worth, it can lash out, believing that someone of higher caliber would not be treated the same way. What the self-absorbed mind fails to see is that even if a prospective partner acts in a way that is not respectful or kind, his actions only speak to his character, not yours.

Jenny, for example, had a habit of frequently feeling disrespected, which lead to many fights with her boyfriend, Jake. On one occasion, Jake's old roommate came to town for a night and wanted to go to the movies with them. When they got to the crowded theatre, Jake's friend sat next to him, blocking Jenny from sitting next to her boyfriend. Jenny immediately assumed the old roommate did this because he didn't like her and wasn't happy she was there. After the movie, they all went for ice cream, but Jenny hardly said a word. She completely withdrew because of the seating arrangement. Her boyfriend quickly became annoyed that she had disengaged from the conversation and told her she was overly upset for little reason. They ended up having a big fight in the middle of Ben and Jerry's, which embarrassed Jake and his friend and made the situation even worse.

When I asked Jenny why she didn't ask her boyfriend to change seats and sit in the middle, she said she was too upset to say anything and wasn't sure if she was overreacting or not. I asked if it was possible that

Cursed?

Jake and his friend were so caught up in spending time together that they didn't realize she might feel awkward with their seating arrangement, but she was adamant that they purposefully wanted her to feel foolish because they didn't respect her.

When you are so consumed with your own level of worth and how others perceive you, the most unfavorable situations come off as slights against you, and you believe that another girl who is "better" than you would have been treated differently. It doesn't occur to you that other people are acting out of their own wants for themselves or simply didn't think of you at all. On the rare occasion when someone does try to intentionally belittle you, it's likely that you are dating a person who is emotionally immature and there is little you can do to change that person. They are likely *Cursed* and unaware themselves, and your only choice is to either accept them or move on.

The irony of this *Curse* is that the very women who take things so personally and claim they are sensitive, sometimes have trouble seeing how their own attitudes and mood affect the people they love. They are too busy being concerned about how others can hurt them to consider the possibility of upsetting or offending someone else. This is because the Inferior Mind doesn't think it has the ability to hurt someone with its words or actions. After all, it is less; it is insignificant—how can it possibly cause pain to another person, it thinks!

Marissa, who is twenty-eight, often complained that her boyfriend was not sensitive enough to her feelings. According to her, she's very thin-skinned and wanted her boyfriend to be more cognizant of how his words and actions made her feel. She asked him repeatedly to be mindful of his tone when speaking with her. In the same breath, however, Marissa also told me that she is a moody person who can be sulky and somewhat bitchy if she is having a bad day. I asked her why it was okay for her to give in to her negative self-absorbed thinking, while at the same time expecting her boyfriend to watch how his own attitude affected her. She replied, "I guess I just don't think I have the power to ruin another persons day."

Expecting everyone else to be understanding and sympathetic to you and your situation is a common self-deception of this *Curse*. When a man hurts you, you might become extremely mean and vengeful because you feel so small on the inside that you believe you must cut deep on the outside to make a point. You may not think your words have the power to damage, but they do just as much as anyone else's. Even though you feel inferior on the inside doesn't mean you are seen as inferior from the outside. You aren't because you're not.

Men might tell you that having a relationship with you means choosing words carefully, rarely speaking freely, and always being on high alert that anything said can be misconstrued. Being in a relationship like that can feel restrictive. Even worse, your partner might claim he has to walk on eggshells to avoid a fight or ward off a meltdown because any little misspeak can set off a windstorm of emotions. Anyone would tire of having to be cautious of their words and actions in tandem with routinely reassuring you of their feelings. A relationship is about having fun, sharing life, and experiencing its ups and downs together—it's not to provide constant happiness to one person and assurance of their value. This is why it is vitally important to let go of the need to feel relevant or worthy, which can only be done when your mind is free of *Cursed* thinking.

Wake Yourself

Nothing is more painful to the human body than the mind telling it that it's not enough. The Inferior Mind can use any romantic situation, no matter how small or insignificant, to make that point, and our being will take its word without question. The consequence can be observed not just in our relationships but also in our health and overall wellness. Tell yourself you are lacking or not worthy too often, and your entire body feels the impact. People with this *Curse* are prone to physical illnesses such as stomachaches, nausea, heartburn, eating disorders, and other mind-body health conditions like panic attacks and depression. Dealing with these physical ramifications is another layer of difficulty that impairs or debilitates those with this Face of the *Cursed Mind* from reaching their life or love goals. Only when you wake up to the realization that it is not your value but *your thoughts about your value* that are keeping love out of reach will you be able to switch focus and begin working on the primary disease that is plaguing you.

You can begin the process of self-transformation right now by asking yourself, why you think you aren't good enough. What about you is so extraordinarily different from other people in the world that it makes you less of a person than they are? You might come up with an answer, but it will never be the truth. Although you think you need to be more or be something else, let's face the real reason you feel bad about yourself: You have been living life absorbed in you, and when you do that, you cannot possibly feel good. As I said in Chapter One, the more you think about yourself, the worse you feel about yourself. We were not built to obsess, question, and contemplate every detail about who we are and continually assess our value. While you might blame other factors for your low self-worth, like your weight, appearance, or some personality trait, it is your self-absorbed thinking that is causing you to feel so low and undeserving; you just haven't been keenly aware of it until now. As human beings, it is in our nature to love and give to other people. Once you begin shifting focus onto the world around you, your negative feelings will subside, and you will become more authentically confident and comfortable with who you are. Then the gift you've been waiting for can happen unencumbered by the *Curse*: to find love, to be in love, and to stay in love.

The first Cure of the *Curse,* Be Present, will be the most helpful in ceasing all self-focused thoughts, but because your mind is intelligent, thoughtful, creative and splendidly capable, you will naturally have to use your brain throughout your day and within your relationships. When you take away *Cursed* thoughts, there will be a lot of space for the right kind of thinking—that is what the second Cure, Be Grateful, will assist you in. More on that in Chapter Ten!

REFLECTION

Take the time now to reflect on this chapter. If necessary, go back and reread it one more time to fully understand the Inferior Mind. Then, put the book down for a day and see if you notice that you think or talk about yourself in the negative sense. Do you feel you are the cause of other people's bad behavior?

Chapter Six

The Wanter Mind

Karen and Eddie had a crazy, passionate love affair from the get-go. They met while Eddie was dating a friend of Karen's and felt an instant chemistry with each other. Whenever they were at the same party, they would run off to a secluded area and make out. It was fun sneaking around and knowing they weren't supposed to be together. When the relationship was finally out in the open, Karen's friend was understandably upset. Karen was sympathetic, but since she believed she and Eddie were soul mates, she never entertained the thought of not being with him.

They married quickly, barely dating a year. For a while, things were great. Eddie worked hard at his law practice, and Karen was busy running a thriving boutique business. The passion between them wasn't quite as strong as it was in the beginning, but Karen kept herself happy by regularly planning fancy dates and exotic vacations.

Then they had their first child, which is when Karen said everything changed. Routine set in, and suddenly life wasn't as exciting. After their second child was born, their relationship unraveled further. Karen resented Eddie because he often had to work late and she was left caring for the children. Eddie began to resent Karen for always being in a bad mood when he came home from a long, exhausting workday. When the kids finally went to bed, Karen was glued to her computer, trying to keep her business afloat, and would reject Eddie's invitation to cuddle in bed and watch prerecorded episodes of *The Voice*—a show he loved but Karen found to be a waste of her precious "me" time. As the years passed, they grew further and further apart. The hot, spicy affair was soon long gone. Karen found herself daydreaming about past boyfriends, and Eddie started noticing the summer interns at his office.

How did this happen? Was it avoidable? Why is it that so many relationships start off passionate and symbiotic but end up flat lining a few short years later? In this particular story, the culprit lies in the third Face of the *Curse,* the Wanter Mind.

The Curse of the Wanter Mind

When I tell women that the reason they have relationship problems is because they are self-absorbed, many of them can see that instantly—except for those with a predominately Wanter Mind. "Wanters," as I like to call them, are unique in that they are unaware of exactly how self-centered they are and how routinely they search for boosts to their sense of worth. In other words, women who possess this Face of the *Cursed Mind* might not tell you that they struggle with worthiness or feel inadequate because they often don't consciously realize it is how they feel. Like those with the Inferior Mind, they have a deep-rooted sense that they are not good enough; however, a woman whose *Cursed Mind* mainly resides in the Inferior Face recognizes this in herself, but someone with a Wanter Mind as their dominate Face, will not. Because a Wanter is unaware (or avoidant) of her feelings of not being enough, her *Cursed Mind* presents in a completely different way: Instead of focusing on protecting her sense of worth, she experiences a constant feeling of *wanting*. Her unconscious mind craves one thing after the next because it provides a temporary feeling of self-validation to obtain whatever it is she has set her sights on.

For instance, some women with a Wanter Mind have a compulsive shopping habit. They feel an increased sense of self-worth when they buy the latest handbag or pair of shoes. If you asked them, they would tell you they have a shopping addiction, but their addiction is not to the apparel but to the feeling of value that comes from wanting and obtaining it. Because the sense of fulfillment from the purse or shoes is only placating the *Cursed Mind*, the feeling is only temporary. The Wanter then needs to buy a new handbag or another pair of shoes shortly after to feel good about herself once again. It's a cycle of wanting and getting that never reaches an end. The Wanter is unaware as to why she keeps wanting or that it's even a problem. She is too busy chasing the next designer shoe, luxury car, technical gadget, or fabulous vacation to take a moment and reflect on why she is always in this state.

Although you may not have recognized this before, constant or excessive wanting is not a feeling; it's an unconscious thought pattern, and one that occurs when you unknowingly feel as if you are not yet enough and desire to be more worthy than you believe you are now. The Wanter Mind thinks that by *getting* more, you *become more* or *become enough*; thus, its focus is in pursuit of external objects to acquire. You don't realize you are searching for self-fulfillment or validation, but that is what perpetual wanting is: the self-absorbed mind's unrecognized hunt for "being enough" that it thinks lies outside itself. In the context of relationships, this means that once you decide that you like someone, you become attached to the idea that getting that person means you are worthy (or at least worthy enough to have him.) Much like the luxury apparel, the more that person makes you want him, the stronger your attachment. There doesn't need to be a real viable chance of a relationship; there only needs to be deep, sustained wanting to keep you interested. Therefore, you might continue to pursue someone despite everyone in your inner circle telling you that the relationship has no chance of materializing. Wanting can also be the reason you stay with someone who never fully commits or does not meets your needs, hence making you always want something more from them.

Cursed wanting is what sparked Karen and Eddie's relationship at the start. The fact that they were not supposed to be together was fuel for

Karen's *Curse*. But Karen showed signs of being a Wanter even before her taboo relationship with Eddie. She had a history of chasing men who ignited wanting; mostly players that had no interest in monogamy. They would court her appropriately for a date or two, taking her to expensive restaurants and lavishing her with compliments, but after a couple of weeks, their interest level would drop. Instead of accepting that these men were not quality prospects and moving on, Karen's Wanter Mind would hijack her entire being. She would plot and plan how she could get them more interested in her. She would send photos of herself in sexy lingerie or promise them mind-blowing oral sex if they were to take her out again. The guys would oblige her sporadically, but they never came close to having a real relationship or loving her.

Every guy Karen dated was like the last. She was never interested in anyone who was nice and into her. If she went out with someone who fit that description, they only got one date before Karen claimed they were too boring. And although some might not have been a good match, the fact that she showed such a strong pattern of disinterest in men who were emotionally available and an unwavering attraction to those who treated her poorly or were non-committal was proof in the Wanter pudding. When she met Eddie, it was obvious he was not a player, but because he was dating Karen's friend it made him technically unavailable, stimulating her mind to *want* him.

In this chapter, we will take a close look how the Wanter Mind becomes addicted to the feeling of wanting, which attracts you to people and relationships that provide a challenge or element of chase (which is, in essence, wanting) and consequently scares you away from anyone who is available and ready for a commitment. We will explore how *Cursed* wanting can make dating extremely painful at any stage, as well as how it can easily sabotage an otherwise normal, healthy relationship.

How Wanting Creates Self-Sabotage

At the onset of love, there is usually strong desire. A feeling of butterflies or knots in your stomach is natural and normal when you first meet someone of interest. Relationships that are healthy and involve two loving people, however, evolve and transition from that feeling into one that is more comfortable and contented. The usual uncertainty of how one person feels for the other goes away, and both sides develop an easy, relaxed, and happy rapport when together. That maturation to a more contented place rarely happens for those with a predominately Wanter Mind. Many Wanters are not able to get to the next level in their relationships because the habit to want creates a huge roadblock that most do not know how to overcome. That roadblock is this: When a Wanter gets the person she wants, it isn't long before she doesn't want that person anymore. As with the new handbag, the guy and the relationship become dull and need renewing.

If being with someone becomes easy and comfortable, and the proverbial roller coaster of emotions comes to an end, uncertainty and dread will seep into the Wanter Mind. *"He doesn't give me butterflies like he did before. I must not be in love anymore! I'm bored! I'm unhappy! He's not what I want."* This happens because if there is no wanting, the Wanter Mind thinks there is no attraction or love. It believes the desire to be with her partner has disappeared, when in reality, the *Cursed Mind* doesn't know how to transition to the next phase of love: *just being* with someone. It's impossible for anyone who is under the control of the Wanter Mind to *just be* in a relationship without wanting because that would mean the journey to worth and validation is over, that she is finally enough and her life is fulfilled. Those feelings only occur when the *Curse* is broken and wanting is seen for what it truly is. Until then, a Wanters reaction to any leveling off of emotions will be to ignite wanting again. She may distance herself from her partner, start an argument, or even cheat to create turmoil. If her partner reacts with anger and pulls away, she is back where she feels most comfortable, wanting him. If that doesn't work, she will move on to someone new.

This is why happy, long-term commitments are rare for this *Curse*. After the first phase of love dissipates (what people call infatuation or falling in love), a Wanter will assume she is not in love anymore. The feeling of falling in love naturally fades, but instead of embracing the next stage of love, she fights or runs from it. This is why Wanters have very short relationships. The one exception to this rule is when a Wanter gets involved with another Wanter, and an "on-again, off-again" relationship ensues. The hot-and-cold, push-and-pull effect happens on both sides, which means no one is ever fully satisfied, and no one is bored, either. That type of relationship retains a longer shelf life because through the ups and downs, makeups and breakups, the feeling of wanting can sustain by itself. Of course, once the couple makes a real commitment and gets married to each other, they often quickly decide they've made a mistake and end up divorcing. (When you are fully and legally committed, you can't want!) *Cursed* wanting is frequently the reason a couple may be together for 10 years before tying the knot, but once they do, the marriage rapidly deteriorates. From the outside no one sees the truth of the couple, but if you could look into their minds and understand how they each felt about themselves individually, you would have heard their struggle for wholeness, which they mistakenly assumed the other person would fill once they wed.

Wanters who realize that they get bored with people and constantly vacillate between wanting a relationship and then running from it eventually start targeting people who are unattainable in order to keep the feeling of wanting alive much longer. Although they garner satisfaction when they obtain the object of their affection that gratification doesn't last, and the *Cursed Mind* would prefer to keep itself in constant wanting. It knows that the boost from having someone will not sustain, but the excitement, thrill, promise, and hope that comes from wanting an unattainable person can last years, or even a lifetime. This all happens on a completely unconscious level and leads some Wanters to become addicted to the feeling of wanting itself, ever rejecting true feelings of love like comfort, peace, and contentment. If you have ever asked yourself if the reason you want someone is because you can't have them, you are more aware of your own Wanter Mind than you might even realize.

You may be a Wanter if you have often said to yourself: *"Why is it that when a guy likes me, I don't like him, and the guys that I like are never interested in return?"* This is not an ironic coincidence. Wanters who are single can fall into the chasing trap, in which they are only attracted to people who present a challenge or a chase for them. You might have a thing for guys who are married or taken, notorious players, or highly sought-after bachelors. Any guy that fits into a typical non-committal or hard-to-get profile will do. Because "having" does not make you feel as good as "wanting", you might run from men who are too available or show too much interest. Once you know you can get someone, your Wanter Mind will no longer consider that person a prize to be won and a boost to your worth; thus, it will quickly lose interest.

If you asked a Wanter what the attraction is to someone who is unreliable or non-committal, she would site some other alluring trait, such as the man's confidence or charm. She might gush about his passion, humor, or brilliance, but none of those qualities have real weight in a relationship where there is no love or even moderate mutual feelings of affection.

Julie, for example, is a smart, driven, and beautiful 26-year-old. She is a catch by anyone's standards, but she has never been in a real relationship—not because guys haven't pursued her (she's had many admirers throughout her lifetime), but because she unknowingly has a Wanter Mind and therefore is only attracted to men she can't have. Ever since high school, she has been in love with Mark, a guy she hooked up with a few times and who then moved on to another girl. She says the draw to Mark is unexplainable, and Julie is convinced they are soul mates. Over the years, she and Mark have kept in touch, and every once in a while they fool around, which only strengthens Julie's feelings. Mark secretly likes that Julie is smitten with him and contacts her whenever he's not involved with anyone. When Mark is busy in a relationship, Julie does go on dates in an attempt to move on but says she feels nothing for other men.

The reality is that Julie does not want to have a normal relationship. There is excitement and unpredictability in Wanter relationships, and that rush of emotion is intoxicating. This is what makes it such a hard habit to break. Julie might feel low and rejected when Mark pulls away from her or stops answering her texts, but the minute he becomes responsive again, the emotional high is euphoric, almost akin to being on drugs. She feels confident, attractive, and full of self-worth. Julie thinks she and Mark are "meant to be," but that's only because she mistakenly thinks that the high she gets from wanting is love.

You might be wondering if learning you are a Wanter means that you need to go out with men who seem boring to you. You might worry that I'm telling you to date people who are available and interested regardless of how attracted you are to them. That's not it at all. What I am telling you is that the reason you might find so many men boring and unattractive in the first place is because you have a Wanter Mind and are only interested in people that put you in a state of craving. If you learn to rid yourself of this Face, your *Core Self* will clearly see which guys you connect with and which you don't. The Wanter Mind cannot extract worth and validation from guys who do not make it want. It classifies those guys as boring, but what it really means is *"I can't become more than I am by dating you."*

It doesn't have to be that someone isn't available or interested enough, though. A guy who is selfish, damaged, or unstable can trigger wanting because those types of men are also unable to love and commit as a healthy individual could. A past client of mine was notoriously attracted to men who were addicts. She thought she fell in love with people of such nature because she was drawn to their vulnerable sides and wanted to help them, but truthfully, it was because they were so impaired by their own mental anguish that they could not commit to her. Her *Cursed Mind* would hear the words, *"I'm sorry, I can't be in a relationship right now. I need to focus on getting myself better,"* and immediately she was in wanting and would not let them go.

Even if a Wanter is aware of her attraction to unrequited love, she often believes she cannot do anything about it. Wanters think they simply want who they want, and suggesting otherwise would be like telling them to change their favorite color or food. They don't think they can control who they find attractive or fall in love with. In some ways, there is a bit of truth to that. An addiction to wanting is as powerful as an addiction to food, alcohol, or anything else. Feeling overwhelmed and powerless against the craving can easily resign someone to the adage, *"I can't help how I feel."* A Wanter might meet someone who has a girlfriend or displays some other unavailable quality, and be totally enamored within a few minutes of chatting. But it's not the guy; it's the situation that reels her in. And being drawn to a situation is not the same as falling in love. If a Wanter can begin to see and understand the difference, she has a chance to change her pattern.

An Addiction to Pain
Women will ask me, "How do I know if I really want to be with someone because I am genuinely interested, versus being 'in wanting'? How do I know if I love him or I just love to crave him?" It is a valid question, as many relationships start out as crushes, which are very bittersweet. The answer lies in how you react to the one thing that follows the excitement, thrill, or enjoyment of wanting, and that is pain. Wanting and pain go hand in hand. This is because wanting someone for the benefit of self-fulfillment means that you have attached all of your hope for happiness and being enough to someone else, and when that person makes a move counter to what you expect of them, you automatically feel disappointed, devalued, and rejected. This is why, at the very preliminary level, dating can be so painful for those with a Wanter Mind. They anchor their dream to finally experience peace within and become enough in a fledgling relationship with unknown odds of working out. Therefore, the minute a guy redirects his interest, even slightly, it causes an enormous amount of pain. The second he fails to respond to a text, pain again. The day that he decides to date someone

else, all that craving turns to excruciating pain. *"I was on my way to being good enough and now this happens,"* the mind might say. The Wanter cannot do what other women can and accept that they need to move on because the person they wanted still holds their chance for being something of more value.

Luna, for example, had a whirlwind romance with a guy named Gianni. For two weeks he heavily pursued her, texting every day, taking her out every night, and gushing about his amorous feelings. She liked him and was beginning to get excited about where the relationship could go. Then, out of the blue, Gianni told Luna he couldn't see her anymore – that their relationship wouldn't work due to differences in their values and upbringing. Luna was shocked at first and then the terrible pain set in. Instead of moving on as all her friends and family suggested, her Wanter Mind completely took over. For the next year, she tried to bait Gianni into being with her. She would strategically go silent for a while, then pop up at a bar he was hanging out in, or text him to come over and hook up. Sometimes Gianni would comply and sometimes he wouldn't. When he did, Luna was happy for a few days and hopeful that things would work out. But most of the time she was in terrible agony, crying over why they weren't together and what could she do to change his mind. I told her many times, "It's *your* mind that needs changing, Luna" but her *Curse* would not let her hear me. To this day, she still wants Gianni even though he's now married to someone else.

If you are interested in someone and he begins to pull away or treat you badly, your reaction to his behavior will tell you if you are a Wanter. Do you sadly walk away, but know that you will find someone else, or move on because you know you deserve to be treated well? Or, through the agony, do you hang on and strategize a way to keep yourself in that person's life? Do you fall into a deep depression, convinced that he was the only person for you? Do you vow to get him re-interested, even if it will take months or years of effort and no promise of success? In short, does the pain caused by wanting make you want the person more?

Answer these things, and you will know if your feelings are real or *Cursed*.

As excruciating as it might be, a Wanter will always choose the pain that comes with wanting over the comfort of peace. Few would readily admit they like the pain, but Wanters know that it comes with the territory and often grow to depend on it. If they don't feel pain, they feel numb, and to them, that is an even worse feeling. The *Cursed Mind* cannot sit idle because its purpose is to continually think about and search for ways to obtain more value. Therefore, a Wanter would rather hang on to someone with little promise for a future than to give up hope and live without wanting.

Rebecca held on to a relationship with Ben for this very reason. He told her up front he didn't want a relationship with her but would have sex with her frequently. Rebecca's Wanter Mind loved pining after Ben and imagining that one day he would change his mind, and they would be together. She slept with him regularly for years until Ben fell madly in love with another woman. Rebecca was devastated but continued to tempt Ben to cheat on his girlfriend. Then Ben got married, and Rebecca had to accept her chance was over (even though she never truly had one to begin with). "Ben is gone and now my life feels so empty," Rebecca told me one day on the phone. But since she never had a real relationship with Ben, what she thought was a feeling of emptiness was really the absence of wanting.

Most Wanters won't accept a relationship is over (or accept that one will never happen) until they are forced by circumstance (the guy marries or moves away, for instance) or another relationship is on the horizon. Being completely single without any prospects at all is torture, so it isn't unusual for the Wanter Mind to randomly pick someone to want. To stop searching and hoping to obtain someone would feel like giving up and resigning herself to insignificance. *"That would be so boring! I can't do it. I need someone to want!"* The Wanter Mind thinks. Ironically, giving up the search for worth and identity through a relationship is the only way to find peace and learn how to truly love. A Wanter has to learn to *just be* which often means accepting being single until the right person comes along.

In order to break the Wanter's *Curse,* you have to be comfortable on your own and embrace what might feel like the vacancy or numbness that occurs when you aren't wanting, because *in that void lies true peace within.* You only have to give yourself the time to adjust to it. Your *Cursed Mind* might fight the feeling, but your *Core Self* can flourish if you learn to *be* without wanting. Only when this is accomplished will love stop being painful for you.

Acting From Wanting

Now that we've discussed how wanting causes an attraction to certain men, let's break down how wanting can affect your daily decision-making and interfere with the progress of a potentially good relationship. Although satisfying *Cursed* wants may only be temporary, not satisfying them at all usually brings a new level of frustration, anger, and misery. For this reason, wanting can completely control you despite being smart, savvy, and disciplined in other areas of your life.

Jeanette, who was a very successful real estate agent, spent years being controlled by her Wanter Mind. She was very methodical with her business and religious about her health, but when it came to men, all of her logic and self-control fell to the wayside. Whoever she wanted, she had to have. There was no plan B. When she recently joined a dating site, she didn't find many of the men attractive—except for one man in particular who did pique her interest. Immediately, her Wanter mentality kicked in. She had to meet him. Despite her friends advising her to wait a bit and let him ask her out, Jeanette grew impatient, sent a message, and asked him. They met and had a wonderful date. She was smitten, and the desire to "have him" took over, so rather than say goodnight and leave at the height of impulse, she slept with him and spent the night at his place. The next day, she waited for him to contact her, but the desire to be with him nearly drove her crazy. To her relief, he sent her a quick message that evening saying he had a nice time and hoped to see her soon.

Jeanette was elated that they were on track for a second date, but as another day passed with no follow-up on a time or place, her wanting kicked in once again. She checked his online profile every 10 minutes, thought about how she could run into him accidentally, and strategized what she could message him that would allow her to spark up conversation again. Finally, when the wanting became unbearable, she composed a short message and sent it. The guy took almost 12 hours to respond, and it wasn't what she was hoping for. He didn't make mention of getting together again, and now Jeanette was even more depressed, anxious, and confused. She felt terrible and sick to her stomach. What now? How could she rid herself of the awful feeling inside? Her stomach ached, her head pounded, and she felt so nauseated that she was on the verge of throwing up. There was only one way out of this misery, she thought, and that was to somehow see him again. She had to figure out a way. She sent him a text and invited him to a concert for which she already had tickets. It took a few days, but he responded that he would go with her. Immediately, the painful feeling subsided within her, replace by excitement and validation. They had a great time at the concert, slept together again afterward, but then he vanished from her life for good. Despite sending several texts and a few emails, Jeanette never heard from him. She suffered, agonized, and stalked him for almost a year after he ghosted.

Because wanting is an overwhelming thought pattern, it is very hard to sit with or ignore. When an event occurs that moves the Wanter further from her desire, wanting can turn into such a painful emotion that the person often feels she must. do. something. Her *Cursed Mind* jumps into hyperdrive and has only one mission: get closer to obtaining the object she desires by any means possible. This is what causes many women to push for a relationship too fast or make a move they shouldn't. Many clients have told me they knew they were making a mistake with a guy but did it anyway because at the time, they could not fight the incredible urge that is wanting.

Wanters are usually very ambitious women who go after what they want in life, making it very hard for them to play by any dating rules where they have to wait for someone else to take action. If Jeanette had been able to pace the relationship appropriately, it may have played out very differently. Perhaps if she had let the guy initiate more or hadn't seemed as eager when they were together, an alternate outcome would have occurred. Or, if Jeanette was not *Cursed*, she might have said to herself, *"Oh well, he's not that interested. I need to find someone else"* and continued to fill her funnel instead of hounding and luring this particular guy out with her. In a new relationship, timing your interactions and crafting appropriate responses with someone is extremely important. It can either give the impression you are cool and collected, or demanding and "crazy."

Unfortunately, being patient or accepting someone's low interest is almost impossible for the Wanter Mind because it is more fixated on getting who it wants than assessing how the other person feels. What that person needs or wants is never part of the equation. Some Wanters will even try to bargain their way into a relationship, promising certain benefits or arguing their case. The self-absorbed mind doesn't realize that while it's fighting to be with someone, it is also completely ignoring the other person in the relationship. This often happens at the end of a relationship, when a Wanter senses it's about to suffer a loss and therefore will desperately try to coerce the person not to leave.

Not often having felt real romantic love and not understanding that it is almost the exact opposite sensation of wanting keeps women with this *Curse* in a pattern of precipitous attachment. The attachment happens very quickly, which is why Wanters are known for falling hard and fast for people they don't know well or haven't known long. But love is never desperate, nor does it produce a painful urge to obtain someone. Love is selfless and freeing, whereas attachment is selfish and controlling. Can you see the difference? When you love someone and they don't love you back, your heart is sad but you accept the other person's feelings. When you *want* someone and they don't love you back, you just try harder and that causes more pain or problems for you.

Redirecting Wanting

A person with this *Curse* has a difficult time committing to someone who is available and loving, but it does happen. This doesn't mean the person is then cured, however. The *Cursed Mind* is very clever and will work to stay alive. If a woman with a Wanter Mind is smart, once she loses her craving for her partner, she will redirect her wanting to other things in order to keep her search for value going.

After Karen and Eddie married, the wanting between them dwindled, but because Karen had no intention of being single again, she directed her wanting to other things. One of Karen's big wants, for instance, was to be taken out to a nice dinner downtown. She didn't particularly like cooking and loved the social aspect of dining out. It made her feel good and provided a self-worth boost to eat at nice restaurants. Eddie often obliged in taking her out, but as soon as a day or two passed, Karen was already itching to go out again. At first Eddie didn't mind placating her requests, but as they continued in their marriage, and especially once they had kids, he became tired of having to keep up with her social needs. Eddie felt he never got a break from them and that Karen's appetite for going out was bottomless. He began to resent the fact that she couldn't just be happy at home eating a meal with him and that an evening out didn't satisfy her for more than a day. He felt like everything he did to make her happy was fleeting and never enough. Karen, on the other hand, believed that Eddie was becoming more selfish and spiteful in his reluctance to appease her. She felt he was robbing her of her happiness and wasn't being loving. Karen didn't see that her indirect wanting was draining the love right out of her marriage.

Karen's *Curse* did target Eddie directly from time to time as well. She began wanting Eddie to "be more." It was as if he had to constantly up his game. She wanted him to wear better clothes, take more responsibility with the kids, make more money, lose more weight, and so on. Eddie, and their relationship, was never just fine the why he was. Karen claimed she was only trying to bring out the best version of him and saw no harm in doing so. She believed that if she didn't love him, she wouldn't have taken such an interest in him. Of course, Eddie didn't see it that way at all.

To be in a commitment with a Wanter feels like you can never relax. You must forever be dangling a carrot for your partner to chase after or you have to keep life interesting by perpetually raising the bar one way or another. There always has to be something to want. When marriage, children, and the stresses of life are thrown in, it can be very difficult to keep that up. Some Wanters will cope with the monotony of married life by developing new addictions: shopping, gambling, binge eating, drinking, or even cheating. All of these habits are meant to satiate the Wanter mind from looking for fulfillment outside itself in a new way, now that it has the relationship it thought would make it feel whole but hasn't.

Even though a Wanter can redirect her wanting, the constant need for external indulgences still negatively affects her relationships. Wanters can be exhausting as partners because no matter what you do or give to them, they want more from you. Despite having the relationship or marriage they craved, they don't know how to be at peace—and if a woman isn't at peace, her partner cannot be, either.

How to Stop Wanting

You can stop this *Curse* once you recognize what it truly is. It is not an attraction to a certain type of guy or the belief that you simply love a challenge or like to "fix" people. When you are not at peace with yourself, you do not want peace in your relationships. You want to chase; you want hot-and-cold; you want unattainability. To change your failed relationship patterns, you must eradicate the *Cursed Mind* and its need for more value. You have to become conscious of why wanting happens within you, instead of blindly chasing who you want out of habit. And most importantly, you have to learn to accept yourself and your life as it is right now. Without doing that first, you will never be able to accept the interest and love that another person has to give you. This is why the third Cure of the *Curse* is "be accepting." When you accept yourself, you accept peace, and not only does the wanting within fade but so does the painful attachment to men. Without self-acceptance, you will look for ways to enhance your worth through things, experiences, and people. You will believe that the more that you have means the more that you are, and you will unconsciously want your way through your whole life.

The *Curse* will fight you in your quest to be accepting, making you feel awkward and uncomfortable when you first try to change. But in order to find a loving and caring relationship, you must find your way out of the habit to want because wanting and love cannot coexist. They are competing emotions, and each will take you in a different direction. Only you can determine which one will ultimately win.

Don't worry if you feel overwhelmed or confused right now because you are half way through the *Faces* and learning a lot about your potential thought habits without knowing the solution yet. Take a few deep breaths and continue on to the last two Faces. The answers you need are coming, so please don't despair. Use the tool you have to persevere through the next several pages: "The wound is where the light enters you."

REFLECTION

Reflect again on this chapter. If necessary, go back and reread it one more time. Then, put the book down for a day and try to catch yourself in "wanting." What is it that you want? How does wanting make you feel? What does wanting make you do?

Chapter Seven

The Superior Mind

Reina was not thrilled about having to contact me for help. Admitting she had a problem she couldn't fix herself was annoying for her. She had every area of her life under control and going just the way she wanted—except when it came to relationships. Reina had recently broken up with a guy named Danny, with whom she had fun and tremendous physical chemistry but not much else. It became clear Danny wasn't going to commit when one of her friends spotted him on a dating app, even though he had been sleeping with Reina for 10 months. When she decided to end it, she went to his workplace and yelled at him in front of his coworkers. Since then, she had been on a handful of app dates, none of which were good, in her opinion. She hired me to help her figure out how to get a guy who was more "her type" interested in her, as well as just reaffirm that app dating was worth her time and energy.

"I am starting to think the caliber of man I want doesn't exist, and that's why I'm alone," Reina lamented. "I guess that makes me feel better though. It's not me; it's the guys."

"What kind of guy was Danny?" I asked her that day in a coffee shop.

"God, Danny was perfect," she began. "He had these green sparkling eyes that melted me. His body is sick; he works out six days a week, and you can tell. The sex was amazing. I still think about it even now.

Sometimes I want to text him just to hook up one more time. I don't know if I'll ever find someone I have that kind of chemistry with again."

"It's interesting you call him perfect, even though he never really committed to you," I pointed out.

"Oh, I mean he's perfect in the sense that he's exactly my type," she corrected herself.

"Yes, but it sounds like he's only your type physically," I said. "I would imagine you would not like to date another guy who has sex with you while pursuing other women on Tinder."

Reina laughed as if I had made a joke.

"You have a lot of clients on these dating sites, right?" she asked. "I mean, am I going to find someone who meets my standards? I know how that must sound, but I'm highly educated, I make a great salary, and I'm the youngest looking 34-year-old I know. I just want to make sure if I put in the time to date this way, it's going to pay off by me finding a guy who matches my high value."

The Curse of the Superior Mind

Of all the *Faces of the Curse,* this is the one that can keep you single the longest. When the *Cursed Mind* shifts into Superior mode, your self-absorbed thinking is concentrated on how you can feel good about yourself and enhance your feelings of self-worth. The mind looks for opportunities where it can achieve the feeling of being better than others and the two most obvious ways it attempts to accomplish this is by urging you to show off or brag. *"I am so great and here is why,"* the Superior Mind declares. However, those are extreme tactics used by the *Cursed Mind*. There are other more subtle yet common habits that also create the feeling of superiority for which it uses to self-enhance. We will discuss those habits in this chapter as well as how they work against relationship building.

This *Face* functions similarly to, and often in tandem with, the Inferior Mind, only instead of looking for proof of your inadequacy, the Superior Mind hunts for ways it can prove its superiority. It can do this in a very loud and obvious way: *"Look at that! I'm the thinnest person in my office! The cute guy at the party last night complimented me and no one else! I am super smart, beautiful, and successful!"* Or, it can do this in a more inconspicuous way: *"Most guys just don't keep my attention. I can't believe he thought it was okay to wait three days to text me – I'll show him. I don't want to sound snobby, but I am not going to settle for just any guy who is interested in me. I'm very picky."* Regardless of how overt or insidious, this type of self-absorbed thinking is concentrated on making you feel as if you are better or more important than other people.

Although some of the aforementioned thoughts may sound like the effects of good self-esteem, there is a difference between having confidence in oneself and operating under the influence of the Superior Mind. High self-esteem is defined as having a positive but healthy and realistic view of yourself and your abilities. A woman with this quality acknowledges and accepts the good and not-so-good parts of herself. She is quick to recognize when she is wrong or someone else is better at something, and it doesn't affect her overall feelings about herself. Most telling, a person with high self-esteem does not rank other people's worth or believe that anyone is beneath her.

On the contrary, a person whose mind is habituated to self-absorbed, superior thinking might deny or downplay any unflattering qualities she might possess in order to keep her high worth intact. She can feel threatened when she is wrong or perceives someone as having more than her because that makes her feel like she is less. Most tellingly, she does not like to fraternize with men (or anyone else) whom she deems having "low value" or whom she has no use for.

Women who are highly conditioned to superior thinking are typically the most confused as to why they haven't found love. Many see themselves as being total catches and are therefore mystified as to how they are still single. But when the mind engages in superior thinking it often alienates others without any awareness of doing so. The simmering desire to feel important and be seen as important in every situation becomes your priority, which distracts you from taking real notice of how the people around you are feeling. Failing to recognize the emotions of others, and therefore, show empathy to them, makes connecting with anyone very difficult.

In a relationship, a woman with a Superior Mind might know how her partner feels (because she's told), but because she has been habituated to superior thinking, she will rarely indulge any request from him if it doesn't benefit her. This *Face* of the *Cursed Mind* is conditioned to the belief that making itself happy always takes precedence; and that conceding to someone else or putting that person's needs ahead of its own is a burden. It does not know and cannot fathom the innate and natural joy that comes from serving others or making them happy without gaining something for itself. Only our *Core Self* knows that.

Today, nearly everyone spends some time ruminating in the Superior Mind. How much time and to what degree determines the level of destruction it can do to our relationships. The thought habits stemming from this type of self-absorbed thinking create a number of behavioral tendencies that frequently put you at odds with others; even those with whom you might be attracted. When you regularly look for ways to build yourself up, you often end up putting others down, which is a relationship killer at any stage. We will explore these habits, which include the following: extreme pickiness, the tendency to judge and complain, and the need to be right. I will also explain how they prevent you from developing a deep or lasting relationship with another person.

How Superior Thinking Creates Self-Sabotage

Most of us know at least one person who has fallen under the Superior Mind *Curse*: She is the woman who openly and frequently touts her accomplishments or credentials so other people can bear witness to all her great qualities: "I got another A on my test, everyone! Did you know that people tell me how smart and beautiful I am all the time? I am so successful that men are intimidated by me." However, not all women with this *Curse* are cut from the same cloth. While most seem overly confident and self-congratulatory on the outside, the reason for their boasting and bragging can vary on the inside. Some were raised to look out for themselves and told they possessed a higher value than others, but a surprising number of women who parade a level of self-importance actually feel inadequate and worry they are not enough. Essentially, they possess an Inferior Mind, but instead of indulging in negative self-absorbed thinking, they fight these feelings by engaging the Superior Mind. To cope with feelings of inadequacy, they attempt to exhibit a level of superiority, hoping to show the world and themselves that they are just as good as the next person. This can lead some people to constantly seek "the best" in life: the best clothes, the best cars, the best tables at restaurants, the best vacations, the best jobs, and yes—the best partner. The Superior Mind believes, *"If I have the best, I am the best!"* not realizing that your true value can't be heightened or diminished no matter what or who you obtain.

Women who compensate for feelings of inferiority by employing the Superior Mind, can eventually draw a rigid line between what they see as worthy and acceptable for themselves and what is not. When this theoretical boundary is set, one of the most self-sabotaging dating patterns materializes: The mind convinces you to only consent to dating someone who elevates or at least matches its own perceived or desired level of high value, thus attaining high worth by association. Much in the same way as a name-dropper feels a sense of superiority when they tell people they are friends with a celebrity, the *Cursed Mind* looks to gain or reflect higher value by the people it dates. Each Superior Mind makes its own decisions on what qualifies as "worthy"; but once it sets its standard, being with anyone outside of that standard is unthinkable. Few women would openly acknowledge this, but it is the reason many find themselves uttering words like, "Why does this guy think he has a chance with me?" Or, "I'm not going to go out with someone *like that!*" And, "I'm just really picky."

When the Superior Mind wants you to be picky, it is always to the detriment of finding love. Not only does your pool of potential prospects become incredibly small, but more value is placed on the superficial qualities of a partner. To put it another way, the Superior Mind cares less about who someone is on the inside and what characteristics make him a good partner and is instead focused on a guy's outward image. Not just what he looks like—because image includes more than physical appearance—the guy must ultimately look "good on paper" and demonstrate worth in an area the Superior Mind has decided has noticeable value. In today's society that often means a guy who meets a certain height criteria, level of attractiveness, or status (career or otherwise), but it can include a particular income level, ethnicity, religion, or as made popular by social media, his amount of followers, likes, or even passport stamps. Dating someone who makes only an average salary or isn't tall enough, for example, would not be an option because the Superior Mind would consider that "settling" (if income and height were its embodiment of value.) Unfortunately, the qualities that actually matter in a partner such as kindness, generosity, integrity, and reliability never register on the *Cursed Mind's* must-have list—because while extremely important for a healthy relationship, these traits do not help maintain or elevate the Superior Mind's own feelings of worth.

A woman who is battling feelings of inferiority will often withstand serious relationship issues in order to attain high value by association. She often won't recognize that a relationship is unloving or toxic and may tolerate a man's poor treatment because she doesn't realize the ego boost that comes from being with him is not love.

Beverly, for example, is a paralegal who is smart and attractive. She wanted to be a lawyer but failed passing the bar. Her parents were perfectionists and hard on her growing up, so when she had to settle for what she thought of as a lesser career path, her *Cursed Mind* wrestled with her sense of worth. Subconsciously, she felt she needed to compensate for her shortcomings in order to validate that she was as good as her parents said. This led to Beverly's big downfall in love. She only dated highly successful men and refused to give anyone else a chance unless they sat on top of an organizational chart. She insisted she was only attracted to guys who were smart and powerful, but in reality, she was deathly afraid of dating someone she saw as "average" because her *Cursed Mind* would see herself as average, too. She did not realize this until she broke her *Curse*, of course. Even when I gently pointed out this fear within her, she scoffed and disagreed about feeling that way. For years, she found herself in the same type of relationship where these highly successful men prioritized themselves and their work over her, and she accepted it because deep down she felt she was the subordinate one in the relationship and it was the only way for her to elevate her own feelings of self-value. She eventually realized she was using the wrong metric to evaluate someone's potential when the last guy she dated yelled at her for getting up in the middle of the night to use the bathroom, disturbing the sleep he needed for work the next day. Finally, she asked herself, why am I always repeating this pattern? The truth of what I had been saying became clear, and the pattern ended. Beverly is now happily married to a very nice man and can use the bathroom whenever she wants.

The Superior Mind is only interested in gaining value from the guys it associates with, and for that reason, you can unwittingly prioritize qualities that don't really matter in a person and discount those that truly do. The feeling of associated high worth is often confused with love and attraction because superiority is a fix or a high for the mind, just as romantic love is high for our *Core Self*. If you aren't able to discern which part of you is experiencing the high, you can involve yourself in a relationship that isn't right for you. Ironically, most women with this *Curse* who are setting out to feel good about themselves, choose men who only make them feel bad in the end.

With so few guys meeting the dating standard for the Superior Mind, another negative pattern frequently arises – the tendency to hold tight to the person who does meet all necessary requirements, regardless of how unhealthy or imbalanced the relationship might be. A guy might be wrong for you in every way, but your *Cursed Mind* won't move on from him despite a lousy or lonely relationship because you think viable prospects are few and far between. Reina put up with Danny's noncommittal behavior for this very reason. She only wanted to date attractive, younger men. If she didn't have that instant attraction to someone, she quickly rejected him, claiming there wasn't any spark. When she met Danny, she fell for him instantaneously because he fulfilled the requirement set by her Superior Mind. She loved seeing his gorgeous face walk through her door; reveled in knowing her friends swooned over his incredible physique; and got a thrill knowing that wherever they went, heads would turn. But he rarely answered her phone calls, frequently cancelled plans, and only spent time with her on his terms. Reina was a typical example of the relationship mentality brought on by the Superior Mind. She would have rather had a "non-relationship" with someone she thought was worthy then a real relationship with someone she considered to be average.

It needs to be said that there is nothing wrong with dating men who are good-looking. Nor is it wrong to date men who are highly successful, drive nice cars, or are more than six feet tall. But those things have nothing to do with love and rapport in a relationship, so if they are your leading criteria, don't you have to ask yourself why they are the standard by which you measure potential? If you have this *Curse*, you may have never experienced a case in which a guy became more attractive as you got to know him, and that will likely continue until you recognize your own Superior Mind and awaken to its motives. If someone's image is what matters most to you, then integrity, kindness, or even humor are not going to enhance your attraction.

Without acknowledging that love might come in a different package than expected, and allowing your *Core Self* to quarterback your search, the Superior Mind can reach a point where it decides no one will ever be good enough for you to date – that every man you meet is average or uninteresting, and you would be better off alone. If you don't question this mentality and observe how it is hurting your ability to find love, the *Cursed Mind* can and will turn your single status into yet another way to exhibit high value: *"At least I didn't settle"* or, *"I'm the smart one! I don't have the headache of a husband like all my friends!"* This is how the Superior Mind can avoid rejection by telling you that you aren't a "needy girl who can't live without a man." If you arrive at this thought, often the next step is pushing men away to keep yourself from being rejected by them first. If you have told yourself you are of higher value for so long, you won't want to run the risk of ever having evidence to the contrary.

When you become aware of your Superior Mind and stop letting it choose who you should be with, your *Core Self* begins to naturally focus more on what is really important: a man's character, the connection and chemistry between you, and your shared values. When you bring your *Core Self* to the center of your being, those qualities become far more important to you, and the type of packaging becomes less critical. The truth about dating can be boiled down to this: The shallower and narrower you are about what image you want your partner to have, the more opportunities for love you end up missing, and the more likely you are to stay single.

The Superior Vibe

The Superior Mind's constant thinking on you and your importance can eventually trick you into a false belief that you are the exception to most rules in life and more deserving than other people. The thoughts of a woman with a Superior Mind who is single and dating might sound like this: *"I deserve to be treated like a queen. I deserve a man who will pay every time."* Or, *"I shouldn't have to waste time messaging so many guys. I shouldn't have to sit through so many mediocre dates."* It's not that wanting to be treated well is wrong or app dating isn't tiring; it is the thought that you are entitled to special treatment and are "above" doing what other people have to do that causes trouble. The Superior Mind singles you out, making you feel special and different, but sabotaging your chances for building rapport with anyone. For instance, a woman with a Superior Mind might feel she shouldn't have to work as hard as other women in order to meet people. She might strive for the bare minimum and put herself online or go to a busy happy hour, but doing anything more than just being there would be doing too much. *"Guys should come to me, not the other way around,"* her Superior Mind might say. If the person she zeroes in on doesn't make a move, she might go into self-protection mode, citing the guy as not being confident enough so she wouldn't like him anyway. Or, if he asks for her number but then doesn't call, the Superior Mind will conclude that he was simply intimidated by her beauty, brains, or other superior trait.

This *Face* of the Curse won't take responsibility when things don't happen the way you want, or allow you to self-reflect on what you could have done better to change the outcome. Instead it will spin any poor results into something positive to keep your feelings of high value intact. While that can make you feel good instead of feeling rejected, it doesn't help get you a date or into a relationship. The vibe you give off when you believe you are too good to engage in some average or menial task is snobby or pretentious, which some guys might view as confidence at first, but many will quickly catch on to the underlying entitled belief.

Of course some women do get further in the process and actually go on dates, but dating with an attitude of entitlement rarely produces great results. Because of it's urge to show its high value to other people, some women with this mindset might find themselves making comments that sound pompous, arrogant, or completely detached from the conversation because their focus is not on the other person. Many women with this *Curse* put their feet in their mouth when they are around someone they are interested in. Sometimes they realize it after the fact, and sometimes they don't. Either way, the energy emanating from someone with a Superior Mind is typically more chilly and antagonistic than warm and inviting, and that can really make or break a date.

For example, last year I received an email from a woman who was frustrated with her love life. She was beautiful and confident, but she complained that in the year and a half she had been going on app dates, she had only encountered two guys she found interesting. Consequently, they were the only two who were not interested in her. She wrote that she felt cursed with bad luck and wanted my help to figure out why the only men she even remotely wanted to see again didn't reciprocate her feelings. When we met, I asked her to first describe the men she was not interested in.

She sighed heavily. "What can I say? I don't mean to be rude, but they were just awful. They were not attractive or interesting. Some of them practically put me to sleep. It was a huge waste of my time. I know within a few seconds if I'm going to click with someone or not, and it's annoying when you meet someone you thought might be a possibility only to lay eyes on them and know you will be counting the minutes until you can leave."

She proceeded to then tell me about the two men she actually liked; how she was super flirty, taught both of them about wine, and was able to show off a little by speaking French to their waiter. She said she did tease the guys about not knowing a second language, but they thought the comment was funny. She said both men asked for her number but failed to follow up.

"After all the time I spent sorting through the duds to have the only two men with potential not want to see me again is so disappointing," she said dejectedly. "I don't know what happened! All the other guys were totally smitten with me—some of them so much so I couldn't get rid of them! It doesn't make any sense that I can have any guy I want except the two who interest me. I swear I'm just somehow cursed."

The woman was definitely *Cursed*, but not the way she thought. It was clear to me that her "high-valued" Superior mindset was the reason for her ironic results. Through the 18 months of dinner and coffee dates, she only thought about how much work the process was for her. When a prospective date turned out to be less than what she expected, she brooded and complained about it, irritated they had taken up her time. She called most of the men boring and unattractive, and callously disregarded anyone who didn't wow her. In the same breath, she whined about the two men who treated her in the same regard. She spent no time appreciating the guys who spent their time, money, and attention on her, and her entitled attitude was something that permeated her being, whether she was with someone she liked or not.

"I can sum up the problem very simply," I told her. "If you are not appreciative for every man who shows real interest in you, especially for the guys who pay you the compliment of taking you on a date, you won't earn the chance with the two men that you want. You might think your demeanor changes with the people you are interested in, but I assure you that when you assume a state of entitlement, believing your time is more valuable than anyone else's or that you are above sitting through a date with someone you consider 'mediocre,' those thoughts permeate your being and create an energy that sticks with you at all times; it just comes off differently depending on how you feel about the person you are with. With the men you don't like, it comes off negative and bitchy, but with the men you do like, it comes off as arrogant and entitled. Neither vibe is attractive."

The woman looked stunned for a minute. She had not ever thought about how her mindset affected the men she had gone out with. She had not put herself in their shoes and recognized they had their own high hopes of seeing her again and potentially finding love. When she abruptly ended a date or ungraciously declined a second one, she never considered how she was making the men feel. As the *Cursed Mind* does, it only thought about itself and what it was or was not getting.

The Superior Mind feels excited and reacts with "wanting" when it finds someone it desires to obtain. However, it has the opposite reaction when it encounters someone it can't use for enhancement, treating those people with indifference or disdain, which is what the woman in the previous example had done. Once the Superior Mind decides a man has lower value, it has no use for him and promptly disregards him. This is why many women who exude *Cursed* confidence are labeled as cold, rude, selfish, or simply a "bitch." The Superior Mind only acknowledges people it finds beneficial for itself, and everyone else is ignored.

You might be thinking, but don't men love bitches? There was even a series of books by Sherry Argov dedicated to this idea. Maybe you read them, and it even worked for you. I won't argue that being confident is an attractive quality, and bitches have no shortage of confidence. A "bitch" doesn't crave a man, seek his approval, or worry if he's going to commit. *Acting* like a confident bitch might make it seems as if you are at peace with yourself, and peace within is the most alluring quality. But *being* a bitch is a different story. A bitch (operating under the Superior Mind) doesn't care about her partner's needs or know how to love him without certain conditions. She puts herself first and ultimately hinders growth and love in her relationship. The *perception* of being at peace with yourself really only charms people at the preliminary stage of dating. Once the relationship deepens, the self-absorbed mind becomes more visible, causing big problems. Therefore, a bitch may be able to land more men than other women, but that doesn't mean she will experience real love. In many cases, she won't.

For anyone who identifies with this *Face,* the key to connecting with more people and growing opportunities for love is to stop looking at men as being worthy or unworthy of you. When you call men names, describing them as "boring," "stupid," or "weird" it is your Superior Mind diminishing them in order to build yourself up. The mind likes to label people because doing so makes it feel "above" them, but your *Core Self* respects everyone and doesn't seek to inflate your sense of worth by association with one kind of person or rejection of another. When we appreciate the innate good in everyone, we awaken to the truth of ourselves: We are not more or less than anyone else, and there is no reason to continue striving for high value, as it isn't bringing us love nor does it fill us with any joy. The only task that is accomplished by the Superior Mind is creating a vibe of self-importance that most people eventually retreat from.

Acting From Superior Thinking

As I mentioned, the Superior Mind uses several tactics in order to enhance itself other than the obvious inclination to brag and show off. Two of the most pervasive habits are also the most unrecognized –

judging and the need to be right. Both of these thought-habits typically go unnoticed by the person engaging in them, which is unfortunate because they can easily sabotage that person's dating life or intimate relationship.

The first habit of judging is one of the Superior Mind's favorites. When the mind makes you a judge, it feels superior over others. Sure, you could land a higher-paying job, marry a prince, or become Instafamous, but picking people apart and judging what could be better about them is a much faster and easier way for the self-absorbed mind to experience the sensation of superiority. Some women eventually form a habit of looking at everything in life with a judging eye, while others stick to playing magistrate solely in the dating sphere.

Most people never realize they're being judgmental, however, I see it all the time in single women today, especially because I was someone who used to be judgmental as well. Judgment can be positive or negative but the negative tends to strengthen the minds feeling of superiority much more and therefore that is the form of preferred judging by this *Face*. One of the most noticeable places I see constant judging is with the assessment of people on dating apps. The Superior Mind loves to judge guys at a glance, swiping left on any profile that needs improvement or seems not worthy enough. It's not unusual for the Superior Mind to declare that there isn't anyone good online without you having gone on a single date. This is another example of how the mind uses other people as a vehicle to build itself up, but consequentially distances you from connecting with anyone when it does so. As the mind judges what is wrong with the guy it's considering, it feels a sense of "rightness" in itself. That feeling is addicting which is why it continues to judge, not noticing or caring that it's ruling out all contenders in the running for your heart in the process. In fact, it thinks it's doing you a favor!

Remember Reina? She had a very hard time finding any guy that she wanted to go out with. With almost every profile she found a quality she disliked. When she did match with someone and agreed to a meeting, she would scrutinize every detail of the guy; from the brand of his shoes to the way he chewed his food. *"Ugh,"* she would think. *"I can't go out with him again. Look how he sits with his legs crossed. It's effeminate. And look at his eyebrows! I can't spend the rest of my life with those eyebrows. What does he do for a living? That can't make much money."* Because she was unaware of her habit to judge, Reina only saw what needed to be better when seated across from a man. The Superior Mind would not allow her to wait and see if love could blossom because it began judging him before even knowing him. The only men that passed her judgment test were those whose image and looks were perfect, which was why Reina was only ever attracted to men who were charmers and players—guys who looked great on the outside but didn't want to commit.

Women that are prone to judging often have difficulty getting second dates. Judgment is palpable, and most guys will pick up on critiques, whether they are vocalized or merely communicated with a disapproving look. Over the years I've had numerous clients retell first dates that were, in their opinion, "nothing special"; citing numerous things about the guy they didn't like. However, these same women are always caught off guard when the guy doesn't follow up and ask them out again. They have a hard time grasping how their judgment could be the reason, but most men won't want to get involved with a woman he feels looks down on him in some way, no matter how attractive or successful she might be. As a whole, most men don't suffer from negative self-absorbed thinking, and therefore, don't seek approval when they are judged. They just move on.

Breaking this thought habit is key for not only finding someone but also preserving a committed relationship. When you meet someone of interest and start dating him, it may not be long before the Superior Mind starts to judge what isn't perfect or good enough about him. That thought often opens the door to wonder if you could find someone cuter or more successful, maybe a better dresser with less baggage? Or perhaps someone who would make the bed or not leave towels on the floor? As you ponder these things, you fail to see what you are doing to the relationship you are already involved in; you create space and begin to neglect it. Then it's just a short while before the *Curse* has once again put an end to something that could have been so good.

Marcy was an example of this. At 36, she was tired of dating and wanted to get married and start a family. However, anytime she got into a relationship with a man, it wasn't long before she was picking him apart and asking herself if he was all the things she really wanted in a partner. As soon as the honeymoon period was over and the relationship started to really take off, Marcy would begin to look at her boyfriends with a judgmental eye. If she found one or two things she didn't like, she convinced herself she was settling for less and became increasingly annoyed—she was a catch, after all. She didn't have to settle for just anyone and would rather be alone than compromise and be with someone who didn't meet her criteria. And that's exactly what happened: Marcy's attitude destroyed every relationship she was ever in, and 10 years later, at 45, she is still very much single.

Even if you do take a trip down the aisle, your marriage is not safe if you allow it to cohabitate with the Superior Mind. You will find new ways to be picky and new things to judge that may be more directed at your partner's abilities than his image. *"Cook it this way,"* the *Cursed Mind* might say. *"Clean it that way. Buy this kind of detergent, not that kind!"* And when it comes to the more important issues, your opinion might be even more judgmental: "Your brother is driving me crazy. You need to speak to him immediately! You gave little Timmy a cookie after dinner? Don't you know what having sugar this late will do to him? I can't believe you haven't opened an IRA yet. Do you want to just flush money down the toilet?" Most women with this *Curse* become the unspoken boss in the marriage, which really means, "I'm exercising my superiority." Unfortunately for the spouse, days are filled with strict direction and nagging—which certainly makes a fun marriage for any man (is my sarcasm coming through?).

When you apply a negative judgment to someone, either directly to his being or indirectly at his ability, the Superior Mind feels a sense of righteous superiority. The act of judging, however, separates you and your partner further and further apart because as you feel more elevated in your stance, your partner feels belittled. This can lead him to ponder the question, "Can I ever make her happy?" The bottom line is this: The necessary qualities of love like understanding, empathy, and forgiveness are pushed aside when you are busy being a judge and your partner can feel the absence of those elements.

The second subtle habit of the Superior Mind is closely related to judgment; it is the need to be right. Nothing makes the self-absorbed mind happier than being right because that is the ultimate display of superiority over another person. Unfortunately, in order to be right, you have to make someone else wrong, which never feels good to the other person. You can also make a situation wrong by complaining about it and putting it down. Very little people notice this but complaints are the way the mind declares, *"This situation is not right or should not be happening to me,"* making you feel as if you are above or too good for whatever is happening.

Make your boyfriend or spouse wrong too many times, and you will end up alienating him completely. This is especially evident in the face of disagreements, which all couples have. Most healthy partnerships learn to compromise and give a little so they can reach an agreement. But if you have a Superior Mind, you are more likely to keep fighting because your desire to be right often overrules your desire for relationship peace.

One example of a relationship that nearly failed due to the need to be right: Kenny and Jill, who had only been married a year. Kenny was a smart, high profile lawyer who had spent years fighting for his clients and built his reputation on winning arguments. This deep-rooted need to be right seeped into his personal life, and when it came to decorating their house, Kenny wanted Jill to do things the way he thought made sense. Jill had her own ideas of what she wanted and tried to express them to Kenny but was repeatedly met with an argument: "That makes no sense. My way is much more logical." (Code for, "I'm right; you're wrong.") For months, they argued about the house, and at one point, Jill was so upset by what she called Kenny's "controlling behavior" that she left for a week to stay with her mother. What the couple did not realize was Kenny's Superior Mind *Curse* had him believing he was right about how they should go about decorating—and therefore, Jill was wrong. Although there are better and worse ways to decorate a house, there really isn't a right or wrong way; it comes down to preference. Jill thought Kenny needed to be in control, and Kenny thought Jill was emotional and nonsensical. When I sat down with them, they were on the verge of a divorce as a result of all the fighting during the past year. It wasn't until Kenny had the epiphany that making Jill happy had to be more important than doing what he thought was "the right way" to furnish a house that their relationship completely turned around. They are still very much in love today and recently celebrated their five-year anniversary—but it is only because Kenny awoke to his *Curse* of the Superior Mind and works every day to put love ahead of being right.

The Superior Mind will often do whatever it can to avoid admitting fault. Taking blame for a mistake is something only our *Core Self* can do; hence, you know you are living as your *Cursed Self* if you cannot accept responsibility for your errors. The *Cursed Mind* will never accept blame for mistakes because then it would have to accept it wasn't in the right and is therefore not superior to the other person in the conversation. It will try every trick in the book to avoid being wrong including joking, deflecting, or creating an entirely new problem just to avoid actually saying those two apologetic words—I'm sorry—thus accepting blame. Arguments can last for days, weeks, or even years because the Superior Mind will hold on to its original belief and not waver, even if it's at the expense of love. If you have this *Curse*, all that really matters is being right, and if love is lost in that quest, the Superior Mind will find a reason why that wasn't your fault, either.

The first year of marriage with my husband was undoubtedly the most difficult. We fought quite a bit and the reason was almost entirely my fault. I didn't see it at the time but whenever my husband attempted to tell me something he wished I'd improve upon, he was met with an argument about why I didn't need to oblige his request. Case in point; he asked me to find a good spot to always put my keys so that I wouldn't lose them. Back then, I wasn't as present as I am now and I lost keys and various other items quite a bit. Instead of saying, "Thanks for the idea, honey. I'll give that a try", my Superior Mind heard his suggestion as an attack on my worth. In attempt to continue being right, I balked, "I don't lose my keys that much!" And added, "You are trying to micromanage me. Just worry about your own keys!"

What I learned was that a person who lives through the Superior Mind doesn't notice how defensive they are, day in and day out. I didn't stop to notice that when my husband pointed the finger at me, I automatically pointed a finger right back. Why did I do that? Why was it so important to deflect blame and make him wrong? Why could I not accept that maybe I had faltered and, instead of fighting it, learn and grow from it? The answer is because the *Cursed Mind* is not interested in making sacrifices of itself for the good of a relationship. It doesn't want to admit fault and have to face the fact we are not superior to anyone else. It would rather ruin the love we have with someone than to be vulnerable, admit mistakes, and work to be better for your partner. That would be the loving thing to do but would defy the identity of being perfect or better than most—and you cannot be both at the same time. Repeat: You cannot be loving and be superior. Putting the person you love first and looking to improve yourself is vital in any relationship. If you have this *Curse*, you don't want to do those things. Instead you think, *"Why should I 'bow' to someone else? He should concede to me!"* Or, *"Why do I have to be the one to say sorry? He should say it first!"* Sadly, it took some time for me to truly grasp that my husband was only ever trying to help me, and he absolutely reserved the right to also tell me when something I did was bothersome to him. Luckily, I came to practice listening and ingesting constructive criticism instead of immediately defending myself against it, which made a big difference in the way we communicated.

Being right is the more dangerous of the two habits because it is self-perpetuating. The more the Superior Mind is right, the more it wants and seek to be right. Without much awareness, a person can become conditioned to looking for opportunities where others are wrong, just to be able to point it out. *"Ah! What he said/did was wrong! I'm so excited to be able to show him that,"* the mind thinks. On a date that can mean drawing attention to a mistake or error which then feels humiliating to the other person. In a relationship it can mean constantly identifying imperfections, or pointing out a miscalculation which, overtime, can be demoralizing. And, as I found out the hard way, the more you hold on to the idea that you do not have to be the one to change or give in, the more your partner will do the same. The *Curse* has a way of rubbing off on the people around you, and soon it will have your partner digging in his heels and acting in the right himself. The good news is that the minute you surrender to the possibility of being wrong, their defenses come down and compassion and empathy kick in!

Change Can Be Hard
This Face of the *Curse* is the most difficult to break of them all. Because the Superior Mind believes you are better than others, it also thinks you know better, too. Therefore someone saying you are using the wrong metric to date will have you reacting defensively, in most cases. You might listen to opposing opinions and may even see the point, but this *Curse* won't let you easily bend on your belief of who is right for you or how you should behave with them.

Coaching a woman with a Superior Mind is by far the hardest for me, because while they want help with dating or their relationship, they do not want to change or self-improve. In their mind, they are fine the way they are, and it's the men in the world who need improving. In a way, they only want counsel on how to cope with a world that never meets their expectations, or they want direction on how to better influence it with certain dating techniques from my other books. I understand it because I've walked in their shoes, but penetrating the *Cursed Mind* is still hard regardless.

Reina had a hard time with our coaching sessions because although she longed to be married and have a family, she didn't want to hear any constructive criticism. Her *Cursed Mind* fought to protect her superior mindset, and so any suggestion I made that pointed to her being the cause of her problems was met with a strong defense. I could almost hear her Superior Mind yell, *"Stop saying I'm doing something wrong! I'm never wrong! I have 10 examples I can think of off the top of my head where I'm right!"* When I explained she had to put emphasis on the more important qualities of a man instead of being so focused on their looks, she felt I was telling her to settle for someone she didn't find attractive. Her *Cursed Self* had made her so shallow that even the suggestion to reprioritize her relationship criteria annoyed her. Our conversations remained gridlocked because she would not recognize herself as a large part of the problem.

But then we had a breakthrough.

Reina was coming up on her 35th birthday. A week beforehand, she had a rare moment of vulnerability during one of our sessions. She broke down in tears and admitted that she thought her life would have turned out differently. She thought she would be married and have children of her own by now. She sobbed uncontrollably and in a momentary outburst became angry and yelled, "This wasn't supposed to happen to me!"

I asked her what was supposed to happen.

"I'm supposed to have a husband. I'm supposed to live in a big house and have two children. I have so much to offer someone, and yet here I sit completely alone. It doesn't make any sense," she cried.

I asked Reina how she felt right now, and she said she mostly felt angry. She was angry that she didn't have what she wanted and deserved, and other women with far less did.

"Why do you deserve it?" I asked her.

This caught Reina off guard. "Why? Because I'm a good person," she answered. "I'm smart. I have an awesome job. I have a great life. I deserve it because ... I just do."

"Is it something everyone deserves?" I asked.

"No, not everyone. I don't know, really," she admitted. "I guess I feel deep inside that I should have it."

"You mean you feel entitled to it?" I asked.

Reina became angry. "No, that's not what I'm saying!" she insisted.

"What are you saying then?" I asked.

Reina was at a loss for words. She struggled to find a comeback, but she couldn't.

I jumped in. "Instead of fighting what I said and trying to find a reason to make me wrong, why don't you think about it for a second. Why don't you see if there is any truth to what I'm saying, that you feel entitled to whatever you want? There is no need to get defensive. I'm not judging you. I just think we should explore this feeling."

"Fine," she said reluctantly. "I guess I can do that."

I sat quietly and watched her. She started to cry a little more.

"Do you think that me believing I am entitled to a family is the reason I don't have one now?" she asked me.

I began carefully; knowing this small break in her defenses was what I needed to help her see what was going on inside of her.

"If you think you deserve a man's love and are owed a great life, what sort of energy do you think you put out there?" I prodded. "What vibe do you think you give people, especially men?"

"I have not had a relationship in so long, I really could not answer that," Reina sulked.

"And why is that? Why do you think a real relationship has not come out of the last several years of dating?" I asked.

"I just have not found anyone I like. I have high standards, and I've always found something wrong with the men who do ask me out," she said.

"If you've always found something wrong," I said, "do you think it's possibly because you're always looking for something to be wrong?"

"Why would I do that? Then I'd be shooting myself in the foot. I don't want to be alone; I want to find someone," she argued.

"Yes, but you said yourself you have 'high standards,' which means you are looking for a specific idea of a person that you have in your head, and if a guy doesn't measure up to that idea, you aren't interested. Is it possible that who you are searching for is just a concocted idea of a person, and not a real person?" I asked. "In our heads, we never factor in flaws or imperfections, or even things we may not necessarily like. We dream with our own idea of perfection, which does not hold up in real life. Maybe you would rather be alone than compromise this idea you have because it's what you think you deserve, and you have a fear of being with someone who isn't 'perfect' or 'ideal,' in your opinion. Because then you might have to face the fact that you aren't those things, either."

I could almost hear her *Curse* say, *"Ouch."*

"What would I have to do differently?" she asked me quietly.

Now we were getting somewhere. "You have to start really looking for love, instead of looking for the kind of man who fits some image criteria," I told her. "It's a subtle shift in thinking, but a very important one! If you stop dating with your mind and start dating with your heart, I promise you will find love. Right now, you see yourself as more deserving and better than other people because you are smart and beautiful, but that mentality is what is holding you back from the most wonderful and fulfilling experience humans can have. Yes, you have a pretty face; yes, you have a high-paying job and several degrees, but what you *have* doesn't matter to love, Reina. Once you detach your sense of self from all the things you think make you who you are and focus on becoming the most loving version of yourself, you'll finally find what you have been looking for all this time."

"You're telling me to settle again," she said, deflated.

"No, I'm telling you to throw away the 'box' you have created that says if a guy doesn't fit inside, he's not worthy of you," I corrected her. "I'm actually telling you to raise your standards. I'm saying you should place importance on qualities that are important instead of qualities that are superficial and, in the long run, do not matter. I'm telling you to follow your heart, and not the mind."

REFLECTION

Reflect for a moment on what you've just learned. Reread this chapter if needed. Put the book down, and for a day, see if you can hear yourself judging, complaining, or looking for evidence to feel a sense of high value. How does it make you feel? What energy are you putting out to the world when you engage in those thoughts, and what choices does it lead you to make?

Chapter Eight

The Contestant Mind

Darcy is a fashion consultant living in New York City. Like most people in the industry, she not only works in fashion, she lives for it and goes to great lengths to make sure her image is perfect. Every extra penny in her paycheck goes to enhancing her wardrobe or maintaining her appearance. She's a petite brunette with a very outgoing personality, and last year she decided to get breast implants. From the outside she looks like a girl that men would notice, so you might be surprised to learn she has a chronic dating problem. However, Darcy has been on dozens of first dates in the last two years, and none of them have resulted in a second. She is active on dating apps and often approached when she is out, but recently, a pattern has emerged, and the initial attraction she gets from guys never results in a relationship.

One day, Darcy called me, crying hysterically. "It happened again!" she sobbed.

"Tell me what happened," I said.

She took a deep breath. "The guy I went out with on Thursday hasn't texted me," she said. "We had a great time. He was so funny and cute. He even said we should go out again. I don't understand it. This happens every time! What am I going to do? Everyone around me is getting married, and here I am without a boyfriend. My friend Jackie isn't even that attractive, and she is dating this unbelievable guy! If she gets married before I do, I am going to move out of the country!"

I tried to calm Darcy down and reminded her that racing Jackie to the altar would only put pressure on herself, which would lead to putting pressure on the guys she was dating. Darcy was not lacking in initial attraction; she matched with many guys on Bumble and Tinder and was asked out quite often. However, something she was doing or saying on the first date was turning guys off so much that they didn't want to sit through round two and get to know her better and I had to figure out what it was.

Darcy wasn't a "mean girl" and she never shied away from meeting new people, but she did have a habit of constantly talking about herself. She also had a tendency to compare herself to those around her and this had a big impact on her life, both socially and romantically. She was jealous of friends who easily met their significant others. It seemed unfair that she struggled with love while others found it effortlessly. It wasn't uncommon for her to skip bridal showers or engagement parties because it was difficult for her to act happy for others when she was miserable about her own situation. Even just seeing a couple holding hands on the street was enough to send her into a tailspin.

Before she went on dates, Darcy prepped herself for hours. She devoted half the day to doing her hair and makeup, and she would text pictures of herself to her friends asking how she looked. When she arrived on the date, Darcy was excited but equally consumed with nervous energy. While she tried to be engaging and personable, most of the time she rambled on about herself without realizing it.

Darcy would do a little Google searching before and after each date. She would click through the guy's photos on Instagram, looking for any signs of him hanging out with other women. Then, Darcy would obsessively compare and analyze them. After many hours of scrutinizing, she was always quite sure her date was not going to call her again. And although he never did, it wasn't for the reason she thought. What I came to understand after only a few sessions of coaching with her was that

Darcy was suffering from the last Face of the *Curse*, the Contestant Mind.

The Curse of the Contestant Mind
This *Curse* is the easiest to spot because it is the most noticeable to outside observers. The reason I call it the *Curse* of the Contestant Mind is because women with this type of self-absorbed thinking view life as a contest. Their mind is unconsciously conditioned to function two ways: It compares itself to others in an attempt to gauge its own level of worth, and it constantly seeks attention. The first habit of comparing is yet another way the self-absorbed mind keeps the focus on itself by constantly asking *"am I good enough today compared to this person or that person?"* The mind loves to play the game of deciding who is superior and who is inferior so it can toggle between both *Faces*. Making comparisons to other women leads to competition once a guy enters the equation and that stimulates the *Curse Mind* further because it creates the possibility of you becoming a clear winner should the guy chose you, which makes the mind feel superior.

Although it may not seem like comparing yourself to others would be that damaging to your love life, especially given the fact you only do it in your head, the truth is that when you engage in comparison habits, you cause yourself to vacillate between feeling really good and really bad about yourself. Your self-absorbed mind ping-pongs between believing its worthy and worthless, depending on the situation. One day it tells you that you're ahead of the class and the next day it says you're behind the curve, which causes your emotions to fluctuate regularly. Like all the *Curses,* the mind then looks for an external approach to make you feel better, which is almost always counterproductive to growing and fostering a real relationship.

For instance, maybe you recently met someone and you are just getting to know each other. Then, your best friend, who met someone at nearly the same time, is asked to be in an exclusive relationship. Suddenly, your Contestant Mind starts comparing and tells you that your friend is more worthy because she now has a serious boyfriend. You feel jealous, sad, and unable to shake the feeling of not being good enough. Instead of recognizing that your mind has fallen into a conditioned thought pattern and acknowledging that your *Cursed* thinking is the cause of these bad feelings, you take action in an effort to feel better and heighten your sense of worth. You might text the guy you were seeing, hinting that you need to have a talk, or asking him to be exclusive. If he isn't ready to do so, he could feel pressured by your suggestion and back off which is the opposite outcome that you wanted. More severe tactics might ensue from this situation as well, like rushing into sex in the hopes you further the relationship, or lashing out at your friend because you're envious, both of which are self-sabotaging.

The second habit of attention-seeking is how the Contestant Mind draws notice to itself in order to feel significant. *"Look! Notice me. When you do, I feel important! When you don't, I feel nonexistent,"* it seems to say. Attention from others fuels the feeling of value and being enough. Once the attention fades, however, the Contestant Mind will start to suffer from withdraw and pursue another fix. For this reason, those habituated to this Face are often addicted to social media where they can easily fish for positive feedback by posting selfies and other self-focused messages. But gaining followers and receiving likes based on superficial qualities creates a vicious cycle. Because you can get instant attention, you can create an addiction to post more often, thus becoming even more dependent on feedback. Soon, you can be dedicating massive amounts of time to your social media image, not realizing that the attention you're getting is fleeting and mostly depthless. That is to say, it never amounts to anything more substantial with any guy, and it never makes you happy for long.

Emily is 22 years old and admittedly addicted to her social media accounts. She wants to be in a relationship with someone, but she spends most of her time each day thinking about what she's going to post online. She takes more than 50 selfies attempting to create the perfect one. She constantly checks to see what people, mainly guys, are saying about her pictures and stresses about replying to them in a timely fashion. I asked Emily if she thought that she spent too much time online, thinking and posting about herself, during one of our coaching sessions. She said yes but protested that everyone else does the same thing. I followed up by asking if everyone else had trouble connecting with guys and maintaining a good relationship, to which she also replied yes.

The Contestant Mind thinks the more people who see and agree with your worthiness, the better, and doesn't pause to question how attention-seeking, especially online, can hurt your self-esteem. Your *Core Self* knows the danger, which is why you may have considered shutting down your accounts, but can't find the will power with the *Cursed Mind* running your life. When you do get involved in a relationship, you are likely to be disappointed by the amount of attention you're granted because the adoration of one cannot hold a candle to attention from many. You might expect the other person to nourish you with heaping doses of positive feedback, and when he doesn't, you can feel unsatisfied or empty. Instead of understanding why you feel that way, your *Cursed Mind* will just blame your partner for not doing his job to fulfill you. Or you might even seek to supplement attention from other sources by having side relationships with other guys.

In this chapter, we will investigate the main thought habits of this *Curse*. The need for attention, the desire to compare and compete, and striving for the upper hand in a relationship, are all unconscious mind patterns that spawn unbefitting behaviors which could keep you single, unfulfilled, and unhappy unless you recognize and work to change them.

How Attention-Seeking Creates Self-Sabotage

The desire to continuously stream positive feedback to themselves leads most women with the Contestant Mind to spend an enormous amount of time on their appearances. Since physical attraction is what men notice first and what easily solicits attention, you can get sucked into the idea that whoever is the hottest, wins. Wins what, though? Yes, you might win more "likes" on your photos or get more swipes on dating apps, but devoting hours to perfecting your image rarely produces lasting relationship results. The Contestant Mind never sees this, though. Instead, it regularly urges you to up your game, attempting to be more of what it thinks is attractive. *"If I am thinner, prettier, more outgoing, more perfect than other girls my age, it will keep people focusing on me and I will be happy and be loved,"* it seems to say. Although the amount of attention might increase with each self-enhancement, the quality of attention often does not. There has to be more substance behind a pretty face for a deep relationship to develop. Since attributes like good character and intellect aren't attention grabbing or post-worthy, the *Cursed Mind* usually neglects developing them. For this reason many women who strongly identify with this Face of the *Curse* are good at generating interest, but struggle to grow their relationship from "like" to love.

What is just as crippling to a budding romance is that although a wealth of attention is required, it is often unreciprocated. When you are caught up in what everyone thinks of you and how much love or attention you are receiving, your concentration is rarely aimed at giving those things to anyone else. Even if you only care about what one person, one guy thinks of you, the boundless need to satiate the self-absorbed mind by way of his attention can deprive him of feeling loved and appreciated in return. Some guys might feel this imbalance after a few weeks or months of dating you, but others can actually feel it right away.

Darcy, for instance, was never asked out twice. After spending thousands of dollars on her appearance, and hours getting ready for each coffee date, her perfected image couldn't close the deal. When seated across from a guy, she not only talked too much, she also talked about things that were so centered on her own interests and motivated by her attention-seeking nature that men quickly became bored with the conversation. She repeatedly suffered from the most frequent effect of the Contestant *Curse*: When you spend most of your time thinking about yourself, you automatically spend most of your time talking about yourself.

If you asked her, Darcy would deny monopolizing any conversations. She knew to ask her dates questions and felt she did a good job inquiring about their lives. What she didn't realize was as soon as the guy started talking, her Contestant Mind immediately related whatever he was saying to her own experiences and opinions. *"I have something to say about that!"* she thought. Or, *"I can impress him with my story!"* This made the conversation another contest of who has a better story, all while she was hoping the guy would respond with affirming words about her value. Before her date could even finish completing a sentence, Darcy would jump in with her thoughts, leaving him feeling like she really didn't care what he had to say. She was never fully engaged as a listener and therefore never really connected with any man she went out with. Paying attention to someone else, even someone she liked, was momentary because her mind would unconsciously wander back to, *"How can I show him I'm interesting,"* or *"How do I get him to really fall for me?"* This attention-seeking thought habit was the predominate factor preventing second dates.

Of course, not all who possess a Contestant Mind fall into the trap of losing interest by the time the check is paid. Some women with this *Curse* master the initial stages of dating; they have the right packaging, are good at flirting, and know how to play a little hard to get. Unfortunately, just because they can skillfully maneuver the "getting him interested" phase doesn't mean they sail effortlessly into a serious relationship. Many find it quite difficult to get to the next level because they are only confident in the beginning, when the guy is in hot pursuit of them. If the chase slows, even for a brief second, they begin to question themselves as well as the guy's feelings.

My client Betsy had a history of two- to three-month relationships. When she reached out to me for the first time, it was because she had recently met someone she liked and was worried his interest was starting to fade. When I asked her what signs she was getting that indicated a loss of interest, she said it was mostly a feeling that she was losing the upper hand (which is often code for "I'm not getting enough attention to feel good about myself"). After two months of dating, she felt that her boyfriend wasn't trying as hard to win her over anymore. Even though he was still in regular contact with her, and they hung out many times a week, she felt he wasn't being as attentive as he used to be and certainly wasn't complimenting her enough.

Normally, when Betsy began feeling this way, her *Curse* would flare up and her self-focused thoughts would take over. She perceived relaxed behavior on the guy's part as disinterest and would frantically attempt to stir up his emotions. In previous relationships, she would start playing harder to get in order to provoke attention. She would spontaneously get mad at little things or pretend she was sad and needed to be alone. Most boyfriends interpreted these attention-getting attempts on her part as drama and backed away. Now, Betsy wanted to know what she should do to make her boyfriend "want her more and focus more attention on her."

What Betsy did not realize was that she was fighting the normal progression of any relationship. At some point, the chase must end so the real relationship can begin and true love can develop. I told her she needed to recognize that her focus was concentrated on how much attention she was getting from her boyfriend, and her attempts to incite jealousy or worry was all in order to feed a self-absorbed craving. It's only natural that men will relax a little and be more themselves the longer you date them. The courting process doesn't last a lifetime. If you expect someone to bring you flowers every week, plan lavish dates your entire life, or focus 100 percent of their attention on you every day, you are in for major disappointment. The truth was that some of the men Betsy dated were not truly losing interest like she assumed; she just didn't understand the transition period from dating to a relationship, nor did her Contestant Mind want to accept less attentiveness. Betsy had to stop making the man chase her and start giving back, but do to that, she had to notice and then resist the self-absorbed mind's cry for attention.

In the courting phase, most decent guys don't mind that the relationship is one-sided and they are expected to do the heavy lifting. As time progresses, however, they expect the relationship to balance out.

After all, a relationship, and especially a marriage, is a partnership, and men are looking for potential partners—someone they can love, who will genuinely love them back; someone who will think about them. Having a Contestant Mind inhibits your ability to accept a balanced relationship because it confuses receiving attention with love. Therefore, if you aren't getting large amounts of attention, you think you aren't being loved, and your *Cursed Self* gets very upset.

Attention can become an addiction, just like wanting. It can feel as if you have no control over the yearning for feedback on yourself. Much like any other addiction, this one will take time to quit. Once you have cleared your mind of the habit to think about yourself and unconsciously seek to enhance or protect your sense of worth, the desire for attention will begin to fade gradually on its own. However, if you are hooked on social media, it will be difficult, if not impossible to conquer this Face because platforms like Instagram or Snap Chat are designed to keep you focused on yourself, rewarding you with social validation when you do so. Continuing to use your online presence in a manner that self-promotes can easily negate any improvement you make in breaking the addiction. Therefore, a social media diet is strongly recommended in order to truly create lasting, inner change. You will learn in the Cures that the first step is noticing the need for self-validation rising within you before you have a chance to act on it. Then, knowing that it comes from a place that is hurting you, attempt to do nothing about it.

The Contestant Vibe

Your mind being conditioned to crave self feedback can compel you to perceive any guy you are interested in, not as a potential partner or equal, but almost as a judge. Rather than go on a date thinking, *"let's get to know each other"*, you sweat and stew over the question, *"what does he think of me?"* Unconsciously, you assume if someone deems you good enough, a relationship will ensue. If he doesn't, it won't. Seeing the human dynamic this way causes an immediate inequality between the two of you, and many guys will be instantly aware of it although unable to put a finger on the vibe. No normal, healthy man wants to feel like he has that much authority over a woman's feeling of worthiness, and achieving it after just a few hours at dinner together feels odd.

Your perception of men being the judge and you being the contestant is also why you might feel the pressure to be perfect. Going on dates becomes akin to participating in a talent show where you could either win or lose. Your mind thinks, *"If I look, talk and act perfectly, he will score me as a 10 and fall in love with me!"* In reality, the opposite usually occurs. Too much thought about yourself lowers your self-esteem, heightens your fear of rejection, and produces a vibe that is insecure, or even phony, if you attempt to conceal self-doubt with seeming perfection. Either you won't open up about yourself, or you will talk way too much, depending on how your *Cursed Mind* wants to handle the situation. The guy, feeling bored, disconnected, or both, may only see you again if he's highly attracted to you. If he does, it might be in small doses or when he has been drinking, perpetuating your fear that you are not good enough to have a real relationship with.

This is how those with a Contestant Mind wind up in a non-relationship, or a friends-with-benefits situation. Guys keep them in their funnel because there is physical attraction, but they don't have enough of a connection to take the relationship to the next level. After having this scenario repeat itself several times, a woman with this *Curse* may become anxious and develop a kind of stage fright when meeting someone new, making dating more challenging with each attempt. *"I try so hard to be perfect and yet I'm still single after all these years,"* the mind thinks. It is only when a woman stops trying with the mind and starts dating with her heart does her vibe, finally, feel natural.

The real troubling affect of the Contestant Mind is that its influence can grow over time if you indulge its need for attention long enough. It can dominate your thinking to a point where you inherently believe there is no alternative source of happiness for you other than attention from men. Women who feel this way often insist they aren't in control of their thoughts, claiming that their mind is who they are, so instead of wanting to rid themselves of the *Curse* and their attention-seeking, they see only one option—and that is to satisfy it.

The result of this extreme identification with the *Cursed Mind* is very harmful. Because it wants attention so badly, it can convince a woman that she needs to be in a relationship in order to be happy, causing her metric for gauging a guy's "datability" to become far more lenient than most. To an outsider, it may seem like she would entertain being with just about anyone that shows interest. It's not that the woman is foolish or unintelligent; she's simply under the complete rule of her *Cursed Mind* and its notion that outside attention brings inner fulfillment. Several unproductive and toxic dating patterns arise from this mistaken belief, such as feeling terrified to be alone and using men for completely self-serving purposes. Most unfortunately, it can lead to being taken advantage of by people who have nefarious agendas because the woman does not care to investigate the source of the attention or his motives. To her, almost any relationship is better than no relationship.

When the *Curse* gets this bad, an awakening must occur, or the consequences can be catastrophic. Contestants are the most likely victims of *Love bombing*, a term used when a guy initially comes on very strong, with lots of complimentary words and romantic gestures, but either turns the tables or disappears after he gets what he wants. Rather than be suspicious when this happens or recognizing the guy was no good from the start, the Contestant Mind becomes obsessed with holding his interest. Many women in this situation are then susceptible to mental, physical, or financial abuse, and repeatedly so. The men who take advantage of them can sense the vibe of attention- seeking and feed that addiction to get what they want.

How Comparing and Competing Create Self-Sabotage

The Contestant Mind is very attracted to romantic situations where there can be winners and losers. Men who are already in a relationship are prime candidates, as nothing makes the Contestant Mind feel more like a winner than stealing a guy away from another woman. If it is successful in luring him away from his relationship, the Contestant Mind will not only fulfill its quest to have a boyfriend or husband, but it will also become the triumphant victor—and will congratulate you on being "better than" the other woman.

Of course, when you play the comparison game, there is always the chance you might be defeated. If you lose the guy to another girl, the mind will drag you down to rock bottom, especially if it perceived her as being inferior. *"I'm so much prettier,"* it might complain. Or, *"He likes smart women, and she's not half as smart as I am."* The fact that a man could pick someone of lower in rank is confusing to the Contestant Mind, which is perpetually ranking everybody. It doesn't understand that love is not based on who scores higher in certain categories, or who is more physically attractive. Rather than accept defeat, the mind will urge you to try and win the person back in order to feel worthy again. This is why some women can't determine if their emotions stem from really loving someone or from an aversion to losing. The answer is the latter, of course, because when you love someone, you don't need to question if you love him. The inquiry itself arises because your *Cursed Mind* is asking your *Core Self,* who is listening.

Darcy held on to her last boyfriend for two years, despite the fact that he did not treat her well and cheated on her twice. When I asked why she persisted in trying to work things out with him, she admitted that if he finally decided to be faithful to her she would feel like she was good enough to change him. She wanted to be the girl who was so special that he reformed—a *Cursed* motivation if I ever heard one! Darcy felt if she let him go without accomplishing that, however, it meant she was a loser, and the next girl he got involved with would ultimately be dubbed the winner. In the same breath, Darcy told me her worth was not tied to being in a relationship with her boyfriend, which just points to how unconscious the *Cursed Mind* can truly be.

The reality of the situation was that Darcy's boyfriend was a selfish man with his own *Curse*. He believed he was superior to women, and because of that, he thought he was above fidelity. Because Darcy was

Cursed, too, she couldn't see this. She wasn't looking to make her relationship work because she loved her boyfriend; she was looking to make it work so she could feel like she was a winner. Is a woman using a man to heighten her feelings of worthiness any better than a guy cheating on her? In Darcy's eyes, she didn't see it that way, but the truth is she did not love her boyfriend any more than he loved her. For love to happen between two people, they can't both be completely functioning through their self-absorbed minds, because the self-absorbed mind has no interest in real love. It only cares about gaining or protecting the feeling of worth for itself.

Case in point, if a relationship does go well and starts feeling like love, it usually won't last for long. Much like the Wanter Mind, the Contestant Mind will cause its own trouble when things become too comfortable. Normal, healthy relationships do not provide competition, and therefore, there is no opportunity to win; so if someone you're dating turns out to be a nice, normal guy and a loving, harmonious relationship follows, the mind may create problems in order to create a win-lose situation for itself. It might not have another woman to contend with, so instead, it will make the very guy you are dating your opponent. It might want you to accuse him of flirting with another woman, or overreact about some small disappointment, all so you can be at the center of a chaotic battle again and hopefully come out feeling like a winner.

Gisele was a client who signed up for coaching because she was tired of her volatile relationship patterns. Every boyfriend she had brought problems or challenges into their relationships and she wanted to find the right person and settle down. Soon she was dating Eric, who seemed like a nice, genuine guy. After they became exclusive, Gisele kept saying that she was worried she wasn't seeing something. She told me she felt like there was something missing and couldn't relax around Eric. "It's too quiet," she said during a coaching session. One night, she went through his phone, searching for evidence to confirm her uneasy feeling. She didn't find much, but she did see a few texts from a coworker that made her cringe. She asked me if she should be upset and confront Eric, to which I told her, no. I didn't think there was anything inappropriate about the texts and the fact that Gisele even questioned their importance was more proof to my point. Gisele seemed disappointed and said, "Ok, I'll just keep looking for whatever it is that is making me feel this way."

After a few more weeks of coaching, we uncovered the cause of her uneasy feeling. It wasn't anything Eric was doing, rather it was Gisele's Contestant Mind becoming restless and wanting to exert itself. It was not use to the peace that Eric brought to the relationship, which is why she said, "It's too quiet," and saw that as a negative! Gisele was actually hoping to find something to get upset about when she looked through Eric's phone because then she would have a reason to start a battle. Without any battling in their relationship, she had no chance to feel like a winner, or "in the right", as she had with her past boyfriends.

Another word for all this winning and losing is drama. Whether it chooses a situation that already has drama or generates the drama itself, the Contestant Mind loves it, and doesn't care that it sabotages your relationships with others. If you feel that drama follows you, you have to stop and ask yourself who the common thread is in all your dramatic situations. It's not coincidence that you cannot escape it—you are the one who creates it. Why would you create drama? If you looked closely, you would see that all drama is actually a comparison contest between you and others. In *A New Earth: Awakening to Your Life's Purpose*, Eckhart Tolle asked, "Can you feel that there is something in you that is at war, something that feels threatened and wants to survive at all cost? Something that needs the drama in order to assert its identity as the victorious character within a theatrical production?" "Without the dramatic stage, you have no place to be on display, no opportunity to show yourself in all your glory once the struggle is over. At the end of the production, you are hoping to come out as the winner or the star."

That "something" in you that needs the drama is the *Cursed Mind* wanting to show itself so it can remain relevant and important.

Very often, clients who identify heavily with this particular Face say to me, "I'm exhausted from dating! I have tried for years and have overcome so many issues, yet I'm still single." The reality is that they aren't exhausted from trying to find love; it's their constant battle for the feeling of worth, validation, or importance in the atmosphere of drama and disarray that fatigues them. It would fatigue anyone. Until they acknowledge their own self-absorbed mind, and peace in a relationship becomes a priority, drama will continue to prevail and the rollercoaster that is their love life will ride on.

The Biggest Contest of All
The Contestant Mind is the most prone to feeling pressure to get married because it wants its life to be comparable to others and often considers marriage the final test of worth. Only those who are married achieve real worthiness, it thinks. Therefore, lagging behind its peers or falling short of cultural expectations makes the Contestant Mind believe it is not as good as other people. If all your friends have boyfriends, it will want a boyfriend as well and may even coax you to commit to someone you don't like that much. Once your friends begin to get engaged, the social pressure really sets in, and the race to altar is officially on because this Face of the *Curse* does not want to come in last. That would be humiliating for the self-absorbed mind.

Women with this *Curse* sometimes admit that they're not sure if they want a commitment because they want to be in one, or because they don't want to be the only person in their squad who's not married. Their *Core Self* wants love and will wait, but their *Cursed Mind* is more concerned about keeping up with their friends in order to show a perception of equal value. Succumbing to this kind of *Cursed* thinking usually leads to choosing a partner based on availability or out of desperation, which is regretful given there is no greater decision in life than choosing who you marry.

People might see your desperation and warn you that wanting to marry because "everyone else is doing it" is not a prudent reason. They might even say the words, "It isn't a competition. People find love and get married when the time is right for them." Those sentiments usually don't penetrate the Contestant Mind because it is *always* comparing your life with others. Realizing the habit of comparing and competing is of the utmost importance because then you can tackle changing the habits instead of indulging it and suffering the consequences. And the consequences are, indeed, everlasting.

For example, comparing and competing will still be prominent post-marriage if you don't consciously work to stop engaging in the habit; it will simply involve other couples. Your mind might measure your relationship against your friend's in order to see who has the superior marriage. Are you as happy and loved as all of your friends? Do you have what they have? Does your husband stack up to the other husbands? If the answer is yes, the comparing mind can relax. If the answer is no, the fear of being beneath or behind can drive you to act. The action might placate your self-absorbed mind, but will likely hurt your relationship.

Helen, a former client, would become very jealous whenever she would see her friends post pictures with their spouses in cool locations or trendy restaurants. She would feel bad about her relationship and immediately demand that her husband take her on vacation or buy her something new that she could show off. If her friends' husbands posted something sweet for everyone to read, Helen would get mad at her own husband for not being effusive enough about his feelings. Nearly every day, she was upset about something in her relationship because her comparing mind felt the need to keep up with everyone else. Her husband would sometimes comply, but always did so with a sigh and an eye-roll. He would often lament to his friends that Helen was so high-maintenance and eventually began avoiding her by staying at work late.

As long as other people see it as having the ideal life, the Contestant Mind draws all satisfaction from that. It doesn't care as much about what's happening on the inside of your relationship as much as it is concerned with the perception on the outside. While you are busy spending all your mental energy comparing, competing, and attempting to win another contest of worth, think about what your heart is doing? Where is the love and daily goodwill needed to sustain that one lasting, meaningful relationship in your life? How much time do you dedicate to being happy and peaceful with your significant other without some struggle or drama inside or outside your relationship, taking your focus away? Whether you involve your partner in the drama, or make him an opponent in it, it is ultimately an ego-driven distraction that feeds our Contestant Mind, but creates distance from our *Core Self,* as well as distance from love.

Free Yourself Before It's Too Late
If you aren't currently dating anyone, the habits of the Contestant Mind can chip away at you, making you sad and bitter any time you hear someone has gotten engaged or married. As the years pass, you can become more jaded and depressed, which will only make it more difficult to meet someone. The pain of envy and not being on par with others can build over time to the point where you always feel that pain, even without a situational trigger. That pain along with the desire to achieve your romantic goals can eventually drive you to take extreme measures when you do get involved in a relationship, like attempting to get pregnant (or lying about it) so the guy you are involved with will feel obligated to marry you. This is when the Contestant *Curse* reaches another pinnacle. In an effort to get *your* way, and fulfill *your* dreams, the self-absorbed mind will disregard the other person in your relationship in order to advance its own agenda. *"I need to do something immediately to get the life I want,"* the Contestant Mind seems says. Other *Faces* of the *Curse* can cause a person to take such action for the same objective, only the motivation changes slightly: A Wanter might do so to possess an unattainable guy who would otherwise never commit, a Worrier will do it to ensure a certain future, and so on. The result of such behavior is the same regardless of where it stems from—no one ends up happy, and the pain is only gone temporarily.

The Contestant Mind thrives by emphatically ignoring one of the basic truths of life: it isn't fair. It won't accept this truth, which is why it regularly ignites jealousy and prompts you to react with anger when someone has more than you. But the pathway to love is never through tactics suggested by the *Cursed Mind*, which takes advantage of others in order to gratify itself. Love is only achieved and maintained through our *Core Self,* who is loving and accepting of life, and therefore, is able to create an environment of love that is attractive and appealing to others.

Trying to change some outside situation in order to remedy jealousy and pain from the *Curse* does not work. Only changes on the inside of you will effect changes on the outside. When you no longer engage in the comparison game and learn comfort in your own self-acceptance, the Contestant Mind will cease to cause you problems. I urge you to take this to heart before you are motivated to do something rooted in the *Cursed Mind* and suffer a repercussion that could last the rest of your life. All the Cures in the next half of the book will help end your self-absorbed thoughts, leaving your *Core Self* to love purely, wholeheartedly, without any agenda—and for the first time, receive the same gift in return. It isn't about doing anything different, it's only about thinking in a new and productive way, which can transform your entire life if you let it.

REFLECTION

Reflect for a moment. Reread this chapter, if needed. Put the book down for a day, and see if you can hear yourself comparing and competing with others in your mind. Do you feel a sense of needing to prove yourself? How does it make you feel? What does the feeling make you do? How often does the need for outside attention arise within you?

Cursed?

PART III: THE CURES

Before you even begin this next section I want to share with you some very good news: Although reading about the *Faces* might have been hard, by doing so you have already accomplished the first Cure! By learning how to recognize the *Cursed Mind*, you have taken the most important step in this journey. You have made yourself aware. Hopefully you now understand how the *Cursed Mind* skews your self-perception and creates unhealthy and unproductive patterns in your love life. Knowing the different ways in which the *Cursed Mind* pursues worthiness or avoids feeling worthless makes it easier to separate *who you are* from *what you think*. By disassociating your being from your conditioned mind, you create space for your *Core Self* to resume its place at the forefront of your essence and character. When your *Core Self* is in the driver seat, the journey for love becomes exponentially faster and easier.

Now, on to the Cures! The Cures are practices designed to either quiet or reframe the *Cursed* voice in your head, thus allowing your *Core Self* to be the guide in your relationships. Remember your *Core Self* is the person who carries the best of you and radiates the kind, loving, and joyful energy you inherently have within you. She is the woman with endless love to give and grace for all love received. She is you, totally at peace with yourself. And as I've said before, peace within is the most attractive, engaging quality that a woman can possess!

Remember, this journey is not about becoming a new or different you. As Eckhart Tolle stated in *The Power of Now*: "You do not become good by trying to be good, but by finding the goodness that is already within you and allowing that goodness to emerge." This is about bringing back your original, loving self, the you who shows up on your best days but often is pushed aside by the fears and wants of *Cursed Mind*. We are going to bring that person back to take full reign over your life and being, and in doing so, put an end to the *Cursed* patterns in your relationships once and for all.

Get ready: This next section is going to really empower you!

Chapter Nine

Be Present

How would you feel if you woke up tomorrow and didn't care if you ever got married? Wouldn't it be nice to take a vacation from the anxiety and pressure that plague you in your relationships? Imagine what life would be like if your mind wasn't constantly thinking about the things that went wrong in the past and all your anger and regret just disappeared. It might seem like it would take a mythical fairy godmother to make these things happen, but the truth is, you have the ability to free yourself from all of those feelings. You can unburden yourself from the worry and remorse that have weighed you down your whole life and take a leap forward in becoming the person you've always wished you could be. You can be happy and at peace with yourself, and in doing so, move closer to your goal of finding the right person and falling in love with each other. The first step in this journey is learning to hear your *Cursed* thinking when it happens and stopping it in its tracks. To do that, you must learn to be present.

Natural Presence

What does it mean to be present? By now, you've probably heard this term before from a health or wellness expert as a necessary practice to reduce stress and increase your overall happiness in life. People throw around the expression "be present" so regularly that the meaning has lost some of its critical significance and is often boiled down to simply living in the moment. While living in the moment is good, that definition doesn't capture the enormity of the mantra, or what it actually helps you to accomplish in terms of breaking your *Curse*. Therefore, I think it's worth explaining the term again even if you think it's self-explanatory or have heard it a hundred times before.

Being present is to fully focus your attention on the moment you are experiencing without analyzing, judging, or resisting it. When you are present, you are not thinking, only feeling and observing. On a date that means when a guy says something to you that is confusing or bothersome, you don't immediately start thinking, *"Why is he saying this to me? Is he trying to fool me? Make me jealous? Piss me off? I can't believe he's saying this! How can I get him to change what he's saying so this relationship will work out for me?"* Instead you listen intently and fully take in his message. You ask questions to get a better understanding, and learn all you can without your self-absorbed mind intruding on the conversation.

It's likely that at some point in your life, you've experienced glimpses of presence, perhaps at the very beginning of your relationships when you're falling in love. When the person you're falling for smiles at, touches, or kisses you, it isn't hard to focus all attention on him: his smile, his eyes, his lips. For that brief period of time, you don't think about yourself; you just experience what it is like to *be where you are*. If you have never been in love, you might experience the same presence when you see something extraordinary and magnificent like the sight of animals in the wild, or an incredible view from a mountaintop. The incessant thinking in your head seems to vanish on its own in the moments that feel miraculous. This is what I call "natural presence," which means connecting with the moment without even trying.

Being present all the time is hard for people because as strong as love is, your self-absorbed mind can be stronger. The habit to retreat into your own head and engage in *Cursed* thinking is so ingrained that it occurs without you even noticing. You start worrying about what's going to happen or how someone feels about you, and before you know it, your body is in the present, but your mind is in the future or past. You start obsessing about your worth or stressing about what you want, and suddenly your *Cursed Mind* is talking so loudly you can't follow or fully understand what is happening in real time. The authentic joy and deep connection you previously had with someone fades, and like clockwork, problems occur.

While natural presence is a wonderful experience, it doesn't last long for most people. The culture and stress of modern life tend to interfere more than ever, and thought habits of the *Cursed Mind* are so deeply rooted that even when you are enjoying a nice moment, the prattling in your head keeps you company. Therefore, you cannot rely on natural presence. You have to work to keep yourself rooted in the very moment you are experiencing. It is not easy, but it is necessary. Of all the self-help tips and techniques, the tactics and strategies, being present will be the best tool in your box when it comes to finding and keeping love. If you can give your full attention to life as it's happening, you can keep your connection with others strong, remain in a *Curse*-free state of mind, and guard your relationship from self-sabotage. When you make it a priority to fully inhabit your experiences when they occur, the *Cursed Mind* and the troubled patterns that come with it weakens and your *Core Self* begins to emerge.

Why Be Present

There is a well-known saying that is attributed to motivational speaker Junia Bretas that goes like this: "If you are depressed, you are living in the past. If you are anxious, you are living in the future. If you are at peace, you are living in the present." On most days, we are not at peace because we leave the present. We do this habitually, without much awareness, because the self-focused mind is more concerned with what happened in the past or what will happen in the future. To put it another way, the *Cursed Mind* doesn't care about right now because most of the time, nothing is wrong with now. Even someone with the most avid Worrier Mind will admit that being single today isn't the problem; it's the fear of remaining single. Or, it's the fear of becoming single again, if she is in a relationship. If you think I'm wrong and being single right now is a problem in the present, ask yourself this: If you had a guarantee that you would find love or have a family in one year, would you still have a problem now? Your *Cursed Mind* needs the future and past in order to make something wrong because without something being wrong, what will it worry about? Lament about? What will it judge? What will it want? Your self-absorbed mind needs these mind-created problems in order to sustain its power and continue its existence. It wants you to keep chasing your worth in the future or believing it has already escaped you in the past. Because if you embrace the present and come to peace within yourself, your *Cursed Mind* will have no control over you and will cease to exist. Without some problem or unresolved situation, you can't focus on *you*. This is why the *Cursed Mind* constantly avoids the present—it has no power there.

Being present sounds pretty simple to do, but ending future and past thinking is hard. Very hard. Especially when thoughts about both seem to pop into your head automatically on their own. Even as you are reading this, you may hear the voice of the Worrier/Lamenter Mind rattling in your head like static, reminding you of what could shake or break you tomorrow. If you have had the Worrier *Curse* for many years, a part of you might believe worrying is useful, and until you change the belief that worrying is helping you, you will continue to do it. You must recognize that it is more harmful to you and your relationships so you want to stop your future thinking. Without the desire to change, your old thought patterns will persist in dominating you, and your cycle of unsuccessful relationships will go on.

The very first step in learning to be present is being aware of when you are not. When the voice in your head begins to cause a panic within, you must have the awareness to know you've let your *Cursed Mind* take over. The minute you become conscious of this happening, you will automatically become present.

Ashlee, our Worrier, learned awareness of her mind quickly. She noticed her *Cursed* thinking one day when she was waiting to hear from Greg, the new guy she was dating. He had mentioned something earlier in the week about getting together on Friday, and it was now Thursday afternoon, and she had not yet heard from him. Immediately, Ashlee began to worry, and her mind flooded with future thoughts. *"Why hasn't he called yet? How could he wait until the last minute? Was he losing interest and not going to follow through? Am I going to be sitting at home all night on a Friday! What if I have to start all over again and find someone else?"* She felt the usual anxiety and stress consume her body. Her heart was racing, and her mouth was dry. She itched to do something to figure out what would happen. She felt the urge to control the situation rise up inside her. *"Text him,"* said the voice in her head. *"I need to know what's going on so I can feel relaxed and have this relationship continue. I can't let it slip away."*

But as she was reaching for her phone, she stopped. Ashlee became aware of her thinking. She realized that her Worrier Mind was creating panic by thinking about the future and worrying about herself. The emotions she was feeling at the time—which vacillated between anxiety, anger, and frustration—were not coming from Greg or from a real situation, at least not yet. They were all coming from her *Cursed Mind*, which feared being dumped again and losing its sense of worth in the process. She walked away from her phone, and for several minutes, she breathed deeply and focused on each breath. She looked around her office. She heard the clock ticking, the sounds of her coworkers chatting, and the traffic outside. She brought her mind back from the future. She told herself none of the worried thoughts and "what-if" problems she had could be dealt with right now. Attempting to fix what hadn't occurred yet would only lead to a mistake. There were no proactive steps she could take in this situation because there really wasn't an actual situation yet. In the past, when she got anxious, she would do something she regretted later. She was not going to do that now. Ashlee calmed herself with the reminder that if her boyfriend stood her up tomorrow night, she would deal with it then, but not a minute before. For now, she could only go about her day and concentrate on the work at hand. It was hard to do since she wanted to worry out of habit, but whenever she felt her mind slip, she cleared it by giving her full attention to the present.

An hour later, the phone chimed, and it was Greg. Because Ashlee was now calm and acting from the present, she was able to interact with him authentically from a good place. If she had continued to let her future thoughts dominate her mind, she may have answered his text with a slightly annoyed or needy reply. She might have even said something snarky or rude because he didn't contact her earlier that day like she had wanted. Thankfully, that didn't happen, and they went out the following night.

Ashlee was able to realize her self-absorbed thinking amidst a *Curse* flare-up. She observed her thoughts instead of reacting to them—this is awareness of mind. It's hearing the *Cursed Mind* and knowing what it is so you don't mistakenly act on it. By recognizing the predicament with her boyfriend had not actually occurred yet, Ashlee was able to see the reality of the situation and behave accordingly. Instead of acting on the fear she would be stood up, she acted on the knowledge that she wasn't being present. If the worst did happen and she was stood up on Friday night, she would have to deal with it on Friday night. She would have been disappointed, of course, but obsessing about it before then would only have caused her to prolong her disappointment unnecessarily. She would have ruined Thursday along with Friday. Or worse, she may have ruined the entire relationship by jumping to the wrong course of action. It only takes one too many anxious remarks or overly eager texts for a guy to feel pressured or drained by another person's self-centered impulses, and in the past, that's exactly what Ashlee would have done.

Recognizing your *Cursed Mind* when it's talking as you is not easy at first. When you have formed a habit, especially one you didn't even know you had, it will take time and practice to change. Most of the time, you will have to catch yourself in a flare-up. You might be out with a guy or at work thinking about him and realize you have not been paying attention to what you were doing for the last few minutes. Or, you may be at home and suddenly feel anxious or down for no real reason. When you notice you have been "in your head" or realize you feel stressed or depressed for seemingly no reason, stop and ask yourself these two questions: Were you thinking about something that is not actually happening now? And is the source of the fear rooted in you boosting your sense of worth or preventing some injury to it? If the answer is yes to one or both, then you can be sure whatever it is you fear is not a true danger to you; it is simply your *Cursed Mind* resurging. Worrying can be a subconscious habit much like biting your nails, which means you will do it automatically until you intentionally take steps to break it. If you identified with the *Face* of the Worrier, and you know your relationship problems begin with your habit to future think, you can now choose to take the right action. Instead of giving in to the worry and saying or doing something inappropriate and potentially being perceived as irrational, overly emotional, or needy to the other person, you can work to clear your mind and create peace within you instead. Knowing the problem you are having is with your mind, and not with any guy or relationship circumstance, is a key shift in your mentality that will save you from making fatal errors that may have ruined your previous relationships.

    Sarah, for example, had a history of letting her anxiety get the best of her. When her Worrier Mind started to run through "What If" scenarios about the future, she would attempt to calm herself by turning to the guy she was dating. The problem was she wanted the guy to assure her that she would not end up alone in life –a strange position for anyone in a new relationship. When Sarah and I started coaching, she realized that asking the guy for help in this situation was only creating more of a problem. They guy didn't want to be her therapist, and he felt pressured to assure her of feelings he wasn't quite sure of yet himself! When Sarah learned to be aware of her *Cursed Mind* taking over her, she was able to identify that her anxiety stemmed from her self-absorbed thoughts engaging in "What If" scenarios. Only she had the power to stop creating those scenarios and make herself feel better. If she needed help to turn off her mind and become present she turned to me as her coach or she used a guided meditation. By using awareness of mind as her coping strategy, she stopped pressuring men to make her feel better and she's now been in a long-term relationship for over a year.

Of course, there will be times when the present moment is truly unpleasant. The guy you wanted to hear from disappears, or the boyfriend you thought was "The One" breaks your heart, and you are left in clear and present heartache. What then? Do you still have to be present? The answer is yes, and here is why: It is impossible to avoid all disappointment and sadness in life. Trying to steer clear of all emotional pain is what has ultimately caused the majority of your mistakes with men thus far. Trying to stay ahead of or avoid self-focused pain is worrying! Although it may seem that grieving the loss of a relationship is too painful to bear, the constant rumination and fear of the pain is actually far worse and lasts much longer. The best thing to do if a relationship ends is to grieve it and work to accept that it's over. As soon as you accept what's happened, despite the hurt, you get closer to healing from it. We will talk more about this in Chapter Twelve: Be Accepting.

Hear the *Cursed You*

Being present means not only keeping your mind out of the future or past but also hearing the *Cursed You*—your worth-searching mind talking—and learning how to quiet her. You've lived with her voice in your head for so long that it will be difficult to kick her out or even recognize when she has taken over. Many people confuse the conditioned voice of the mind with who they are. My client Amber was very good at letting go of her future and past thinking, but she didn't realize her *Curse* had shifted *Faces* in order to stick around.

After she had been coaching with me for a while, she was determined to stop her Worrier/Lamenter Mind. *"Focus on the present!"* she would tell herself. *"Why is this so hard? It's because I'm not smart enough. I know other people would have an easier time with this."* As she would go about her day, her *Cursed Mind* commented about all she encountered, seemingly in the present. *"What is the matter with that guy? Why did he look at me like that? Ugh, is something wrong with me? He's so rude for making me feel this way."* After a month of trying to be present, Amber reported feeling more unhappy and worse about herself. I pointed out that the voice in her head was still her *Cursed Mind*, only now it was vacillating between the Inferior and Superior Mind, judging everyone around her as well as criticizing herself. Once she realized that she was still letting the *Cursed Mind* narrate her life and she was still not truly being present, she was able to reset and practice presence the right way.

Being present means no voice talking to you, about you or your life situation. Being present means to just *be*, without any of the thinking we have identified in the previous chapters. When you notice you are thinking in the form of judging, complaining, stressing, self-protecting, comparing or enhancing, you have reengaged the *Cursed Mind*. Some people try to stop their conditioned thinking by finding a distraction for it like working or staying super busy, but that only temporarily helps. Once you are alone again with little to do, your *Cursed Mind* will be there, waiting to resurge. This is why some people never want to be alone. They don't want to face their *Cursed Mind!* But it's much better to remedy the root of the problem than to simply put a Band Aid on it.

When your mind is engaged in self-absorbed thinking, don't cover it up with a diversion. Instead focus on the moment you are living in, outside your head. If you are vacuuming the house, focus on vacuuming. If you are walking from one class to another, focus on the walk. If you are in bed trying to sleep, focus on being in your bed. Your *Cursed Mind* will think this is boring, but your *Core Self* will find it exhilarating! You just have to give yourself time to adjust from one to the other.

It's important to do these mini-exercises of presently focusing on everyday tasks. If you are reading this book, it's likely that dating and relationships are a trigger for your self-absorbed mind, so before you put yourself in that *Curse*-provoking situation, practice being aware of the *Cursed You* and bringing your attention to the present in a benign environment like house work or exercise. If you have trouble being present during those simple practices, you will really struggle when it's game time.

    Don't expect to be skillfully adept at first. It is going to take lots of practice to get into a groove of being aware of your mind and then shutting it off. When you get frustrated or feel like giving up do to lack of progress, remember that when you are able to stop your self-absorbed mind on a date, the effect is not only amazing, it's multifold! Your vibe will completely change. Instead of seeming nervous, distracted, or over-eager, you will be perceived as relaxed, focused, and at ease. When you are able to relish having a cup of coffee or drink with an eligible guy, instead of furiously worrying about what will happen next or what he thinks of you, the energy you emanate is magnetic! Not only that, but your ability to assess who the guy is will be much more on point. If you are with a guy who is genuine, caring, and thoughtful, your *Core Self* will be able to pick up on that energy as long as your *Cursed Mind* isn't blocking its view. By being present and focusing on *him*, you will able to sense how interested he is in you and feel if there is a real connection. How wonderful will that be? Likewise if a man is selfish, dishonest, and manipulative, your *Core Self* will sense that as well. The feeling you will get with a guy like that will be unpleasant or uneasy. Don't worry; your *Core Self* does not need to think about you in order to keep you safe. You will innately sense real danger, like a truck barreling down the street or standing too close to the edge of a cliff. You don't need to obsessively analyze in order to avoid these perils because when you are present, you feel the danger and take the right action to protect your wellbeing. Unlike the *Cursed Mind*, which might have told you to ignore how your body felt around someone and get in his car or go back to his house because it wanted him to like you!

This is what you are striving for—to live without the *Cursed Mind* creating commentary on life so you can be at peace when you are with another person. When you are at peace, you are unconcerned about how you are being perceived and if you are being liked. Best of all, the other person can feel that ease within you which is a game changer in dating!

Lamenters: Laying the Past to Rest

Now let's talk about the Lamenter Mind. The habit to ruminate on various events that have occurred and hold tight to hurtful experiences creates a big obstacle for love that most people never fully understand. The Lamenter Mind is so stuck on how you were wronged in the past, that it makes you believe that you cannot be happy today. However, if you aren't happy or at peace today, it is extremely hard to attract the love you want. Remember the vibe that radiates from a person who past-thinks is often dismal and draining or combative and agitated; neither is alluring or engaging. So leaving the past completely and rendering it powerless over you is vitally important.

How do you do that, though? Hopefully by understanding why the Lamenter Mind holds on to that past in the first place. It needs the past in order to make something wrong so that it can be resentful, hold grudges and become a victim. It loves to engage in these habits because they help put attention on itself. If you told the *Cursed Mind* that you were going to fully move on from the past it would say something like, *"If I'm not wrestling with the unfairness of my past and trying to make those who wronged me pay for what they have done or at least get others to feel sorry for me, what will I do with myself?"* The answer is the *Cursed Mind* will die, but in doing so, you will be present as your *Core Self* and your love life will flourish.

Remember Nora, who was abandoned by her father? For years she lamented about his decision to leave her and her mother and how it should never have happened. She was mad, she was sad—but mostly she was bitter that she had to endure lasting emotional effects because of his decision. She was a grown woman whose parents divorced 20 years ago, and yet she held on to the injustice, unfairness, and hardship (the self-absorbed pain) allowing it to affect her in the present day. I told Nora that until she decided to move on from what happened and only deal with the present, she would have difficulty not only attracting guys, but also trusting them. Her Lamenter Mind was like a closet where she stored her entire past. It was completely cluttered, and the more she reflected on how unfair her life had been, the more she added to the mess. Anytime she got involved with someone new it was as if she invited him into that closet, shut the door and tried to have their relationship inside. It was stressing her out, making her angry, and causing her to feel hopeless. It was time to clean her mental closet, once and for all.

It was hard for Nora to stop her Lamenter Mind, but with lots of practice, she did it. What helped was waking up in the morning and meditating on a few key mantras that helped her stay aware of her thought habits: *"Only my Cursed Mind wants me to remain bitter, sad, and angry, so I can be in the right and my father (and men) can be wrong. Only my Curse wants me to hold onto the identity of being a victim. My Core Self wants to be free in order to find love, and to be free I must live in today and only today."* Then she took a few deep breaths and stopped thinking. The moment she stopped thinking, she became present. The more times she became present, the cleaner her mental closet became.

When you can finally see that the past is only useful for the *Cursed Mind* and your *Core Self* does not need it, you will begin to see a dramatic difference in your life going forward. Do not try to reconcile a bad experience by way of your mind, or think your way into feeling better about it. That is what Nora tried to do for years. Thinking about the past is likely what created your pattern in the first place. Instead of wanting to be good with whatever happened, strive to be good with the present. It is a much more productive habit to have.

Another client of mine recently told me a wonderful story about how being present helped to stop her past-focused thinking. She was on a camping trip with many other single men and women. As they were hiking on the second day, she remembered why she had booked the trip for that particular weekend: It was because one of her exes was getting married then, and she wanted to be busy doing something else when the day came. She felt herself becoming sad as she continued the hike, reminiscing about the good times she had with her ex and wishing things had turned out differently with him. Typically, these past-focused thoughts created bouts of crying, and she started to worry that she was going to start sobbing in front of everyone on the mountain. But then, she made the conscious choice to end her past thinking. She recalled a quote she liked in *The Power of Now*: "The moment you realize you are not present, you are present." Instead of diving deeper into the past and recalling all her feelings of resentment, she noticed her mind was not present. She focused on the trees in the distance, the mountainous terrain, and the happy chatter among the campers. She took several deep breaths and smelled the fresh air. She kept her focus on what was happening all around her, and she felt better quickly. She didn't cry that day, and every day she cries less and less.

End Your Past Pattern

It's easy to make the past a part of you and not even realize it. Women who constantly repeat old, painful relationship patterns, subconsciously believe the past is a large part of who they are and how worthy they are. They are drawn to guys who satisfy this long-held belief and agree with their assessment of self. But it is just a trick of the *Cursed Mind* that keeps the pattern going; it is not real love, attraction, or even bad luck. Eckhart Tolle so eloquently put it in the *Power of Now,* "The mind conditioned by the past always seeks to re-create what it knows and is familiar with. Even if it is painful, at least it is familiar. The mind always adheres to the known. The unknown is dangerous because it has no control over it." Many women with a Lamenter Mind would rather endure more pain from a toxic relationship than explore a loving one that she might not know how to navigate or fears would feel strange and unusual. Therefore, without knowing why she does this, she chooses the bad boy again and again.

If this sounds like you, and you know that your Lamenter's *Curse* kicks in when you meet someone, being present will help you see the person more accurately. You won't be looking at him with your old, naïve set of eyes. When you meet a guy who is either emotionally or physically unavailable, and you are strongly attracted to him, be acutely aware of what happens inside you. If you learn to be more present, you can understand why you are drawn to someone: Is it because you want their approval, or you think getting them will be a challenge for yourself? Does he resemble a situation from your past or remind you of someone who hurt you before? These are *Cursed* motivations you cannot see without being present. If you find yourself gravitating to someone who is pulling away or not showing you as much effort, wake yourself up. When you are aware of these feelings and understand where they come from, you can stop yourself from blindly following them. You can change your pattern in that moment.

If you find yourself chasing or pursuing a man who is not that interested, stop whatever you are doing and question your attraction. Give your *Core Self* a voice this time. Let her ask this question: *"Why do you want someone who doesn't seem to want you? Why are you more interested in him now that he is less interested in you?"* Your *Core Self* wants to find love, and that means connecting with someone who is ready and open for it. In order to have a happy relationship, you have to begin with mutual attraction and interest. If it's not there, then don't try to force it to happen. This is what the *Cursed Mind* does because it wants its way and doesn't see anything else. Tell yourself that today you are not going to be fooled or seduced by something that is going to hurt you in the end. Right now, you have everything you need to feel good and complete with your life. In this moment, you don't need anything from anyone, and you can be at peace and content on your own. Find the truth in that statement, and it will set you free from your past relationship habits and start new ones going forward.

Single and Present
Many single women are waiting to be in relationship, or waiting to get married so they can enjoy life and finally be happy. They are so concentrated on the future being their salvation that they don't notice the affect that belief has on their present situation: They move through life with an aura of discontent. Because they think, *"I can't be happy until I have the future I want,"* they walk around and interact with others with the *Cursed Mind* humming in their ear that life right now is not good enough for them.

If you feel like you are waiting for the future to get here, you have to acknowledge the consequences that waiting is having on your romantic life. Since guys can only witness and experience you in the present, they will see you as a person who is living in a state of displeasure. They will sense an irritated or unhappy energy from you because you are irritated and unhappy you are here (single) when you want to be somewhere else (married, or in a relationship). Only when you stop rejecting your life as it is right now and start to embrace it will you lighten your being and transform your energy. You must determine that today is a day that's worth your attention and begin to be present for opportunities for love to emerge.

I had the wonderful experience of witnessing Ashlee finally break her *Curse*. She often told me that she would not be happy until she was married and that nothing could make her present situation "okay", as she put it. To her, the present was not okay so why would she embrace it? The present was a reminder of how she was way beyond the age that she had wanted to be married. No, she said, "I would rather just focus on the future." Then one day as I was yet again attempting to urge her to accept the present moment, it clicked with me that Ashlee thought accepting the present situation of being single meant she was accepting being single forever. I told her, "Accepting your life and situation today does not mean accepting it will be this way always. You only have to accept today *for* today." Suddenly, Ashlee understood. She could be okay today and still work towards the goal of meeting someone. She didn't have to reject her life now, and in fact, rejecting it now was the very thing that was hurting her.

In the *Power of Now*, Eckhart Tolle says, "There is nothing wrong with striving to improve your life situation. You can improve your life situation, but you cannot improve your Life. Life is primary. Life is your deepest inner Being. It is already whole, complete, perfect." What he is saying is that your *Core Self* is whole and complete and nothing can add or take away its value. Nothing you achieve or attain will alter the inner joy of your being. You might think getting married will make you feel happy and joyful and it may for a short time, but you will soon find out that the emptiness returns because nothing outside of you, even something as wonderful as romantic love, is the answer breaking the *Cursed Mind*. And *it is the Cursed Mind that is making you unhappy now*. Remember as I said many chapters ago, your unhappiness is not coming from being single, it's coming from your self-absorbed thinking.

You already have joy and peace within you; no other person can give that to you. Once you access that peace and joy by being present, it will attract love into your life – not the other way around. It really is as simple as this: Loving and valuing the day you are in creates a happier and more attractive you. Your *Cursed Mind* cannot exist in the present, so that is where you must reside to be your *Core Self* and have her shine.

Start Presence Now

You will be amazed at what you will see and whom you will meet by living your life in the present. As the saying goes, "There is no time like the present!" So today, right now, is the best time to being your journey to embracing the moment at hand, and in doing so, ceasing your self-absorbed mind.

Instead of standing in line for your coffee, consumed by what happened yesterday or stressing about what might occur tomorrow, take in all that is around you. Notice the people in front of and behind you. Smile at the cashier, and ask how their day is. Drive to work, admire the scenery, and breathe in the fresh air. Notice the people around you in their cars. When you get to work, don't rush past others with only your agenda in mind. Stay present and smile as you enter the elevator or walk the hall. Whatever problem is waiting at your desk, don't start solving it until you arrive at your desk. This is how you can meet someone: by being here and now when they cross your path. You cannot take advantage of an opportunity to make a connection if you are lost in thought and your mind is busy somewhere else when it happens. How sad would it be if the man you were supposed to marry sat right next to you on the subway but never said a word to you because you were distracted with the future worry of never meeting him.

Remember Cara? The client who was never approached by anyone? She had so many friends who met people easily, and yet in her 27 years, a man had never, not even once, initiated a conversation with her. She was rarely present due to her Worrier Mind and she also struggled with disappointments from her past. So, I gave her an experiment. For one whole day, she was to try and find something beautiful in every person (not just men) who passed by her. It could be their smile, their clothes, or even just a tidy haircut. She didn't have to say anything to them. She only had to stay present so she could take notice. I told her I was giving her the day off from thinking about herself, and it was time for her to think about others and look for the beauty that we all inherently have.

As she went through her day, Cara was surprised at how many people smiled and chatted her up. Because she was actively working to stay present in order to notice everyone who walked by her, she created the right environment for people to talk to her. And since she was looking for something beautiful in each of them, her thoughts were loving and translated out from her being. At the very end of her day, a young man approached her and said she had a lovely smile.

If you are someone who knows you have a terrible habit of being stuck in your head, the best thing to do is wake up in the morning and ready your mind for being present all day. As you exercise your body regularly to maintain your physical health, you must exercise your mind daily to maintain presence and keep your thoughts from drifting back to yourself in the future or past tense. Reading this chapter or even this book will not be enough. The real work happens during your average day, doing the things you always do. Before you even brush your teeth, sit up in bed or find a place on your floor and take a few minutes to breathe and remind yourself that the only day you have to deal with is today. You don't have to think about what will happen if you don't get married this year, or next. You don't have to try and accept what life will be like if you never find the right person. Those are future "what-if" problems, and no matter how hard you try, you cannot cope with them because they are not problems that you have today. It is akin to trying to cope with a future cancer diagnosis. How can you cope with a disease you don't have (and may never have). Thinking about "what-if" scenarios will do only one thing—cause anxiety. You won't be able to come to peace with any unknown future outcome, no matter how much you think it over. My favorite quote from Eckhart Tolle sums it up. "You can always cope with the Now, but you can never cope with the future."

    Today is the only day you can work with in regard to being proactive with love. There is something you can do about today, and that is be your *Core Self* so you are open and here for love when it comes your way. Sit for as long as you need to in order to clear any self-focused thoughts in your head. Feel how your body is behaving to just sitting and being. Is it tense, heavy, sad? Whatever emotion is there, breathe it out of your body. With each breath, feel yourself getting lighter. Take a few minutes to stop reading and try this now. You will have to do this many, many times in order to feel the effects and yield the results—but after all, working at being present is a lifelong practice.

    Breathing is a present-oriented action. You cannot breathe in the future or past the way you can think in it. That is why focusing on your breath can help you stay in this moment. You will most likely have to return to this active breathing many times throughout the day until this becomes your new habit and way of life, but it's important to always remind yourself in the morning so you can begin your day on the right foot. If you tend to get down or stressed right before going to bed, add in some breathing then as well. Be conscious throughout the rest of your day of when you feel tension in your body. Remember that when you use your mind for what it is designed for, it doesn't cause negative emotions. If you get a bit panicked or anxious just before you enter social situations or when you are about to meet someone new for a date, stop yourself in your tracks. Pay acute attention to the present: What is happening right now, right before you? If you are outside at a party, hoping to meet someone but growing fearful you won't be approached or will go home rejected, reel your mind back to where you are in this moment. You're outside the door, about to go inside. Nothing you fear has happened yet. If it does happen, then you can deal with it at the end of the night, but not in this moment. Now is when you go inside and only deal with the people and situations that cross you in the present. If you are getting ready for a date and begin to feel sick and tense, stop what you're doing, breathe deeply, and bring your mind back to right now. Remind yourself that whatever happens on this date is going to happen, and you will cope with it in real time. Trying to cope with it now, before it happens, could ruin your opportunity for love. Close your eyes and breathe again. As you sit or stand there quietly, exhaling your self-absorbed thoughts and accompanying emotions, feel your true, loving self that is deep inside you. With each breath, call her out more and more. Don't think about your *Core Self*; just feel her inside of you. She is there. It may be hard to do at first, but if you stop thinking long enough and focus on feeling the love in your heart, she will emerge and grow stronger each time you do this.

I encourage you to find a mantra that can assist you in these breathing exercises. A mantra can help you center yourself, while reminding you why you're working so hard to be present. Here are a few that I used to use, as well as some from my clients.

"Today is the only day that I have to deal with. It's the only day I can deal with."

"I am one with the present moment."

"I don't have to accept the situation in my life forever. I only have to accept it today."

"The past happened months (or years) ago, I do not have to relive it today."

"Who I am is not my mind; I am my heart and being."

"My love and my power is in the present and nowhere else."

"Something wonderful can happen today. I only have to show up ready for it."

Being Present in a Relationship

When you are present on a date, you can trust without question that you gave the other person the best "you" possible. You can feel confident that you fully focused on him, providing him with the gift of your undivided attention. In doing so, you will be able to feel the connection you have with that person, or feel if it isn't there. You won't have to stress post-date that you said or did something that was misperceived. You will be able to leave the date and know you were at your very best.

If you don't hear from a guy and you thought you would, you will still be disappointed. You will feel sad, and that is normal and healthy. Just be careful that your *Cursed Mind* doesn't seize the opportunity to jump on those emotions and aggravate the situation, making it so much worse than needed. *"Ah! You weren't good enough! You said something dumb. You should have done this, or said that."* Use the power of presence to let those thoughts go and return to just feeling how you feel. Don't let the *Cursed Mind* create a story around your feelings, which will take you from disappointed to depressed.

Once you are in a relationship, being present will allow you to see the events in your life more clearly and accurately. Without your thinking distracting you, you are free to recognize the *Curse* rising in someone else, which is an amazing gift for a relationship. Most people simply react to their partner's mood swings or attacks without little thought of where they are coming from, or if their own response is appropriate. But when you are present, you notice the *Cursed Mind* instead of blindly reacting to it. You can see that your partner is just feeling not good enough, for instance. You can tell his mind is stuck in a self-absorbed place that is worried or lamenting, or caught up in wanting. Rather than taking it personally, you simply say to yourself, *"This is merely a Curse flare-up. I think I'll decide to not react to it."* Or, at the very least, you'll know how to not feed into it further.

At first, it is hard not to react to someone else's *Cursed Mind* with defense and attack (which is what your own *Cursed Mind* wants to do), but when you refrain from doing so, you will see that your arguments disintegrate within minutes. Even if your partner is genuinely upset at something you did, you can keep the conversation above board by not self-protecting or attempting to assert your worthiness. You can simply listen and take note to be better. When you no longer worry about your worth being threatened, you aren't as affected by people's moods and can identify what is really going on inside your significant other. To be clear, this does not mean you should be a pincushion and let someone berate you over and over again. It means you don't engage in *"Cursed* fighting." Stay above it, and if you need to, remove yourself from the situation.

In my own relationship, I have learned to let my *Core Self* do the reacting when my husband gets a little "moody". Recently he came home from a long and frustrating workday. He had been stressed for months and perpetually worried about something at the office. He asked me a question about an upcoming social event we had to attend (one he was not excited about) and wanted to know how to get there. I am not the best with explaining things directionally, and he became quite annoyed that after a few minutes he still didn't know where the event was being held. As his frustration grew, he started picking at my ability to give directions. The old, non-present me would have reacted to this in a defensive way, protecting my self-worth. I would have possibly attacked him back to prove the point that he isn't perfect either, and a fight would have ensued from there. However, I could now see what was happening in the moment and not take his criticism personally. I knew the *Cursed Mind* was emerging as a result of his recent work dealings, and his aggravation had little to do with me. I looked at him and said, "You must have had a really bad day. I'm sorry. Please, let's not turn this into a fight. You are starting to hurt my feelings." Immediately, my husband became present and apologized. He realized his mind had been in such a worried and frustrated state that my struggle with giving directions happened to provoke his *Curse*, which had not yet abated from the workday.

If you are present with your partner, you are able to really hear what he is saying. You hear the story behind the story, which is what I was able to do with my husband. I didn't hear "I'm annoyed with your directions". I heard, "I had such a terrible day and I feel so defeated and unsure of myself, *and* someone at work is driving me nuts." I heard his *Core Self* under the *Cursed Mind*.

"Most people don't know how to listen because a major part of their attention is taken up by thinking. They pay more attention to that than what the other person is saying, and no attention to what really matters – the Being of the other person underneath the words and mind." Another spot-on quote from Eckhart Tolle and *"The Power of Now"* that explains just what is truly needed to stay connected in a relationship, and especially in a marriage. What a gift you can give not only to your partner, but also to yourself! You can concentrate on his *Core Self* and help bring it to presence with your own presence.

Moving Forward Presently

Existing in the same moment in time as everyone else is a key element in connecting with others, and as I've said more than a few times, connection is the first step to love. Staying connected is what makes marriages last. Take that first step to breaking your *Curse* by practicing presence every day. If you learn to stop thinking in the future and past and do your best to live life in the present, a stillness and inner joy will wash over you like you have not felt before. All the uncertainty and anxiety will float away, leaving peacefulness behind. It is then that you are able to experience love on a level unlike any you have until now. Buy a book on meditation or read works by others who are experts in this field, such as Eckhart Tolle. Download a meditation app and learn through a guide until you are able to be present on your own. There are many ways to meditate, so don't give up if the one you try doesn't seem to work. Some people need spiritual meditation, but others might gravitate and greatly benefit from transcendental meditation. Whichever form you choose, remember why you are doing it in the first place: to learn to embrace now so that when your *Cursed Mind* surges, you can use awareness of it along with the power of the present moment to defeat it. You will know you are really on your way to change when you can sit in a room for 20 minutes, be silent and, for the most part, free of thoughts.

Don't worry if it sounds impossible right now; that is the Worrier in you resurfacing. She wants you to say this is too hard, will take too much time, or won't work. She wants to worry that you will fail and be back in the same place you were before reading this book. Listen to me: You will not fail. You can do this, and you can do it quickly, if you make it a true priority. Being present is magical, but it doesn't happen magically. Now that you have finished this chapter, take the first step. Close this book, set the timer on your phone, and attempt to be fully present for five minutes. Concentrate on breathing air into your body and feeling whatever emotions are stored inside you. Then, with each exhale, blow those old emotions right out so you can find your center—which also means to find your peace.

Start your journey to being more present right now. Learn to fully engage with the moment you're in so that when the right person enters your present, you are there to meet him.

REFLECTION

Reflect for a moment on what you've just learned. Then, consider stepping away from this book and working to clear your thoughts for five minutes. Set a timer on your phone and begin a short mediation free of thinking. When you feel yourself wondering how much longer you have, realize this is your *Cursed Mind*, attempting to leave the present moment. Take some deep breaths and focus on feeling your body and emotions. Embrace *your feelings* to stop your thinking. Try saying the word, "Om" in order to assist you in this effort.

Chapter Ten

Be Grateful

Now that you've explored how to be more present in your life and end the habit of living in the past or waiting for the future, you have to turn your focus to the relationship you have with the moments in which you exist. Since the present is the only time you truly interact with other people, it is important to not let the *Cursed Mind* interfere with those interactions. Old thought patterns can creep into your head and give birth to misperception, creating confusion, anxiety, and doubt in your relationships. Those feelings greatly affect your warm, loving, natural energy and also cause you to say and do many things you later regret.

Gratitude is widely discussed in today's culture as a recipe for becoming happier. There are hundreds of books, blogs, and articles explaining the benefits and teaching the practice. While I agree it is an effective way to increase overall positivity in life, it is more than an exercise to help you feel content. Learning to be grateful is a necessity if you want to combat your *Cursed Mind*. Because you are now going to live more presently and use your brain for various tasks at home, work, and play, the relationship you have with the moment you are in is vitally important. Is it a good relationship, one that is content and comfortable? Or is your relationship with the present marked with dissatisfaction and craving for something else? The way you perceive different events in the days, hours, and minutes of your life not only effect your overall wellness but also have a tremendous effect on your relationships with other people. Therefore, being grateful is a fundamental requirement for breaking the *Curse*. It cannot be beaten without it.

The Cure for Lacking

When I was growing up, gratitude was not something often talked about. In fact, I was taught to visualize what I wanted and formulate a plan to get it. My mother never took "no" for an answer, and she made it a point to show me the rewards of her determination whenever they materialized. It wasn't a bad lesson. Truthfully, there were times in life where it served me well and assisted me in tackling productive goals, but something else rubbed off on me more than the drive to persevere: Throughout my adolescence and in young adulthood, as I learned to go after my dreams with unwavering focus, my mind had also become conditioned to *want* things. It didn't matter what it was—new shoes, new clothes, new car, new job. My mind was constantly striving for what was next on my wish list. Boys included.

Unbeknownst to me, my habit to want created the belief that I was lacking in my life and in myself. Wanting by definition is to suffer from lack of something and I felt that was incomplete and deficient in some unexplainable way. The *Curse* of the Wanter and the Inferior Mind had set up camp in my head, and only now can look back and see so clearly how the *Cursed Mind* affected my thoughts and feelings about relationships and my worth. I can vividly recall how I would see this particular guy on my college campus, for example, and a visceral urge to be with him would come over me. I never spoke more than a few words to him, yet the wanting I experienced was tremendous. I would learn his class schedule, try to pass him on the quad, and then spend the whole day suffering if he didn't say hi when he walked by me. A few other guys took interest in me, nice guys who wanted to know me better, but I had no desire to entertain their advances. I would sulk in my room, thinking of the mysterious boy with the leather jacket and sandy brown hair and what it would feel like to hold his hand, to kiss him, to be with him.

For years, I repeated this pattern of wanting the guy who didn't know I existed. Each time I would think to myself, *"What is it about me that is not good enough to grab his attention?"* I believed if something about me was better, I could have what I wanted. If only I had known the truth then. It's not that I was lacking in some way, and therefore I couldn't get the guy. It's that my *Cursed Mind* chose the guy who would reaffirm my feelings of lacking.

The power of wanting and the accessory feeling of deep "lack" that accompanies it cannot be underestimated. How it subconsciously attracts you to someone who is unavailable to you is one of its greatest strengths. Yes, I thought the boy on campus was cute, and that is what initially caught my eye. But my Inferior and Wanter Mind was perceptibly tuned into his energy and the subtle signs he was giving off that told me he was a challenge, and I would need to work for his approval—mainly because upon our first encounter he hardly acknowledged my existence.

Of course, my feelings of lack didn't just affect my attraction to him. They also influenced his attraction to me. As I encountered him at parties or in the lunch hall, my thoughts about myself were blatantly visible to him through my choice of words, actions, and body language. As confident as I feigned to be, and as cool as I tried to play it, my *Cursed Mind* could not be concealed. Each time we interacted, I reaffirmed to him that I thought he was the answer to my incompleteness.

Once feelings of lack are noticed, they often cannot be unseen or compensated for, no matter how pretty, fun, or sweet any woman may be. Most clients who wrestle with the Wanter or the Inferior Mind are blindsided when a man has a sudden change of heart and walks away from them. "I played by all the rules," they will say. "We had such a great time on our dates. I've said nothing to pressure him into commitment! I never told him I love him!" Nonetheless, when I peel back the layers of the relationship, the answer is frequently the same: If the guy was a good person and by all accounts ready for a relationship, it is usually the woman's own feelings of wanting or not being enough (lacking) that prevented him from falling in love.

You could be the total package, and you could be playing by all the dating rules, but the mere thought of getting what you want and filling the void of lack could be invoking a *Cursed* longing in you that supersedes all your good qualities. *"If I get him, I won't be lacking anymore!"* the Wanter and the Inferior Mind thinks. Or, *"If I get to be his girlfriend, I will finally have what I need to be happy and feel good about myself!"* Of course, you may not even hear your *Cursed Mind* saying these words; you just feel them in your bones. The energy from those feelings can overwhelm the person you are fixated on. He might feel that energy immediately upon meeting you, like most guys felt from me, or he may feel it six months down the line when you are knee-deep into the relationship. Whatever the case, it is nearly inevitable that at some point he will sense the belief that he solves the aching of emptiness you're carrying around. And when he does, his attraction will start to fade, and the connection between you will follow soon after. A *Cursed Mind* never goes undetected for long.

All of the *Faces* of the *Curse* function in a state of lack: The Inferior Mind believes it lacks what's needed to be worthy and have love. The Wanter Mind believes it lacks everything, which is why it's always *wanting* and never feels fulfilled. The Worrier/Lamenter Mind lacks something now that it had in the past or hopes to have in the future, and the Contestant and the Superior Mind fight its fear of lack by constantly striving for external proof to the contrary. This is why it is so important to feel satisfied and complete with yourself in the present. You cannot solely rely on strategy to find love; you must have the right mentality as well. No man wants to cure your feelings of lack and most are keenly aware that they cannot cure it even if they tried. As demonstrated throughout time, and certainly throughout this book, a connection cannot grow and love cannot survive when it is being used for the purpose of fulfilling a sense of incompleteness.

If you have spent most of your adult life wrestling with feeling dissatisfied, empty, lonely, or frustrated because you have not yet found love or find it difficult to celebrate other people's engagements or marriages because you don't have that yourself, I can tell you those emotions are not due to lack of your own relationship. They are from the *Cursed* belief that you, yourself, are lacking. Your self-absorbed mind has decided you can't be at peace until it has what it wants; that you aren't complete, worthy, or "enough" until someone approves of you, loves you, or marries you. On the surface, it might seem your desire for love is altruistic, and you will be at peace once you have it. But if you are lying awake at night, tormented over your single status, crying to your friends, or jealous of people who have what you don't, the real problem is not with your romantic situation—it's within your mind. You don't need a man or a relationship. What you need is gratitude.

Gratitude is the true cure for lack. It is the single tool that can remedy the *Cursed Mind*'s habit to only see what is missing or what could be better in your circumstances and in yourself. You cannot ache to be more if you feel you already have plenty, and gratitude is what bridges that gap. Without learning to be grateful, your relationship with the present will feel perpetually empty and lacking because you'll forever see life in terms of what you don't have for yourself instead of what you do have. Being grateful makes what you have and who you are *enough*.

Think About Your Thinking

A few years ago, two of my single clients happened to be going to their 10-year high school reunions on the same night. They both struggled with the Inferior and the Wanter Mind, but one woman had started to practice gratitude while the other had not. Leading up to the night of their reunions, each woman was feeling down. Neither of them wanted to be the only attendee who wasn't married, and they were worried what their old classmates would say about their single statuses. The client who was practicing gratitude asked me for a phone call right before the party, and we talked about all the wonderful things going on her life that she could share with the people who asked. At the end of our call, she felt more excited about reuniting with her former friends, and as I reminded her, the reunion was not about her and her perceived value. It was about reconnecting with others and finding out how they were doing.

When she walked through the door, she was nervous but immediately greeted with warm hugs and big smiles that put her at ease. She spent the night chatting, dancing, and laughing with her old crew. She never once thought about how people appraised her because she was focused on them and how grateful she was to be there. Because of how she chose to handle the present situation (with gratitude), she actually enjoyed the reunion. As a nice bonus, a guy from that reunion who was divorced reached out to her a few days later on Facebook and asked her to get coffee.

The other client went to her reunion as well. She sat quietly at a table, chatting with friends, but every time someone who had a spouse came to talk to her, she sunk deeper into a depressed state of mind. *"You're married, too? I can't believe you got married before me!"* her self-absorbed mind would sulk. She counted how many people in the room were single and found two other women, each of whom she considered to be nerdy. *"OMG, now I'm like those girls!"* her *Cursed Mind* whispered. After about an hour, she couldn't take it anymore and left the reunion fighting back tears. She spent the rest of the night on the phone with her sister, crying about how hopeless her life was.

Two women in two similar situations, yet their thinking caused two very different outcomes that night. This is the perfect example of how most people perceive their lives: either focusing on the moment and appreciating whatever it is or thinking about themselves and what they, or the situation, lacks. As you can see, the perception you choose for yourself can spur different results.

"The primary cause of unhappiness is never the situation but your thoughts about it," said Eckhart Tolle in his book *A New Earth*. If you identify with the second woman in the reunion story, it is likely that you often feel alone and unlucky and only experience happiness when something positive is happening to you, particularly in your love life. But there is a difference in *Cursed* happiness and real happiness derived from your *Core Self*. *Cursed* happiness is the satisfaction the self-absorbed mind gets from a situation. Something goes its way, like a guy showing interest or asking you on a date, and it's happy about it. This kind of happiness is short-lived and dependent on the other person in the equation, which can change at any moment and cannot be controlled. This type of happiness comes with an equal or larger amount of unhappiness. Real happiness that comes from your *Core Self*—what most would call inner joy—is not situational. It doesn't turn on or off depending on what happens to you and is separate from any other person in your life. You might get down or sad when something really bad occurs, but you don't sink into utter despair if you are rooted in inner joy. Most importantly, you don't use someone's love or affection as fuel to keep you happy, which is what feels draining and clingy to the other person.

It may not seem possible to you yet, but I assure you that you can be single and be happy. You don't have to be happy *about* being single, but you do need to be joyful as you are right now, which happens to be a single person. Being joyful is the easiest and fastest way to attract real love into your life. People who are full of joy exude an easy and engaging energy that everyone loves to be around. Joy can fill the void of lack and quickly change the circumstances in your life. No matter what is or is not happening right now, there is a reason to be joyful. You only need to disconnect with your *Cursed Mind* in order to know that and truly feel it. As Shakespeare said, *"There is nothing either good or bad, but thinking makes it so."*

If It Was Easy, You Wouldn't Need It

I realize that for some people being consistently grateful sounds like a monumental feat. If your *Cursed Mind* has been running the show, it is hard to imagine how you will ever change focus and stop wanting a relationship or feel joy with life right now. Some of my clients complain that they would rather do anything else but practice gratitude. They simply don't believe they can carry out the task, especially given their pattern of disappointment and feelings of hopelessness. To which I tell them this: The very reason you are citing as to why you cannot be grateful is precisely why you have to do it. If it were easy for you, you would not need to do it.

If you are waiting for something to happen in order to kick-start your grateful mindset, I have to warn you that you might get your wish; however, it may not be the happy "win" you were hoping for. Much of the time, for people who are *Cursed*, gratitude is learned the hard way—when life shows you how good you had it to begin with.

Mary, for instance, had always felt incredibly insecure and was usually overwhelmed with sadness. She cried frequently because she felt she wasn't as pretty and smart as her friends, wasn't confident at her job, and felt sure she would never meet anyone she liked. She told me that most days she felt sad and sometimes didn't even know why. For Mary, feeling grateful for her life was not in the realm of possibility.

Then something terrible really did happen. One of Mary's older sisters, who was married with a newborn baby, was diagnosed with cancer. Within six months, her sister passed away, leaving her husband without a wife and their baby without a mother. Mary was grief-stricken at her loss, and for a time, completely inconsolable. But through this awful life circumstance she learned the lesson she didn't think she could ever learn. She came to me two years after her sister's passing and seemed like a completely different person.

"I will always miss my sister and be sad she's gone," Mary told me. "But whenever I get sad about something in my own life, usually something silly like not liking my body or feeling like I won't ever meet someone, I think of how insulting this is to my sister. How can I not be grateful that I am here on this earth, able to see my family, talk with my friends, and enjoy just being alive. How can I not make the most of the day I've been given, a day that she would give anything to be here for? I get to watch her daughter grow up, and she doesn't. To be sad about things that are not life and death seems incredibly self-centered and disrespectful to her."

The daily self-loathing and sadness that Mary had carried with her before was gone. She was still grieving her sister, but she no longer had the self-absorbed pain of wanting what other people had and focusing on herself. It took a tragic event for her to recognize and stop her Wanter and Inferior Mind, but then she was able to be grateful every day in the name of her sister.

There is beauty and opportunity in each day that you have, but the *Cursed Mind* stands in your way, blocking that view. Whenever you feel frustrated or jealous because someone has a better life circumstance or you hear your *Curse* asking for something good to happen, remind yourself that instead of a gift, you may get a lesson.

Get Grateful

Every study on gratitude will tell you that you are more apt to perform better and succeed in your endeavors when you get grateful, and finding love is no different. Even if you are single and embracing your life right now seems to contradict your dream of having a partner and family in the future, achieving that goal is far more probable with the right attitude. You don't need to worry and stress about attaining love in order to find it. You only need trust that your *Cursed* mentality is the problem and not your lack of a relationship so you don't waste time attempting to fix the wrong problem.

This does not mean you should stop putting yourself out there or cease all efforts to meet someone. You can absolutely work toward the objective of finding and keeping love and feel a strong sense of gratitude at the same time. These two ideas do not conflict because one is an action and the other is your mentality. You have a choice: You can go on many dates, searching for the right person for you, grumbling the whole way and frustrated by your lack of progress, or you can meet each new prospect with a cheery disposition and an appreciation for yet another opportunity. You—and only you—can make the choice about which approach you take.

Now it's time to get started. If being present means to fully inhabit the moment you are experiencing, then being grateful is the positive relationship you should have with that moment. This means you must first be present enough to rise above *Cursed* thoughts like these: *"I need this," "I cannot wait until I have that," "I wish this was different,"* or *"I wish my date was more like this."* Dwelling in these thoughts puts you right back in that old, familiar state of lack and dissatisfaction. You have to be aware when your self-absorbed mind starts to ruminate, and not ignore that you are allowing it to do so or indulge in it what it's saying.

Your goal now is to create a new way of perceiving situations so that you see what you have instead of what you do not. This way, your *Cursed Mind* won't surreptitiously take over when you aren't paying careful attention to it. It's very easy to let yourself fall into old wanting thought habits when you are tired or stressed or encounter certain triggers.

I believe it's best to begin by officially committing yourself to the task of practicing gratitude. That means take action! Tell as many people as you can, write the words "be grateful" on your bathroom mirror or refrigerator, and enlist a close friend or relative to join you in this journey. Don't merely mumble, "I'll try to be more grateful" and fool yourself into thinking that will suffice. You are going against the *Cursed Mind*—you will need lots of reinforcements.

Remember that gratitude is called a practice for a reason. You will not be great at it at first, and it might be hard to get started, but like anything else in life practice makes perfect. After you announce to the world that you are going to get more grateful, you have to take the second-most important step in this process and actually write down what you are grateful for each day. While journaling might seem like a small action, it takes at least three times as long to write something as it does to think it. This amplifies the experience of practicing gratitude and makes it resonate more. I cannot stress this enough: It is unlikely you will be able to break the *Curse* without the physical component of journaling your gratitude.

How long do you have to journal? Three months—and no shortcuts. Sit down at the end of your day, when you can reflect back upon the last 12 hours and think about what gifts you enjoyed that day. Perhaps you had a good night's sleep the night before and woke up early, feeling energetic. Maybe you have a comfy bed in a nice house or apartment. If that sounds minor, lest you forget that some people in other countries sleep on the ground! As you continue thinking about your morning, consider all the things that make life easy for you: a hot shower, steaming cup of coffee, or a mode of transportation that got you to work safely. As simple as these things are, they didn't always exist, and not everyone has them.

As your day progressed, think about the people you came in contact with, whether friends, family, or co-workers. Did someone smile and say hello to you first, or ask you about your day? Did a friend wish you a happy birthday or a great weekend? Appreciate the people who take an interest in you and care about your well-being. They certainly aren't obligated to do it. Write down a few things you appreciate about those people and how they positively affect your life.

As your thoughts of the day draw to the end, think about some of the more profound blessings you have. Do you have a mother who is alive and loves you, a father who is supportive and present? What about children? If you have kids, as tough as it is to raise them, you have already experienced love on the deepest level possible. And what about your health? Are you able to walk, run, talk, visit friends, and go out to dinner? These are things not everyone is able to do. The gifts that come with good health are often taken for granted, until one day they are taken away by illness or injury. Write down all these blessings, and before you go to sleep, email this gratitude summary to one of your friends or someone you trust. This is my favorite part of this exercise because inviting another person on this journey with you will not only keep you on track but having them join you in this process and email you their gratitude journal in return will also enhance the whole experience that much more. Reading someone else's grateful thoughts will strengthen your ability to be grateful, too.

Again, do this for three months, even if you are tired and don't feel like doing it. The only way to cure yourself of the *Curse* is to power through and do what is right, even when it's not easy. You are attempting to exhume and resurrect your *Core Self* from deep entombment, so you cannot let your *Cursed Mind* talk you into cheating the process. This will be work, and it will get hard in moments of dating or relationship difficulty—but that is exactly when you need to focus even more on this exercise. At the end of the quarter, decide if you must continue journaling or have effectively reframed your thinking. If it's the latter, you can switch to simply praying or meditating in gratitude before going to bed or when you rise in the morning. Do not let a day pass where you don't reflect on something for which to be grateful. This is a practice you must keep for the rest of your life. Gratitude is not like a diet you go on in order to shed some excess weight, only sticking with it until you accomplish your short-term goal. It's a complete lifestyle change that you have to commit to from this day forward, if you want to prevent your *Cursed Mind* from returning with its many problems in tow.

What will hopefully transpire by the end of three months is that you will have retrained your brain to be grateful in real time. While you are being present, you should feel an appreciation for what is happening in your life now. Let's be honest: It does no good to feel lack and dissatisfaction all day long and then force 10 minutes of gratefulness at night. Real-time gratitude is your ultimate goal so that whatever you are doing throughout the day, regardless of what may or may not happen, you see and feel the gifts that grace and enrich your life instead of seeing what is lacking or could be better. Your *Core Self* is able to enjoy the small, but wonderful moments in your life —the nice weather, a beautiful view, a friendly smile —as opposed to your *Cursed Mind* needing some grand and direct ego boost to keep it happy.

When you are able to achieve real time gratitude it will have a significant effect on your energy. Instead of carrying a heavy, dismal, or dissatisfied vibe wherever you go, your aura will be lighter, more content and peaceful. People who come across you will be able to feel the peace, and then the joy, radiating from your *Core Self*—and like a magnet, they will be drawn to that energy. Gratitude can take any vibe with an undercurrent of lack (needy, desperate, over-eager, wanting) and transform it into a vibe of wholeness. To a man, that wholeness looks like security, self-assurance, and resilience. This is how women with the Inferior or the Wanter Mind can finally achieve the sexy, self-confidence that they have struggled with or often felt they did not have. Insecurity comes from the feeling of lack. True confidence comes from the feeling of being whole and at peace with yourself.

Best of all, when you achieve real-time gratitude, it will make a huge difference in how you interact with the world around you. For example, let's say a seemingly single guy smiles at you in line at a coffee shop. Your *Cursed Mind* might normally react with wanting in this situation: *"Please ask for my number! He's so cute and it will make my day if he likes me."* If he doesn't ask, you might pout, *"Ugh, another example of how I'm not good enough to get a date!"* The Lamenter Mind might store that experience and add another layer of negativity to your being, which you would then carry around for the rest of the day, or perhaps even longer. However, if you have been practicing real-time gratitude, your *Core Self* will instead feel the joy of that simple connection in the coffee shop, and think, *"Oh, that guy smiled at me. That felt so nice!"* Although you'd not be opposed to him asking for your number, you no longer voraciously crave something more from other people because you feel peace on your own. You don't take the guy's non-interest in pursuing you further as an indication of your value and sulk about it, or lament about a lost opportunity to enhance yourself and your life; you embrace the experience you had with him in the moment you had it. Your *Core Self* sees and is grateful for what *did* happen, unlike your *Cursed Mind,* which focuses only on what did not.

On a larger scale, appreciating life in real-time and being grateful for all that you already have, prepares you to appreciate a man's availability and interest when it does come your way. You won't give into the *Cursed Mind* telling you to run from anyone who has real love to give because you will have recalibrated your thoughts to gratefulness. Therefore, his strong desire for you will feel good instead of smothering or uncomfortable.

For any healthy relationship to mature from infatuation to love, gratitude must be present. If it's not there, the *Cursed Mind* will incite wanting by creating some problem when the natural excitement of new romance wears off. If you achieve real-time gratitude, that transition will be easy and feel very natural. If you haven't quite hit the real-time goal, and you are still in the process of journaling and retraining your mind, it's equally effective to notice when your thinking turns to wanting, or when your feelings of desire suddenly shift to indifference or aversion. Let your *Core Self* advise you in those moments. Let her watch your thoughts and decide if you are truly with the wrong person, or if your *Cursed Mind* is simply falling into an old pattern. You will know the difference because your *Core Self* will feel if it is right or wrong to be with someone, while your *Cursed Mind* will tell you. *"Ugh, his clothes are terrible. Why is he calling me so much? Does he have no life? I don't like how nice he is, it's like he has no backbone. I need someone who is better..."* If you hear or feel yourself making these types of assessments, that are rooted in lack and what needs to be better about someone, acknowledge that is what you are doing before you take any action and consider telling the person that the relationship is moving a little too fast for you and to request that you both slow the pace. It might save you a mountain of regret later.

The more grateful you are, the more inherently joyful you will feel, the better results you'll get in your romantic life. It is a domino effect! When you end craving and fill your sense of lack with gratitude, you discover the wholeness you've always had within yourself. You can feel the sense of completeness you hoped to find through a relationship but resided within yourself all along. And as you will read later in this chapter, gratitude will help you most of all by opening up the realm of dating possibilities and making more people appealing to you! Yes, that actually happens!

Resisting Gratitude

Before we go any further, it's worth mentioning that it is common to feel a gripping resistance to gratitude when you start. Being grateful is a mind habit of our *Core Self,* which is completely opposite from any habit of the *Cursed Mind.* If you have been indulging in habits like judging and taking things personally, being grateful might feel uncomfortable, awkward, or unnatural at first. At some point in the process, you may even encounter more proof of how lacking you are and how life constantly shortchanges you. For example, maybe you try to put yourself back online, attempting to have a more grateful attitude about dating, only to be emphatically rejected by all the men you find interesting. Or, as you try to appreciate your single life and find the good in being alone, your roommate tells you she's engaged and moving out. Now you feel even lonelier than before. It is normal to feel as if the universe is handing you more reasons to give up on trying to be grateful. This happens to everyone and is not an indication that you are unlucky and life really is out to get you. It is the *Cursed Mind* making its last stance, attempting to tighten its grip on your old thought patterns. When your self-focused mind is threatened with extinction, it subconsciously starts wreaking havoc on you. It's not that gratitude isn't working when these obstacles occur—it is working. What you are experiencing are the growing pains of progress. Your aware mind is battling your unaware mind, and the fight is materializing in different and unpleasant ways. If you accept these pains as setbacks, as the *Cursed Mind* wants to do, you will stay Cursed. *"Look at that! I knew this gratitude journaling wouldn't work. I'm just not good enough and nothing is going to change that fact,"* your self-absorbed mind might say. If you agree with the voice of the mind, your old patterns will continue and you will have more disappointment ahead of you. Expect that your *Curse* is going to make an attempt to stick around so that you can be prepared for that when it happens.

How do you prepare? You prepare by carefully watching your thoughts when they fall into an old pattern. Use awareness of mind and presence. Your *Core Self* would be happy for your roommate's engagement because it is a good circumstance for her, but your *Cursed Mind* would see it as a bad circumstance *for you* and be jealous or angry. I know that being happy for your roommate might be a stretch right now, and that is totally understandable. Just notice your thinking and make a real effort not to judge the circumstance one way or the other. If you don't judge and instead say, "Ok, that happened", and do not label the situation as negative, you will feel the shift in your mentality. You do have a choice on how you handle setbacks. You can give in to old self-centered mind patterns, or you can notice them when they begin to happen and put into practice all that you've learned thus far in this book. If you can catch your mind engaging in a pattern, and work to clear your head, you won't spiral down your old path of self-absorbed pity, jealousy, or anger. You might not necessarily feel grateful for these hurdles in the moment, but withholding judgment when they come your way will help you stay the course. If you can persevere through moments that test you, the payoff will be well worth it, and your love life will continue to steadily improve.

Then What Happens?
Studies show that living in a state of appreciation does a body good. Our overall health is, of course, important, but what about your relationship results? How will being grateful attract love into your life? Can it really help break all the *Cursed* mindsets, not just the Wanter and the Inferior Mind?

We know those with a Contestant Mind have a tendency to compare themselves to others and often feel jealous. At the core, it's because the Contestant Mind believes certain gifts in life are scarce, with love being one of those rare gifts. When it sees another person possessing something it wants—maybe that person is happy in a relationship or simply had a really great first date—the *Cursed* thought is, *"Oh they have what I want! Now there is one less of that to go around."* All of life is seen this way, which is why people with this *Curse* are angry, bitter, or unhappy for others. But love is universally abundant, and a woman who appreciates her life knows this. When she becomes grateful, she starts to realize there is more than enough love in the world and no longer feels the need to compete with others for it. She becomes cooperative instead of competitive, and that is when a real, tangible change occurs. Life begins cooperating for her. Instead of rivaling her friends, she cheers for them, and in turn, one of them introduces her to a guy who later becomes her boyfriend. Or, instead of wasting time trying to win back her ex because she fears it's her only chance for a relationship, she moves on with real hope and understanding that she will fall in love again. Then, because she is open and optimistic, she very quickly does. When you are grateful, you aren't motivated by painful, self-focused emotions like envy and rivalry because you know love is everywhere. When you truly know this, you are able to make choices that benefit you and create prosperous circumstances.

Amy, for instance, spent years feeling jealous of her friends. She made a point to show up late to their showers or engagement parties and sulked at their weddings when she was made to sit at the singles table. Then, she started coaching with me, and the first thing I made her do was start a gratitude journal. Like most women of her mindset, she found this difficult and did not think it would help. It took almost two months to get Amy to consistently put effort into journaling thoughts of appreciation. And then, as if the light bulb went off one day, she wrote and told me she was feeling "happy for no reason," which was completely foreign to her. Around that time, one of her friends was dating a very successful software engineer and invited Amy to a dinner at his house. Normally, Amy would have made an excuse not to attend, as she didn't have a date to bring, but this time she went and chose to be grateful that her friend thought to invite her. She had never truly felt gratitude for her friendships and took them for granted because what she really wanted was romantic love. Now she felt an appreciation for her friend and because of that, she went to the dinner. Then, she went to three more dinners —without a date. Wouldn't you know it but at one of those dinners two very nice single guys sat on each side of her and at the end of the night, both guys asked for her number.

Gratitude helped Amy make a positive choice for herself and that choice eventually lead her to a good circumstance. I recently checked in with her and she's still dating one of the guys she met that night. Had Amy not been practicing gratitude, she would not have gone to the dinner and not been dating him right now.

Although we've spent most of this chapter discussing the life-changing effect of gratitude on the Wanter and the Inferior Mind, an equally radical transformation happens for those with a Superior Mind. Make no mistake about it; everyone spends time in this alcove of the *Curse*. Most women today prospect for a potential partner entirely under the precinct of the Superior Mind. As much as you might not think you identify with this particular *Face,* if you have toiled on any dating app, swiping on men and deciding who is worth meeting and who is not, it is unavoidable that your self-absorbed mind has taken post there.

When your *Cursed Mind* shifts into Superior mode, it first sees you as unique, unusual, or one of a kind. You feel as if you are not part of the general masses. You are separate, and your journey for love is somehow different, perhaps more important, or more difficult than others. Without much notice to you, the Superior Mind convinces you this separation from other people puts you in a special category, which means you need someone equally as special. This is the reason you swipe left way more than you swipe right.

Do not mistakenly believe that you only find a small number of people attractive. It is your Superior Mind that looks at men through the lens of extreme judgment and searches for the person who is equal to how you view yourself—or how you *want* to view yourself—thus eliminating any man who does not fit that mold. What is really happening when you swipe left is your *Cursed Mind* saying, *"He's not worthy of me"* or *"He does not look like who I should be with. He is not my equal"* based on his photo and a couple of lines of text.

When you learn to live in gratitude, you solve the problem of so few men being appealing. Through appreciation of life comes an appreciation of all people, which is how you end superficial judgment. By ceasing to judge, you cut the lifeline needed to feed the Superior Mind, and it loses its hold on you. You are still able to analyze, of course, but the callous, superficial criticism that kept you from giving more people a chance to know you diminishes. Your *Core Self* looks deeper into each individual and evaluates the real and important qualities that make him wonderful and potentially right for you.

One of my favorite client stories is that of Claire. She had a total transformation, shedding her Superior Mind and finding love within a matter of months. Claire was beautiful, smart, and successful. Looking at her, you would say she had it all. She was constantly in and out of relationships, dating men who were at the top of their game. When she started coaching with me, Claire said she was ready to get married and had just met a man named Decker who had everything she wanted. She hired me to help her "land" him, saying he was perfect for her—even though they had only been on one date.

I told Claire I was going to help her find love, and hopefully it would be with Decker. But first I wanted her to start a gratitude journal and read *"The Power of Now."* She agreed and started reading and journaling right away.

Decker would reach out to Claire, but it was sporadic. He would take her on a fabulous date, tell her how beautiful she was, but then disappear for a week or two. This went on for more than a month. Claire quickly identified that her Superior Mind was smitten with Decker, but since the relationship was slow to progress, she decided to keep dating other people. While doing so, she focused on being grateful more than she ever had in her life in order to fight the *Cursed* feelings of wanting Decker, imagining a future with him, and lamenting as to why it wasn't happening faster.

As she was journaling, Claire began to feel something she had never felt before. She felt peaceful. She stopped aching for something to happen with Decker in between their dates. She lived presently and practiced real-time gratitude for each day she had and each new date she went on.

Then one night, she met a man named Calvin for a drink. Calvin was the nicest, most unselfish man Claire had ever met. He was also clever and smart, and they had an easy and fun rapport. They spent the whole evening laughing and swapping stories, and at the end of the night they had a long, passionate kiss.

After that, Claire never thought of Decker again, which was good because she never heard from him again either! She and Calvin became exclusive a mere two weeks after meeting—and after six months of dating, they are talking about moving in together.

What I love most about the story of Calvin and Claire is what she said to me one day on the phone, about two months after they had met. She said, "If it were not for being aware of my *Cursed Mind* and practicing true gratitude every day, I would have missed meeting Calvin, who is the absolute love of my life. I would not have appreciated what a great person he was if I hadn't done the work to break my *Curse*, and I definitely would not have kept dating around. In fact, I'd likely still be hung up on and waiting for what's-his-name, who I thought was so perfect for me." (She was, of course, referring to Decker.)

The Superior Mind is only impressed by what it can see on the surface. It wants to be seen as better than or having more than others, and a visibly flawed or seemingly mediocre partner would hurt that chance and cause the mind to feel lesser. Once gratitude enters the equation, your *Core Self* takes over your search for love and is more curious and open about who you will date. You see beauty in a deeper way, or at the very least, you are more interested in learning if attraction can happen when you know someone better. Most importantly, your *Core Self* is forgiving of insignificant surface flaws that your *Cursed Mind* wouldn't tolerate.

Claire wasn't fully aware of it at the time, but when you become grateful, your perspective on yourself goes from, *"I am different/exceptional"* to *"I am just like everyone else."* You don't feel entitled; you feel humbled, and that caused Claire to really see Calvin when he matched with her online and when he was across from her at the table. No, he wasn't as suave as Decker, but he was cute and a far better match. If she hadn't worked to break her Superior Mind, however, she would have dismissed him at first glance.

Claire said something else to me that was equally as important that day on the phone. She said that Calvin told her what he loved the most about her and what stood out about her on their very first date was how peaceful and happy she was with herself. He had not seen that from any woman he had dated. Would he have seen that without her practicing gratitude?

Continuing Gratitude

Beyond dating, being grateful can help preserve the love and connection between you and your partner over the years. Instead of letting your Superior Mind point out everything that is wrong, your *Core Self* notices what is right. Although you may still like things done your way or remain a perfectionist at heart, the know-it-all demeanor of the *Cursed Mind* in superior mode, or in wanting, will soften, which will make working as a couple more fun and less tense. While you may have barked orders before in an effort to get your way, gratitude will compel you to say "please" and "thank you." At times when you might have rolled your eyes at an opposing point of view, gratitude will keep you smiling and respecting the other person's opinion. It's these kind little gestures that, when added together, make a harmonious and well-connected marriage.

It has been proven that a simple sign of appreciation every day can keep the love alive between two people and foster an even deeper love throughout the years. After years of making the bed, cooking dinner, going to work, and taking out the garbage, it is easy to take for granted the little things your partner does for your relationship. It's all too common to focus on what else someone needs to do for us or what we want them to do instead of acknowledging those seemingly mundane tasks. So, while telling your husband thank you for mowing the lawn, paying the bills, or even just going to work might not be something you would think to do, it can make all the difference between a happy or unhappy marriage. Can you imagine if you cooked dinner every night for 30 years and your spouse only said thank you the first three times you did it? A marriage rooted in appreciation is one that can last the test of time. Men who feel appreciated at home stay emotionally connected to their wives, and that helps guard against real relationship killers such as indifference, neglect, and detachment.

    Begin your journey to being grateful right now. Put this book down, take out a piece of paper or open your computer, and begin journaling your thoughts of gratitude. Remember, your goal is to achieve real-time gratitude while being present so you replace your sense of lack with the wholeness and fulfillment that is already within you, instead of seeking it from a relationship. The more whole you feel, the more joy you radiate, which will invite love into your life with an ease you may not have ever thought possible.

REFLECTION

Reflect for a moment on what you've just learned. Start your gratitude journal by emailing a friend to join you on this journey. Ask them to commit to doing this for the next ninety days. If that is too long of a commitment, ask for thirty and when the time is up, ask another friend to continue with you. If you want to change your recurring relationship pattern, begin the work of practicing gratitude right now. All change that happens will come from the work you do when you are not reading this book.

Chapter Eleven

Be Accepting

Self-absorbed thinking conditions you to believe that you are the defining factor that influences everything in your life, and especially in your relationships. You think that you dictate how a man treats you — whether he calls you or ignores you, loves you or neglects you, uses you or marries you. Nothing is of greater influence than *you*, the *Cursed Mind* thinks. When you assume that you and your value are the major factors at play in any relationship, accepting when that relationship doesn't go according to plan would mean admitting you weren't worthy enough to make that plan happen. Your *Cursed Mind* can't have that, so it has a hard time accepting anything contradictory to what it wants or believes it should have.

This is why some women continue to chase guys they find attractive despite their signs of lukewarm interest or lousy character. Instead of recognizing that a relationship isn't progressing for whatever reason, they ponder and plan ways to make contact in order to spend more time together, hoping to coerce a somewhat-interested person into a relationship. Why not read the signs? Why not move on and try to find someone who shows more reciprocity? It's because the *Cursed Mind* is not only attached to the idea that this particular person holds the key to peace, love and happiness, but that failing to obtain that person would mean it wasn't good enough to have him. How could the mind so easily subject itself to that kind of rejection? It won't – not without a fight. So, it ignores the truth of the situation and forges on, trying to make what it wants come to fruition. Then, when it doesn't —because it was never going to —the woman will shake her head and lament being cursed to be single, yet again.

The same can be said for why women hang on to relationships that are unbalanced, unloving, or even toxic. When the *Cursed Mind* is ruling your love life, your primary function is to get what you want and that sometimes means perpetually trying to make a relationship work despite all signs indicating that it isn't meant to be. Remember, the *Cursed Mind* doesn't care about having real love. It doesn't have any idea what a loving relationships looks or feels like. It is only interested in how it can enhance or protect its sense of value, and there is often no better opportunity to do that than within a relationship that is not yet fulfilling its needs. I would know as I have personally experienced this myself.

When I was 21 years old, I had a boyfriend named Danny. He was attractive, charismatic, and popular, and in the very beginning of our relationship, he was nothing but attentive. After a few weeks passed, he became more distant, irritable, and selfish. He was hot and cold with me, loving me one minute and needing space the next. After seven months, I couldn't take the pain anymore. In a moment of deep misery, I told him I hated him and never wanted to see him again.

Within a week, Danny was dating someone else, and I was inconsolable. My *Cursed Mind* could not accept what was happening. I had stormed out on Danny because my *Core Self* saw his toxicity, but my *Cursed Mind* secretly hoped he would wake up and beg to have me back. Instead, he had found someone who I thought was prettier and more interesting than me, which made me feel terrible. I did everything I could think of to entice him into reconciling. For almost a year, we continued an undefined, on-and-off relationship that was regularly interrupted by

Be Accepting

his trysts with other women. That time in my life was very painful. I couldn't eat, I couldn't sleep, and I would often feel sick to my stomach. I wanted so much for Danny to change his mind and love me again, even though I was the one who ended it with him in the first place. My *Curse* had completely taken over. At the time I believed getting Danny back would stop the pain I was feeling. I thought, *"I feel this bad because I love him, so being with him is the only way to feel better."* I later realized the majority of the pain was coming from my *Cursed Mind's* inability to accept the reality of our relationship, as well as who he was, and move on.

Getting over Danny took moving to another state, starting a new job, and beginning to date someone else. When I came home years later, we met up again, but this time my feelings for him had completely changed. I saw him for who he was: a charming player who had no real interest in monogamy with anyone, a man who did as he pleased regardless of what anyone else thought or wanted from him. I remember thinking as I left the lunch we had together, *"I used to be crazy about him, but now I don't see anything attractive about him at all."* I was mystified as to how I could have ever been so enamored with Danny.

Very early on in that relationship, I saw red flags. Danny said and did things that hurt my feelings and made me cry, but it didn't curb my desire to be with him. Despite how he treated me, I longed for him. I would say it was because my heart was involved, as most people can attest to feeling the same, but I now know that wasn't the reason. A heart wants to love and be loved. It has good intentions and a pure agenda. Almost from the get-go, my agenda with Danny was motivated by an intense attraction and craving for his approval, which later sprouted other emotions such as fear, dejection, insecurity, and jealousy—all of which points to my *Cursed Mind* much more than any other body part. Being with Danny had awakened every one of the self-absorbed thoughts in my brain, and the emotions that sprang from those thoughts were so strong I thought it was love.

People told me Danny was a jerk. My friends all shook their heads when we would briefly get back together. I told myself they didn't understand, but truthfully it was me who didn't get it. I was too *Cursed* to see what was going on in my relationship, and especially with myself.

I am going to tell you what I wish someone had said to me all those years ago. When there is imbalance, volatility, or constant disappointment in a relationship, a large part of the problem lies in either seeing only what you want to see or fighting to make things as you want them to be. Your *Cursed Mind* can be very convincing when it decides what it wants and thinks it needs, which blinds you to the reality of a relationship with someone and the possibility of it ever evolving into love. The self-absorbed mind never wants to accept an unwanted or unfavorable outcome, so it fights to make what it wants to happen, happen —even if the fight is only occurring on the inside. *"No! This can't be happening! I can't believe this. Why! How? I need this situation to go away, to change, to stop. I can't stand how painful this is right now and that I'm not getting what I really want."* It's a common misconception to think that the unfavorable outcome itself is causing the majority of the emotional pain. But it's actually our attachment to the desired outcome, and the inability to accept a change in life's plan that makes us suffer.

In chapter nine, you learned that you have to be present in the moment you are experiencing, and in chapter ten, you learned to be grateful for that moment. Now it's time to go one step further and be accepting of whatever the moment is telling you, even if it is contrary to your original plan. When you become aware of the attachment you have to certain outcomes in your relationships, your *Core Self* becomes more at peace with any situation that happens in your life. You accept what simply *is*, and in doing so, life and love become exponentially easier because you do not fight or ignore the truth of something—or perhaps more accurately, of someone.

Fight or Accept?

Be Accepting

There are times in life when you need to fight for what you want. There are times to fight for love. Relationships and marriages reach rocky points, and without each individual working to improve themselves, the love between them can be ruined beyond repair. However, there are also times when acceptance is the only true option for you. Because only by acceptance will you have peace, and only with peace can you be your *Core Self* and really understand the path you're supposed to take.

My client Rhoda, who was unfairly fired from her job, came to me in tears one day because she felt her life was falling apart. She was dating a co-worker, and their relationship became strained when she was laid off from her job. She spent months fighting to keep things going with him while attempting to find a way for her company to rehire her. One day, after weeks of struggling to hold her job and relationship together, she told me she "…was exhausted and could not do this anymore…" I asked her what she meant specifically, and her answer was, "I have to stop trying. All the trying is killing me inside." Rhoda had come to a moment where she was ready to accept what was happening. She realized fighting was not the answer, and she had to cease the mission to get her position back and let go of her rocky relationship. Her old job was gone, and her relationship was long over; it just took months for her to admit it. Though she was sad, Rhoda also felt a great sense of relief. Accepting what she could not change brought her a surprising amount of peace. The anger and frustration she felt for months finally waned, and her energy level slowly returned. A few months after this shift in her mentality, she was scouted by a big company, and she's now dating someone else.

There are many instances in dating that you may view as negative, and your initial reaction is to fight them. When someone you care about seems to lose interest or the person you thought could be "the one" doesn't feel the same, it is hard to immediately accept the circumstance. The *Cursed Mind* wants to yell, *"No! This wasn't supposed to happen to me. It's not supposed to be this way,"* which motivates you to fight the inevitable with every resource you have. Resisting acceptance feels easier than facing the pain of losing what you want. You think if you keep fighting, you can keep your chances alive, however slim they may be. You're also hoping to ward off the sorrow that comes with a broken heart. In reality, you can end up prolonging the pain you were trying to avoid. Often the only way to reduce emotional pain is to face it head on and trust that once you move through it, you will come out happier and more at ease on the other side.

Yes, acceptance will sometimes make you sad at first. At times it means grieving a relationship lost. But you have a choice: keep the pain going by refusing to accept what has happened or begin healing from it. Rhoda did not want to accept the drastic changes in her life, so for months she cried and struggled to stay the course on what she thought was her road to happiness. Finally, when she became completely deflated, she decided to accept her situation—and only then did things begin to get better.

Think about how often you avoid, ignore, or resist what a situation is telling you. Can you recognize your failure to accept anything you don't want and commit to embracing all circumstances in life so you can deal with them appropriately? When you feel yourself refusing acceptance of something, can you use the power of being present to feel what is happening inside of yourself? Can you sense your refusal and, in that moment, ask yourself why you are fighting it? Quite often the real answer beneath all the arguing, excusing, and justifying is that you are fighting the feeling that you're not good enough to get what you want.

Subconsciously, that is what I thought when my relationship ended with Danny. The breakup was so painful it made me fearful to love again. I know now that the majority of the pain came from my mind being stuck in a self-absorbed loop, berating myself, judging my actions, and ultimately believing I was not good enough for him. Those self-absorbed thoughts cut far deeper into my soul than the actual loss of the relationship. My *Cursed Mind* was fighting to save my worth, and it was wrecking my entire being in the process. The breakup was just the trigger.

Had I listened to my *Core Self* who stormed out on him because he was making me miserable, I would have spent a little time grieving the relationship, but it would have been far less troubling than the year I spent in agony, chasing him down and trying to win him back. I even vividly recall a moment when I had almost accepted the relationship over. I was in Danny's dorm room, having a fight with him, when he turned his back on me and said he wasn't sure what he wanted anymore. My *Core Self*, tired of the rollercoaster of emotions I'd been experiencing, surprisingly spoke up and said to him, "Should I just let you go?" As the words fell out of my mouth, the agony in the pit of my stomach disappeared and a calm washed over me. I had come to a moment of acceptance and was ready to embrace it. It only lasted a minute, but I felt it and remember it to this day. Then Danny said, "I don't know. Part of me thinks so, but another part of me thinks we belong together." And like that, I was sucked back in.

My *Cursed Mind* believed I could end the pain by reconciling my relationship, but my *Core Self* knew peace was only going to come when I accepted that I wasn't supposed to be with Danny. If I had I accepted it in his room that day, I would have saved myself the year of *Cursed* emotional suffering that followed.

There is a beautiful quote by Eckhart Tolle in his book, *The Power of Now* that I love: "Always say 'yes' to the present moment. What could be more futile, more insane, than to create inner resistance to what already is? ... Say 'yes' to life—and see how life suddenly starts working for you rather than against you."

Even when a situation seems negative, it's important not to resist it. The more you practice being accepting in your romantic endeavors, whatever they may be, the more you are able to detach your value from the outcome. Separating your value from your relationships is what protects you from total devastation of a breakup, disappointment, or even betrayal. A clearing opens up between *you* and *what happened* that wasn't there before through the simple act of acceptance. You experience the event (e.g., he didn't call, didn't commit, didn't love you) and you notice if there is a *Cursed* reaction to the event (e.g., I wasn't good enough, I didn't win, I'm not the best). When you are aware of that *Cursed* reaction, you lessen its power over you. The attachment to the situation weakens because you know it was only a mind attachment. Your *Core Self* is then able to react appropriately either with genuine sadness, or in some cases, with the realization that what occurred is truly the best for both of you.

When you learn to be more accepting you free yourself from being at the constant mercy of life's circumstance. Your *Core Self* knows that nothing outside of you could ever enhance or diminish who you are; that regardless of what happens, you and your value are intact, okay, and enough. Dating and relationships become nearly effortless in that moment and your *Core Self* confidently states with gusto, *"Why would I not accept what is happening? After all, it's happening!"*

Accepting Others

All my clients weathering a breakup have told me they saw the very problem that ended their relationship in the first few months of dating. Whether the man was selfish, angry, manipulative, or noncommittal, the evidence was there from the start. Yet despite seeing the red flag, they chose to continue on with the relationship. Sometimes it's because the wanting is so strong the client cannot tell that what she's feeling isn't genuine love; other times, it's due to the Superior Mind reiterating that the guy is exactly the right fit for her. Whatever the *Cursed Mind* is saying in those moments of discord, our *Core Self* never watches passively. It feels that something is not right and tells you so.

It's true that no one is perfect, and you will always find something that could be more to your liking, but there is a difference between tolerating someone's insignificant personality quirks and excusing obvious character flaws that will cripple your relationship. Your *Core Self* knows one from the other. It reacts with wakefulness to someone else's poor behavior, making you fully present and aware of what just happened,

Be Accepting

while your *Cursed Mind* fights to remind you not to make a big deal of this silent "message" you received. *"You've been alone so long,"* it says. *"Finally, here is an opportunity to change that! Do you really want to acknowledge what he did and start all over again?"* Or maybe: *"People will be very impressed by him! Then they will think highly of you! So what if he is a little selfish? He's so cute. You never think anyone is cute. You deserve a guy you're attracted to, and that's so hard to find! Maybe if you hang in there, he will get better."* All these thoughts are *Cursed* motivations attempting to keep you in the relationship and distract you from the reality of who the person is. When you hear yourself coming up with reasons to overlook someone's bad behaviors, know that it's because your self-absorbed mind is trying to win its case.

    To find the right partner for yourself, you have to welcome all you learn in the very beginning of your relationships—as Maya Angelou said, "When someone shows you who they are, believe them." This means, be accepting of what you learn and don't try to spin it! If a guy says he is going to be in touch after a date and then isn't, don't keep initiating contact with him so you can keep the relationship going. Don't make excuses for him like he's just too busy. Accept what his non-action is telling you: He's either not interested, or he's unreliable. Allow yourself to observe men without fear, wanting, or judgment. If you set up a date and the guy is late, don't chastise him, just observe that he's late. Only the Superior Mind wants to call a man out for not being what she thinks is right. If he doesn't pick up the bill, don't call him cheap or get frustrated by his actions. Don't take his gesture as a sign you weren't special enough for him to pay. If he behaves badly, insults you, or hurts your feelings, remember this: When a man does or says something to you in the beginning of your relationship, it speaks more about him and his character than it does about you. Everything he does, or doesn't do, tells you something about who he is.

    Accepting who he is does not mean you have to bite your tongue when you don't like something. You can and should express your feelings when you are getting to know someone. It's when judgment and the desire to control enter the equation that you have to be careful. Both of those feelings come from non-acceptance and are a result of the Superior Mind telling you *"He should not be that way! He needs to respect me and behave better!"* Although you may not agree with how someone acts, it isn't your job to convict them of their crime. Acceptance is acknowledging and respecting who someone is—good or bad—and not wanting them to be different because it will work better for you. You can, therefore, accept who someone is and at the same time kindly voice your opinion.

Remember Darcy, the fashion consultant? She and I worked for years on finding her a relationship. Finally, she started dating someone she liked, but three months in a problem occurred. When Darcy and her boyfriend Manny were out together, he always made comments about other women. He would remark about their physical appearances and overall appeal, which made Darcy uncomfortable and had her questioning his feelings towards her. After talking this over in one of our sessions, Darcy was ready to voice her opinion on this to Manny. She was ready to accept that this was who he was, but she wanted him to know how she felt about it. One day, while taking her dog for a walk, Darcy told him she needed to tell him something that had been bothering her. She explained that she understood he may not be able to change this about himself, but she felt like he should know how his habit to comment on other women in front of her made her feel. She was nonjudgmental and very matter-of-fact about it, and to her surprise, Manny apologized for making her feel bad and promised to be more aware of her feelings. He also said he had no idea he was even making comments!

Had Darcy chastised Manny for his actions, or waited for him to make another comment so she could blow up at him, the result might have been very different. Instead she used all the tools she learned in coaching to approach Manny the right way, with love and acceptance, and it paid off. They just celebrated their one-year anniversary.

Some women ask me how they are supposed to assess the person they are dating without using judgement. How are they to discern if a guy is a good fit or not? The answer is to allow your *Core Self* to go on your dates and feel what it is like to be with someone. Ask questions and get to know them, but when you are listening and observing, be acutely aware of their entire being and all the information you are receiving. You cannot absorb another person's energy and get a read on them if you are too busy judging and analyzing with your *Cursed Mind,* and you definitely can't assess them properly if you are caught up in wanting. The right person feels right, feels easy, feels natural. Your *Core Self* will effectively tell you if someone is good for you or not if you give her the chance.

If you are single and currently app dating, before you walk out the door to meet someone new, remind yourself why you are going on a date in the first place. What is your goal? Is it to get to know the person you are meeting, or are you trying to figure out your future? Get him to fall for you? Assess if he meets your standards? All those motivations are led by the *Cursed Mind.* You can allow your *Core Self* to take charge by gently reminding yourself that a date is a meeting where you find out who someone is — not who they will be *to you*. It's a subtle shift in mentality, but one that is chock-full of acceptance. When your future, your value, and your wants are not on the line, you are more apt to welcome all that you learn about someone, and that is the best approach to knowing who is right for you.

Single and Accepting

Maybe you would love to practice being more tolerant of others, but you never get the opportunity. One possible reason for this might be that, like many single women, you are living in a constant state of non-acceptance without even being aware of it.

Some people fight the reality of their single lives by being angry, sad, and stressed, hoping that resisting the unexpected and unwanted circumstances of still being single will either cause change and make love happen or, at the very least, make them feel justified and relevant. In other words, if they are not getting attention from men or attaining the love they want, the *Cursed Mind* will try and draw attention to itself by playing the victim. *"Poor me, I am the only one who is single! Life is unfair to me!"* Their non-acceptance not only cloaks them in self-focused pain but also inhibits their ability to attract guys and create relationship opportunities.

One client of mine, Lila, was a quintessential example of this. Every day, she felt depressed that she was 32 and single. She told me she couldn't find any joy in life and knew that would not change until she got married. It was as if she opened her eyes each day and said, "No! No! No! This is not my life. I refuse to accept it and be happy about it." She did this for years, and every person she dated sensed her *Cursed* wanting to be in a relationship and have the future she ravenously longed for. After a year of coaching, she finally woke up to see how her non-acceptance of her single status was keeping her *Cursed* and preventing love from growing with anyone who was interested in her. The constant worry of never having the future she wanted was the very obstacle preventing it. Her *Core Self* had broken through, and Lila decided to keep working toward the goal of finding love while also embracing her life as a single person. She joined a running club, started learning Spanish, and volunteered at a nearby children's hospital in her free time, all things she enjoyed doing. She made the present her new focus and acknowledged what she could not change at the moment. She kept dating but stopped sulking about how bad life was being single and did something productive with her circumstance instead. She accepted the present moment. And wouldn't you know it, three months after her shift in mentality she met someone!

Lila's inner resistance to life as a single person was creating a suffering inside of her, and that pain was permeating her being. The men she went out with could feel her pain, as it translated as an eagerness for them to fulfill a void within her. When she embraced her life at present, all the wanting and future thinking subsided and the pain went with it. Then, her fun-loving energy began dominating her persona and that helped get her into a relationship.

Learning to accept that you are single may sound as if you are giving up all control and allowing life to have its way with you. Besides, how will you meet someone if you just accept being alone? How will you connect if you go into a date saying, "whatever will be, will be" and don't even try? Being accepting of your situation or your relationships as they are right now doesn't mean throwing up your hands and saying, "Well, this is my life, and I can't do anything about it." It means accepting the facts, not fighting them or wishing them to be different, so not only do you understand what action to take from there, but also the action itself comes from the right place: your heart.

Accept the uncertainty of where your life is going. Accept that you are single today and learn to be comfortable with your life now in this moment. You can still work toward the goal of changing your life for the better tomorrow. My other books teach the strategy behind finding love, how to start a conversation with someone, what you can do to keep them interested, and what you need to avoid so you don't make a mistake you can't recover from. However, without having the right mentality, none of the techniques will work effectively or for very long. Say yes to your life as it is right now as you meet people, make connections, and forge relationships. If you root yourself in the present moment, with gratitude and acceptance, you will be amazed at how the suffering brought on by the *Cursed Mind* begins to wane, and how much easier dating will become going forward.

The Final Act of Acceptance

Sometimes acceptance is difficult because dating and relationships are, well, confusing! You might want to be more accepting of people and circumstances but those two things are constantly changing direction. For instance, maybe a guy didn't text you for a few days, which you took as non-interest, but then he gave you a decent reason for his lack of communication. What does that mean? What part of this should you accept? Or maybe your boyfriend broke up with you during a heated argument but then wanted to reconcile a week later. Should you accept his apology and take him back, or accept that he broke up with you for a reason? How do you know if he's being genuine or just playing you? There is a reason why you might be frequently puzzled by the trials and tribulations of dating, and more importantly, feel uncertain of a guy's intentions; but it has nothing to do with how smart or capable of a person you are. To be able to sit down with anyone and really grasp who they are and what objectives they have, you first have to remove the barrier that prevents you from accurately assessing other people and their intentions with you. That barrier is yourself and your own non-acceptance.

If you had full acceptance of self, you could easily and fairly accurately get to know anyone because your perspective would not be muddled by your own need to be accepted. How can you really assess anyone if you are busy worrying about their assessment of you? The Contestant and the Inferior Mind have the hardest time with this because outside approval and affirmation is what has always given them some semblance of acceptance; but all *Faces* of the *Cursed Mind* cloud your ability to assess others. When you are so focused on what you want from someone, you aren't able to see what that person really wants from you, and that can leave you scratching your head when the tide turns in your relationship.

It is only when you are accepting of yourself that you can clearly see the truth of someone else because you no longer view that person as a threat or enhancement to your own worth. You don't live in the future, hoping he solves your misery of being single today, or dive deep into wanting hoping he turns out to be who you want. When you are accepting of yourself, you don't sit on a date and obsessively fret if someone you don't even know likes you. Instead, you are completely engaged in the moment while getting to know him, accepting all you learn along the way. When you start off a relationship on that note, the truth of someone and the reality of the situation become a lot clearer and more understandable. This is the reason some people say they found their significant other when they stopped looking or when they gave up their

Be Accepting

search completely. What they really mean is that they accepted themselves and their life as is, and that was when they found love.

But how do you do it? Self-acceptance sounds so easy and yet you might worry it's a task you've not yet figured out. Maybe you've read books and other materials on acceptance and still don't feel you've fully achieved it. I understand because I struggled with acceptance, too. I tried every practice recommended and still found myself wishing I was better and more than I was. Then, I realized I could only truly accept myself when my obsessive self-absorbed thinking ended. In other words, I was never going to *think* my way into self-acceptance because that only resulted in more self-absorbed, *Cursed* thinking.

As I mentioned in the beginning of this book, if you want your self-esteem to increase, your thoughts of self must decrease. What I didn't explain further is why that is. The conduit between those two inverse elements is acceptance. The less you think about yourself, the more accepting you become. The more accepting you become, the higher your self-esteem rises.

The first thing I recommend doing is pinpointing the thought that contributes most to your non-acceptance. For instance, the Contestant Mind regularly compares itself to others, hoping to win the ego award of "most worthy." When it "wins," it feels good and accepted; however, this feeling is fleeting and the acceptance doesn't last. Comparing also leads to frequently "losing," which makes the *Cursed Mind* feel terrible or—yes, you guessed it—unacceptable.

If you have a tendency to compare yourself to others, you have to first realize when you are doing it. This means catching yourself engaging in the contest with others and disqualifying yourself immediately. How do you disqualify yourself? By being present! End the self-thinking about your worth. You must accept that there will be women who are smarter, prettier, more talented, or more successful than you, but that does not diminish any part of you or make you less valuable or unique. It is likely that all the comparing you are doing is in regards to qualities that are superficial, and therefore, not meaningful or fulfilling anyway. Once you resign to the truth that everyone is worthy in their own special way and become present in the moments when your mind starts to compare, you will move you closer to your own acceptance.

Or maybe you have lived in perpetual wanting and have always desired to be something more? The Wanter Mind will subconsciously tell you that you cannot accept yourself as you are now; that you need to be thinner, have bigger breasts or fuller lips, make more money, or achieve more in your career before you can be whole and feel good about yourself. However, whatever it is that you have been wishing or holding out for is not the cause of your non-acceptance. It is the simple thought habit of wanting to be something *else* or something *more* that is blocking you. Whatever attribute you are focusing on really isn't the problem; therefore, fixing it won't likely solve it. This misunderstanding is the reason some women become addicted to plastic surgery. They think that they will have self-acceptance when they improve the imperfection on their face or body, but after they do, they realize they aren't satisfied and need to enhance or repair something else. This can go on until the person becomes almost unrecognizable, and all because they didn't fix the problem in their head. The thought, *"I need to be more or better than I am now"* is the root cause of the Wanter's non-acceptance.

This is not to say outside goals like losing weight or even plastic surgery are unproductive or unhelpful. For many people they are, and I don't want to discount their value. However, if you don't also recognize how wanting affects your ability to be accepting, it won't matter how much weight you lose or what surgery you get because the hunger to be more will still persist.

Be mindful any time you slip into wanting that is pointed at yourself. When you pass a mirror and think, *"Ugh, I look terrible. Why is my nose like this? I should fix that."* Or, *"I still need to lose ten pounds. I wish my body was different,"* recognize that this is non-acceptance. When you encounter people and feel jealous, and think, *"I need to be like her or I won't be happy"*. Or *"I probably won't find love because I'm not cute enough"* – that is non-acceptance. Use what you have learned about being present to see how many times in a day you unconsciously reject yourself as you are now. One client of mine kept track of her self-rejections and counted thirty-one in just 8 hours! Before doing this she wondered why she always felt down and hopeless; but after that exercise, she saw there was no way to feel anything else! In those moments of self-rejection, it is of the utmost importance that you stop what you are doing and work to clear your mindset. Look again in the mirror. Only this time just say to yourself, *"This is who I am."* Don't try to wish it away. Just accept that this is you, right now, today, in this moment. Who you are right now IS who you are right now! No amount of rejection will change that. The *Curse Mind* wants you to believe that resisting what you don't like will somehow create change, but it will not. The only thing it does is generate negativity and frustration inside you. You don't have to love or even like yourself right now, you only have to accept yourself. Maybe you'll be different tomorrow, but for now, this is you. You can work to improve yourself, of course, but you don't need to reject who you are today in order to be a better version of yourself tomorrow. Try it.

The Hidden Habit

There is one last habit that leads to non-acceptance of self, and it is one that often goes unrecognized by individuals, their inner circle, and even some therapists. It is the habit to judge. If you suffer from the Superior Mind and are attempting to compensate for feelings of inferiority, you may spend much of your time judging everything: life, other people, and subsequently yourself. It isn't that you have never felt good enough; you may very well remember moments when you've experienced boosts of high self-esteem. However, your tendency to judge makes it impossible to be at peace with yourself because you are constantly labeling every word, action, and feature of your being. In order to accept yourself, you have to cease the habit to judge on all levels, regardless if the target is inside or outside of you. You cannot be critical, and at the same time, be accepting.

Cursed?

My client Sandra started coaching with me because she was hopeless and depressed about her love life. She was pretty and had a fulfilling job and a loving family, but for some reason she hadn't had a relationship in almost 10 years. Any guy who liked her, she didn't like, and she hardly found anyone of interest. On top of that, she also hated the way she looked, even though she was quite attractive. Sandra's therapist told her that her negativity was what was hurting her; but Sandra struggled with doing positive affirmations and actually felt worse. When we sat down to chat, I pointed out to Sandra that what she and her therapist had identified as "negativity" was actually her mind constantly making judgments on life and other people. Therefore, attempting to be positive wasn't going to help because she was still judging, just in a forced positive way. She agreed and even accepted what I told her next: She often targeted herself with her judgmental habit, and until she ended judgment on all levels, nothing would change in her love life. Judging was not allowing her to accept anything or anyone because she was constantly looking for the flaw, the mistake, or the improvement that was needed so her *Cursed Mind* could say, *"Look at that. That is not good enough!"* That *Cursed* inclination, although it was slight, made her mind feel good enough to carry on and keep judging.

Sandra's journey to self-acceptance took a while. She had to tackle her Superior/Inferior Mind one day at a time, and recognize when she judged. She had to stop mid-thought and say, *"Who am I to judge? Who am I to say this needs to be better?"* Sometimes she asked herself, *"Why am I judging right now? What am I hoping to get from this?"* She woke herself to her *Cursed Mind* by using these questions. She then took deep breaths and became conscious of the two "people" inside her: her *Cursed Self* who was judging and her *Core Self* who was listening.

When she could feel her *Core Self*, she sat with her for a minute, wherever she was—at her desk at work or on a run after hours—it didn't matter. She eventually learned to meditate in order to embody her *Core Self*. She did not think, *"Here is my Core Self"* because you cannot connect with your *Core Self* through thoughts. You can only sense her

Be Accepting

inside you by the calm that grows when you are not thinking. The more Sandra held on to her own *Core Self,* the less she thought and the more present she became. The more she practiced doing this, making it her new habit, the less she judged. As her judgmental thoughts about others decreased, the amount of men she found interesting increased. Guys no longer had to look "perfect" or fit a certain image to pass her "attractive" test. She stopped looking for the flaws, and that allowed more men to have a chance with her. And, as we discussed earlier, as her own self-focused (judgmental) thoughts decreased, her self-esteem began to increase, too.

    I'm happy to report that Sandra is now dating someone for the first time in ten years. It's new, and we can't know the future, but being this far into a relationship with someone is an achievement in itself. If you asked Sandra, she would tell you that being aware of her habit to judge brought her to this relationship. Instead of listening to the *Cursed Mind* when it judged her new boyfriend for something silly and unimportant (His pants are too short! He mispronounced "Acaí") she caught herself and recognized the mind habit as just a habit that she shouldn't put weight behind. When he didn't text her back as quickly as she wanted, she noticed the irritation she felt was from her mind wanting him to act exactly as she expected so she wouldn't feel bad about herself (He must not think I'm not good enough to text back right away!) She practiced being accepting of him without the Superior Mind interfering, while also accepting what each day of their relationship brought to her life.

    Judgment is one of the hardest habits to break, especially if you are a smart, intellectual person who uses their critical thinking skills quite frequently. The key is to be aware of when your Superior Mind is making judgments with no real purpose other than to keep you separated from others. Through that separation you can be "the one in the right" or "the one who suffers most" or "the one who knows best." Sandra's mind loved to judge because her mind liked being special in that way, but that habit kept her single and lonely for a decade. Remember, the judge is often above everyone in some way but always sits alone. There can only be one judge.

The Big Breakup
We have come to the last component of self-acceptance. What I am about to share with you might seem hard to understand and even harder to do. You may need to re-read this section a number of times or come back to it months after you've finished this book. Once you have identified the self-focused thought habit keeping you from self-acceptance, you will be ready to undertake the last practice that will bring you to a deep-seated, intrinsic form of self-acceptance.

You may have heard somewhere that loving yourself is the direct channel to being loved by someone else. Many books, blogs, therapists, and coaches will tell you that self-love is the fundamental element for happiness and relationship success. I do not agree, only because I think the term can easily be misconstrued and lead people down a path toward the Superior Mind. I understand what those touting the self-love mantra are saying, but I think we only need to accept ourselves, as love is something we give not something we need to reserve for our own being. If we aren't at peace and comfortable with ourselves, we certainly cannot be at ease in a relationship with someone else. As the first half of this book explained, not having peace within will cause you to use your relationships to soothe your own feelings of non-acceptance. And when you use a relationship for that purpose, you eventually destroy the love you have with someone because the pain of your non-acceptance is only covered up for a period of time and not truly cured.

Let's go back to Felicity for a moment before we move on. Her intense need for approval from her boyfriend Kevin caused the ultimate demise of their relationship. If she had real self-acceptance, she would not have desperately craved his approval or feared losing him whenever his focus wasn't on her. After they broke up, her feelings of anxiety and approval-seeking shifted into depression and self-loathing. She remained that way for quite some time, hoping Kevin would return and she would

Be Accepting

be happy again. What she could not see, however, was that she was never at ease with herself or actually happy, whether she was in a relationship with Kevin or not. She was either with him and anxious or without him and depressed. Regardless of her romantic situation, she was in a continual state of uneasiness and pain because of her unrecognized feelings of non-acceptance.

I single out this story in the hopes you better understand what I mean by "uneasiness and pain". Many people believe that their discomfort comes from a certain situation or from the actions of others, but the truth is that those external forces just trigger the emotional discomfort already within us. Now is the time to face your own.

Although it might seem difficult and perhaps more scary than anything you've ever done, the truth is that turning toward your emotional discomfort and looking straight at it is the way to resolve it. All the quick fixes like covering your uneasiness with a relationship, ignoring it by keeping busy, or medicating it with drugs, food or alcohol, only treat the symptom of non-acceptance. If you stop treating it, even for a moment, the pain returns and sometimes even worsens. You must go to the source of the problem and cure the non-acceptance instead. Let's do that right now.

You have long thought about yourself. You have been concerned with what you said, what you did, and who you were or are today. When you ruminate so often about you, it's inevitable that you'll pick yourself apart little by little until there is nothing left. It is like looking at a piece of art and instead of seeing it as a whole, you are examining every brush stroke and variant in the piece. You are inspecting it, dissecting it, and obsessing about it, day in and day out, as it grows older and becomes more worn. You have lost perspective and now cannot see the magnificent canvas for what it was to begin with. To be your beautiful, original *Core Self* again and feel true acceptance, you need only accomplish one final act and it's this: Give up the relationship with yourself.

Cursed?

You do not need a relationship with yourself. Having a mind-relationship with yourself is the crux of the *Curse*. When you shut down the relationship you have with *you,* it's possible to effectively end the self-absorbed thought patterns that lead to all your relationship problems. You do not need to think about yourself; you only need to *be*. Don't worry—you'll still eat when you're hungry, sleep when you're tired, and laugh when something is funny. You won't be giving up any critical part of you, nor will you become someone else. On the contrary, you will become your true, best self—the "you" that you've been searching for all along. The "you" that you've always desired to be. I want you to stop looking at the work of art and be the work of art. That means abandoning the need to know yourself or have an identity. Let go of wishing to think highly of yourself or think you are good enough. Thinking those things will never make them so.

Eckhart Tolle said in *A New Earth*, "Any conceptual sense of self – seeing myself as this or that – is Ego, whether predominately positive (I am the greatest) or negative (I am no good)." The *Cursed Mind* is your ego. Knowing that thinking about yourself in terms of identity and worth is a function of ego will hopefully create space between your thoughts and your soul. In that space you can recognize that what you are really giving up is the relationship with your ego, and that's all.

You can ready yourself for real love and commitment by eliminating the other person that lives inside of you. Whether that person is a judge, a victim, a contestant, a wanter, or worrier, she is the *"you"* who has been standing in the way, creating the discomfort within you and causing the disharmony in your relationships. I could not put it any better than Eckhart Tolle in *The Power of Now*, so I am not going to try. When you give up the relationship with yourself, "…you do not judge yourself, you do not feel sorry for yourself, you are not proud of yourself, you do not love yourself, you do not hate yourself…When you are enlightened, there is one relationship that you no longer have: the relationship with yourself. Once you have given that up, all your other relationships will be love relationships…"

Surrender to the imperfection of you and to the fact that you will never come to terms with yourself through self-absorbed thinking. Your *Core Self* is an undefinable, loving, and boundless being — one that can never be explained or described through thoughts or words. Once you give up the relationship with yourself, you ultimately accept never fully knowing who you are—and in that moment, you will feel the joy of real acceptance and finally be at peace.

Continue to Practice

Dating, relationships and, most importantly, love become so much easier when you are accepting. You have a choice: accept what comes your way and feel the deep peace that comes with that concession, or fight whatever happens and feel the misery and pain that comes with that resistance. It might take practice to be completely accepting with all the people and situations that you encounter, but it is a challenge well worth working toward. If you are religious, or perhaps even spiritual, you will be very familiar with the prayer below. I think regardless of your belief system, it is a beautiful reminder that can be recited daily and help you get closer to acceptance of the world and all those who live in it.

There are many versions of the Serenity Prayer; this is the one I think is most helpful in terms of what we're discussing. If you can, print it out, post it on a corkboard, or use it as a screen saver so that you can see it everyday, and remind your *Core Self* that acceptance is always the way to peace.

The Serenity Prayer
God grant me the serenity
To accept the things I cannot change;
Courage to change the things I can;
And wisdom to know the difference.
Living one day at a time;
Enjoying one moment at a time;
Accepting hardships as the pathway to peace;

Cursed?

Taking, as He did, this sinful world
As it is, not as I would have it.
Amen.

REFLECTION

Reflect for a moment on what you've just learned. Reread this chapter if needed. Put the book down, and for a day, see if you can hear yourself resisting what is happening in your relationships. Can you hear your *Cursed Mind* get angry, frustrated, and complaining when it doesn't like what other people do? Can you be present in that moment and work to accept it instead? What happens? Can you feel the peace inside you growing?

Chapter Twelve

Be Forgiving

Without a doubt, you have come to the hardest step in breaking the *Curse*. You might have easily practiced being present; you may have even enjoyed it. It is probable that while being grateful took some concentration, it immediately provided you with a much-needed release from the pain brought on by the feeling of lack. And while acceptance might have been harder than those two put together, nothing thus far will likely be more difficult than reconstructing your mind to do what it has fought against repeatedly for years. Regardless of how challenging it might be or how begrudgingly you feel about it, learning to be forgiving is the final and most important transition you must make in this process.

Why is it necessary to be forgiving? I have found most women who cannot find or keep a loving and healthy relationship do not possess a high level of forgiveness. Their hearts are consumed with anger, fear, sadness, and remorse, all of which fester inside them and regularly appear at some point in their love lives. It is not so surprising that what you hold in your heart is what you give out to the world and the people in it. To attract love, you have to create a hospitable environment in yourself, which invites love in and allows it to flourish. To keep love, you have to live in a constant state of learning and growing as a couple, despite the setbacks or disappointments life will throw at you. Therefore, you have to let go of the remaining self-absorbed habits that have interfered with your ability to have a healthy and loving relationship. You have to clear out the *Cursed* thoughts and emotions you've long carried so that you make room for love. The only way to do that is to forgive.

Why Is It Hard?

Before we dive into how we become more forgiving and the vast importance of it, let's talk about why it is such a challenge to be forgiving in the first place. Why does the word "forgive" itself often seem to conjure feelings against doing it? While it is human to feel sad and disappointed when you are let down or betrayed, your self-absorbed mind ramps up that reaction because it believes we should not have to suffer in life; our lives should be near perfect, or at the very least, without pain and uncertainty. Therefore, when we do experience an upset, our *Cursed Mind* immediately reacts: *"That should not have happened to me! Poor me! Whoever did this or allowed this to happen to me is shameful and won't get away with making me suffer."* When that is how your mind reacts to an unwanted circumstance, it is no wonder you don't want to forgive.

Another reason forgiveness is difficult goes back to the resistance to acceptance. When a real injustice occurs, the *Cursed Mind* finds it difficult to accept it and move on because it views crimes against you, especially crimes of the heart, as a personal attack. When a man cheats on you, for example, you think it's because you weren't worthy of his fidelity or that all men are out to hurt you. Your *Cursed Mind* tells you to feel deceived, disrespected, and unappreciated. *"He wouldn't have done that if I were someone else!"* The Lamenter and the Superior Mind make you the victim and the righteous judge, eliciting attention in the form of pity while condemning the other person. You don't want to accept what happened because acceptance would bring peace, and the *Cursed Mind* would rather hold on to anger so it can continue feeling like the person who wronged you is wrong, making you in the right. While doing this makes your *Cursed Mind* feel good, it smothers your *Core Self* to the point of near extinction.

When acceptance is hard because a situation is truly hurtful, there are only two paths to take. You either stay *Cursed* and hold on to your self-absorbed thoughts, fueling anger and resentment and poisoning yourself just a little more in your relationship (or for the next one), or you pull away from the *Curse* and forgive. By being forgiving, you completely release your *Core Self* from the clutches of the *Cursed Mind*. The pain of a disappointment simply passes through you and is not stored and transformed into negative energy. Forgiveness allows you to be at peace regardless of what happens in your relationships. Then the real miracle occurs, because once you are able to keep peace within yourself, you finally know how to keep peace with someone else.

Forgiving the Little Things
Sometimes we don't realize how unforgiving we really are. How we react to the smallest of slights, broken promises, or annoyances by others can tell us a lot about our level of forgiveness. It's easy to be kind, understanding, and loving when people are that way to us. It is not so simple when they are aggravating or disappointing.

Whenever we blame, criticize, or hold a grudge, we are choosing, even on a small scale, not to forgive. When we are angered by small mistakes or imperfections, our *Cursed Mind* is essentially saying, *"You should not be like that. I don't like that. You should do better!"* I see this occur daily in my coaching practice. Clients will complain as to why a guy did something, even before they have met him. "Why did he tell me to text him when I'm free? He should be texting and asking me! That's so annoying." Or, "He chose this place to meet, and it's so far from my house! He knows it's not convenient for me. I am so irritated I don't even want to meet him now." It is the *Cursed Mind* talking in those moments, judging and condemning what it does not like and assuming anything outside its own method of operating is wrong or a personal slight. As the relationship deepens, their unforgiving nature does as well. "He was late again and I had to wait twenty minutes! He should know to leave work earlier by now. He needs to make this up to me by doing xyz!" The *Cursed Mind* believes there is no other explanation for why someone is behaving the way they are. When you give into the *Curse* and react this way, you are making judgments on others while also saying something about yourself. You are not only expressing that life must be lived according to your own rule book, but you are also pointing out how you feel about your own need for forgiveness—mainly that you do not believe you are ever in need of it.

Amy, for example, never realized how much trouble she had with forgiveness. She was married to Jim, who was a good husband and father. She knew he would never intentionally hurt her, so the thought of forgiving him never entered her mind. But Amy was a perfectionist and liked everything done a particular way. Jim was not, and he often irritated Amy with his lackadaisical behavior. If he forgot to do something she asked or simply procrastinated and didn't do it immediately, Amy would get very upset and a fight would ensue. Jim would call Amy high-strung and overly type-A, and Amy would call Jim lazy. They never got anywhere in their arguments, and over the years, resentment set in and began wearing on their relationship.

One day as I was talking to Amy, I asked her why she had a hard time letting go of these little disappointments in her marriage. Why couldn't she say to Jim, "It's okay that you forgot to take out the trash. If that's the worst thing that happens today, it's not so bad." At first, she came up with 100 reasons why Jim not emptying the garbage hurt her. "It's one more thing I have to do. It's one more way he shows he doesn't love me. It's just not right to let the trash build up like we're street rats." Then I asked her if Jim had ever forgiven her for anything. She thought quietly for a minute and said, "I don't think I've done anything he would need to forgive."

It took some time for Amy to realize that her perfectionist nature made her believe she didn't need forgiveness and therefore she could not pardon Jim for his flaws or mistakes. Because she was so on top of everything, she believed she never had and never would make an error. She strived for perfection, and on most days felt she was achieving it. It wasn't until several months had passed that she realized she did have something to ask Jim to forgive her for — her unforgiving mindset and how she treated him when functioning through her Superior Mind.

When something hurts or offends you, you can choose how to react. You can either respond with selfishness, protecting or bolstering your own interests, which is what your *Cursed Mind* wants you to do, or you can respond with compassion and an eagerness for understanding the person who committed the act. Amy could tell Jim that it bothered her when the trash wasn't taken out on time, but she didn't have to attack or harbor ill will toward him because of it. She softened her approach and started speaking from her *Core Self.* "Jim, we didn't get the trash out on time this morning again. I feel frustrated about the situation but I know you have had a very long week and just forgot. Can we figure out a way to make sure this doesn't keep happening?" Learning that she could be forgiving to these small errors while still expressing what she wanted was helpful for their relationship. Jim began taking the trash out early because he knew it pleased her, and on those times he forgot, he was apologetic instead of defensive.

Is it possible that you also struggle with forgiving others because you think you are not in need of forgiveness yourself? Do you believe you are so careful, so conscious and thoughtful that you would never make a mistake? If you have a hard time maintaining relationships with men because you feel they are always letting you down, ask yourself if it's possible that your inability to forgive stems from feeling you are living in the right or have reached a level of perfection.

How forgiving you are can be seen in how you handle the minor upsets. When life doesn't go your way and people don't act according to your code of conduct, how do you react? Guys will be careless, forgetful, and even thoughtless at times, but it doesn't mean they are all purposefully trying to hurt you. Do you attempt to understand their motive or purpose, or do you automatically respond with irritation and outrage? Can you shrug it off if they don't meet your expectations, or do you feel you need to be constantly teaching a lesson? If your expectation of a partner is so high that no man could ever reach it, then it is likely no man ever will. An unmerciful heart can keep a woman very single.

After years of coaching with Reina, she finally met someone special. His name was Robert, and they fell in love quickly and moved in together. Robert was the first guy who saw through Reina's Superior Mind *Curse*, and instead of running away or attacking back when she criticized and blamed, he lovingly pointed out what she was doing.

One day they had a fight about Robert shrinking some clothes in the laundry. Reina rolled her eyes at him and used harsh words to describe her disappointment and his foolishness for not knowing better. She bemoaned having to buy a new shirt and not being able to find the same one he had ruined. She walked around all day angry about the incident until Robert finally spoke to the heart of the matter.

"I am not perfect," he said to her. "When you crucify me for the mistakes I make, you make me feel bad, but you also give me the impression that you think you are above human error. I would never demean you for being forgetful or not doing something perfectly because I know that you are human, and I have no right to pass judgment on someone who is just like me. You are not perfect. We are not perfect. I'm okay with that. I just need to know that you are, too."

When Robert pointed out that Reina's attitude toward mistakes was rooted in the belief that she was perfect, it woke her to see how toxic her behavior was for their relationship. His mistakes irked her, but her attitude alienated him. Her *Curse* sought excellence and accepted nothing less. Even though Robert was trying to be helpful by washing clothes and linens, Reina's Superior Mind was triggered when the task wasn't done right. She also realized how unforgiving she had been through her entire life, with her friends as well as the men she dated. She always found a reason to be upset and push them away for acting in a manner she didn't like or understand.

It's up to you to remember that no one is perfect. Everyone sins. To be angry with people for acting imperfectly is to be angry, bitter, and cross with life itself. The people you love will let you down from time to time, and you can either harbor resentment toward them or forgive them quickly and move on. Which one makes for a better relationship?

The next time you feel yourself angered by the little things in life, be present enough to realize why you are agitated. Hear your *Cursed Mind* speaking in that moment, attempting to make yourself right or tell you that you are perfect, and have the strength to be your *Core Self* instead. She is the person who doesn't capitalize on another person's errors, or uses them to enhance her self-perception of being superior.

You might argue that you try so hard to do the right thing and be perfect, so it's not easy to forgive someone who hardly tries to do the same for you. But perhaps it's time to stop trying so hard to be perfect and start trying to be forgiving instead. Being perfect is not a requirement for being loved, and in fact, most perfectionists find it very hard to maintain relationships. Only the *Cursed Mind* thinks perfection of self brings you happiness and love. Your *Core Self* knows that isn't the truth, or you would be happy right now and not reading this book. The only thing that brings real love, is love.

Whatever self-absorbed habit you most indulge in is the one you will have the toughest time forgiving in others. The *Cursed Mind* takes the position that there can only be one person that is right, that is the winner, the center of attention, or even the victim, and that person is you. When it comes across someone else who constantly judges, compares and competes, or seeks attention in some way, you will not want to be around that person because they are exhibiting a habit too closely related to your own *Cursed Mind*. *"Ugh, he's always being a victim. It's so annoying,"* says the Lamenter Mind who believes it's the only real victim. *"He was so arrogant and acted like he knew everything. I gave him an ear full so he knows he's not so high and mighty,"* says the Superior Mind that knows all. When you find yourself really struggling to forgive someone for a particular behavior, you can bring more awareness to your own *Curse*. You can ask, "Why does this person irritate me so much? Why do I like to dislike them? Why can't I forgive how they act?" And you can see that the answer is because they are displaying an unconscious mind habit or belief that is similar to one of your own. The *Cursed Mind* believes there is only one of itself in the whole world and is highly agitated when faced with the reality that it's not extraordinary.

Forgiveness is a choice that becomes easier to make the more you practice doing it. Make the commitment to exercise your forgiving muscles on a daily basis because if you cannot forgive the small stuff in life, you will never be able to forgive when it's really necessary. And make no mistake about it, there will come a time in your life when your forgiveness really will be put to the test.

Forgiving the Big Things

You might be so used to being angry or annoyed by others that you don't think it's possible to become a truly forgiving person. You have trouble forgiving the guy who cut you off on the road to work this morning, so how will you really be able to forgive the man who stood you up, the boyfriend who disappeared, or the husband who left you?

Maybe you cannot forgive someone who hurt you because you think it means continuing a relationship with a person you no longer trust. In an effort to protect yourself and your heart, you are holding a firm grudge. But you can forgive someone and at the same time decide it's best not to continue a relationship with them. Forgiveness doesn't mean reconciliation or pretending something didn't happen. You can let someone go from your life and forgive them as they walk away from you.

Forgiving major mistakes and violations in trust isn't easy but holding on to them hurts far worse than the crime committed ever could. As the saying goes, "Not forgiving someone is like drinking poison and waiting for the other person to die." It's perfectly human to be upset and angry with the person who hurt you, and grieving the circumstance is normal and healthy, but if you want to heal from the experience, you have to

Be Forgiving

want to let go of those feelings. The Lamenter Mind does not want to let go, which is how people end up going through life angry. If you never forgive the slights and mistakes people make, the buildup over time will not only make you unloving, it will also make you hard to love.

For instance, a woman recently wrote me about helping her find a new relationship after her husband left her. She wrote, "Jess, I'd like to know where and how to begin to look for my best friend and a lifelong companion. I am very picky at this point in my life, scared and untrusting of men. I was married, but my husband divorced me after 20 years together. I am discouraged and pessimistic that I will find someone who can fill the void he left. Please help me to meet someone smart, nice, handsome, and educated—someone who I can share my life with and be happy again."

The woman wanted to start dating right away and asked me to help her build a profile to attract the right kind of men. I had to tell her, however, that she was not ready to put herself back in the game. Any plan I put in place to meet someone would inevitably fail because she clearly had not forgiven her husband for leaving her. When I told her we must first work to forgive him, she cried and told me she could not do it. Sadly, she held on to her resentment, making her residual animosity palpable to every man she dated. Her Lamenter Mind kept her energy heavy, cold and embittered.

This woman didn't want to forgive because she believed she was punishing her ex by holding the grudge. To her, forgiveness felt like she was letting him off the hook for betraying and hurting her. But he went on to have a happy life—she was the one who suffered for years.

For many people, the hardest person to forgive is the one who is not sorry —the man who is selfish and unremorseful. "He's not worthy of my forgiveness," some women will say. To forgive anyone who acts like they did nothing wrong almost feels like you are accepting their horrible behavior and allowing them to live without consequence. But forgiving someone doesn't mean you are excusing or condoning what they have done. It means you are letting go of the need to be compensated by the hurt they caused. Much of the time, you want them to pay for what they have done by suffering as you have, so you hold a grudge hoping that happens. But not forgiving the person does nothing to them. It does not punish them, nor does it help them reform. If they are selfish, cruel, entitled, or uncaring, your resentment will not fix them. If they are a liar or a cheater, your permanent anger toward them will not straighten them out. In fact, only by being your *Core Self*, and not reacting with your own *Cursed Mind* would you have the chance to help them understand how their behavior affected you. When you react with *Cursed* emotions like anger and shaming which stem from the Superior Mind, you only provoke the other persons Superior Mind. Your need to be right and make them see their error, only causes them to defend their sense of self either directly to you or privately to themselves. Then the situation quickly becomes a battle of who is in the right and who will come out the winner.

It's human to be angry for a time or sad about what happened, but eventually you have to let yourself recover. You do not need to wait for someone to feel sorry in order to forgive them and move on. Some people may never feel bad about something they've done, and you can't let them have power over your forgiveness. You can't wait to allow yourself to be free from the pain and anger only when they say the time is right. You must unchain yourself and remember that forgiveness is within your control alone. It may seem like the desire to forgive arises only when the person who hurt you grovels and pleads for it, but be careful to observe if it's the true feeling of forgiveness calling you to pardon them, or the smug feeling of righteousness or winning.

Forgiving the Past

As you learned in chapter four, holding on to a hurtful experience will not protect you from another hurtful experience. Quite the contrary, it will ensure that pain follows you wherever you go. People repeat patterns that feel familiar and are attracted to experiences in life that seem to offer another do-over from their relationship history. Therefore, if you carry around the painful betrayal of a former lover, you are only ensuring your attraction to another potential cheater. Likewise, if you carry around the last 50 failed app dates, you are guaranteeing that the next 50 will be unsuccessful as well. Holding on to pain just leads to attracting more pain.

If you identify with the *Curse* of the Lamenter Mind and frequently ruminate on the past, forgiveness is going to be a great challenge for you. The reason the *Cursed Mind* keeps replaying certain events in your life is because it is unaccepting, sad, or angry about something and does not know how to get over it—nor does it necessarily want to get over it. If you've kept a running tab of errors and transgressions committed against you over the years, it's likely you have made self-focused resentment your trusty companion. This means you have become so accustomed to feeling pain (in the form of bitterness or anger) that when you don't feel that way, you look for something to be bitter or angry about, whether past or present. It sounds almost insane, but to be comfortable, you need to be uncomfortable! To feel "normal," your *Cursed Mind* needs to be disgruntled because that has become your comfort zone. This is why those who are past-focused are unable to forgive. The Lamenter Mind chooses not to forgive people as a way to keep the past alive and hold on to resentment. This is mostly done in the name of creating a story that makes itself a victim.

So how does someone with a Lamenter Mind forgive? By first being aware of the reason why she doesn't want to do so. By admitting the truth of why she holds on to injustices, slights, and mistakes made by others. The *Cursed Mind* wants to survive, wants her to continue her victim identity because it makes her somebody to have this story of being hurt, snubbed, or wronged. Without the story, who is she? How can she focus on herself without it? Being a victim gives her mind a problem that she can use to continue living in her head, wrestling with her value and concentrating on herself.

Once we see that we don't forgive because we want to continue thinking about ourselves, and what has been done to us, forgiveness can begin to happen more easily because we know it's silly not to forgive. The reason we weren't forgiving all along was because we liked the self-focused attention that came from being a victim…or being the righteous judge. If we allow our *Core Self* to see this is the only reason we haven't forgiven our past, it can help not only reduce the pain of resentment, but allow us to move closer to the present moment and become our most loving self today.

It's important to mention at this point that many people don't realize how the past has affected them; hence, they aren't even aware they are holding on to it. This happens mainly to those who identify with some of the other *Faces* of the *Curse*. Someone with a Lamenter Mind will easily admit to being past-focused, but women who identify more with the Inferior, Superior, or Contestant Mind might not be consciously aware that old experiences are keeping them in a state of constant emotional pain and resentment. Many people do not recognize how the past has shaped their thinking today, but nonetheless it has and continues to do so. Remember, the *Cursed Mind* originates somewhere in everyone's past, but some people repress painful experiences and try to move on without truly learning how to forgive them. Women who are distrusting of men in general and have a long-standing fear of being made a fool by others often fall into this category. They aren't sure why they have constant doubts about people, or are routinely suspicious of their intentions; but when we dive into the past there is usually a profound relationship or experience that points to the reason they feel the way they do today.

Yvette, for example, had a history of short-term relationships that always ended badly. She was constantly worried a man would cheat or take advantage of her. If a guy did anything she didn't like or understand, she automatically assumed he was doing something nefarious that would make her "the fool". Because of this feeling, she questioned her boyfriends constantly and often accused them of being disingenuous.

When Yvette started coaching with me, she had no idea why she hadn't found "the one" yet. She was frustrated as to why all her relationships ended and that men didn't fight for her more. After hearing her story I asked why she had this pervasive fear that her boyfriends were going to embarrass or deceive her. She said she didn't know, but that the feeling had been there for as long as she could remember. When Yvette and I looked into the past, we found she had a very toxic relationship with her sister. Her sister was particularly cruel and constantly embarrassing Yvette. To make matters worse, Yvette's parents didn't step in to help the sisters get along better. They chalked up their fighting to sibling rivalry and figured they would work it out. What they didn't know was that Yvette grew up feeling totally alone, as if the world was against her, because the people she lived with seemed to be confirming this feeling. She carried that through her college years and into adulthood, and whenever she entered a romantic relationship, she had a feeling of, *"At any moment, this person could turn on me."* Her self-absorbed mind was born out of that experience in the past and therefore was always on guard that someone could do or say something that would make her feel inferior again, just as her sister did.

The only way Yvette was going to see better results with her love life was if she rid herself of this fear of being exposed and humiliated, because she was driving guys away by indulging it whenever she felt it triggered. She first had to recognize how her past shaped her present-day relationships and then forgive her sister for her behavior as a child. She also needed to forgive her parents for their non-action.

Although it was not an optimal childhood for Yvette, and she had grown into a smart, sophisticated, independent woman who had a good life. In many ways, she thrived despite her circumstances, so forgiveness was the last component needed so she could truly break free of her *Cursed Mind* and keep the romantic relationship she so badly wanted. Amazingly, with a little coaching, she was able to do this, which immediately made all her relationships in the present, whether romantic and platonic, more loving and accepting.

Regardless if you identify with the habits of the Lamenter Mind or another *Face,* it is highly probable there is someone you need to forgive in order to end your *Cursed* thinking. Do you know who it is? Maybe there are lots of people, or maybe there is just one. Perhaps the person you need to forgive is the one who planted the seed of your *Curse*. It's very likely that you didn't know how to forgive this person because you were too young to know—and now, that refusal to forgive has grown and affected other relationships in your life today. It could be that the person you need to forgive is the one who creates the biggest frenzy inside you when you are communicating with them, or perhaps, when they simply cross your mind. It's the person who gets under your skin, pushes your buttons, or makes you crazy or irritated. Usually, it's the one person you don't want to accept or deal with who needs to be forgiven.

The way you felt about relationships in your formative years has a tremendous effect on how you interact in your romantic relationships as an adult. If you felt like you could not trust your parent, it is likely you feel like you cannot trust your partner. If you feared the person taking care of you would leave you, it's likely you fear the same in any person you date. Even if you had a typical childhood that was loving for the most part, there still may be some residual negative emotion from the past that you didn't recognize then, and haven't forgiven as an adult. Or you may have had many toxic romantic relationships in the past that are making you fearful of loving someone new again today. There is a way to figure out the person or the circumstance that needs your recognition in order to forgive, and that is to look at your current romantic relationship and ask yourself what you're afraid of. Being abandoned? Being betrayed? Being humiliated? After you firmly establish what it is that you fear, you can then ask, "Where did I first feel this feeling?" Was it from a sibling? A friend? A parent? Once you pinpoint who or what situation first made you feel angry, fearful, or resentful, you can look at it now and see how it has lingered in your subconscious, affecting how you interact with people today, people who perhaps are nothing like that person or situation.

Once you've determined the person and situation that needs your absolution, it's time to forgive. If it seems to difficult or impossible at this point, it is likely that you haven't entirely found your way out of the *Cursed Mind* quite yet, but the next section should help you take the final step, freeing your *Core Self* and allowing you to forgive at the same time.

How to Become Forgiving

One of the most beautiful stories of how forgiveness can bring love to the present is that of Tony and Barbara. Both were married before — Barbara to a nice, loving man who died, and Tony to a cold and demanding woman whom he divorced after twenty years. They were two people hoping to find someone who was right for them the second time around. They met on a dating site and were exclusive almost immediately. For six months they spent all their time together and Barbara was the happiest I'd seen her in the many years of coaching together. Although they had not yet declared, "I love you" to each other, she and I both thought, "This is it."

Then, suddenly their relationship became rocky. They began bickering over seemingly small issues. Tony would get upset when Barbara didn't care to watch the TV shows he recommended, or didn't tidy up immediately after cooking. Barbara became annoyed at Tony for making a big deal out these minor issues and began resenting him for not being more easy going. She also became increasingly upset that Tony hadn't introduced her to any of his friends. The more she pressed him to do so, the more withdrawn he became. Then one day, after Barbara left her dish in the sink, Tony abruptly ended their relationship. He said he needed his life back, and wanted to focus on himself and what he wanted now that he was retired and his children were grown.

Barbara took the break-up like most women at first. She was overcome with sadness for a while; then she tried to convince herself their parting was for the best. After all, Tony could be critical over little things and she found that too exhausting. I told her the only way to weather the break-up was to be completely present, and not lament over what went wrong or *want* the future to work out a certain way. Barbara had to keep herself at peace. It was the only way for her to cope with her feelings and find her path to love.

Barbara put herself back online and began dating again, even though she didn't feel completely ready. Tony made moving on difficult because he kept in contact with her regularly. He asked if they could remain friendly and he called her almost every week. Although Barbara loved hearing his voice, being in such close, regular contact was problematical. She felt like she was on an emotional seesaw —one day she loved him, the next day she never wanted to hear from him again.

This went on for a few months until one day Barbara went to church and heard a sermon on Forgiveness, something she and I had been recently talking about. She told me that as she listened to the minister, she realized she had been holding a grudge against Tony for being critical and not letting her meet his friends. As sad as she was about the break-up, she realized she had bitterness that she was holding on to as well. I suggested that she write Tony a letter and let him know that she forgave him for his behavior. I also added that she should ask if there is anything he had not forgiven her for. She liked the idea and wrote the letter.

The next time Tony called he mentioned that he got the letter and very much appreciated it. Barbara asked, "Was there anything that I did that you haven't forgiven me for?" She asked. To her surprise, he said yes. He said that when Barbara pressed to meet his friends, would leave her dishes in the sink, and make negative remarks about the TV shows he loved, it made him angry and was the reason he thought they were not compatible. He added that if he was going to marry again, he was going to be sure that he chose wisely this time and not ignore signs to the contrary.

When Barbara relayed the information back to me on the phone during one of our sessions, everything began to make sense. Tony was so worried that Barbara was going to manipulate him like his ex wife that whenever she did something that could be interpreted as selfish — even something as simple as not wanting to watch a program he recommended

Be Forgiving

— he would become more convinced Barbara was also selfish and thus, not for him.

I told her, "Barbara, Tony loves you. He's just fighting it because he's afraid. His Lamenter Mind is replaying the past and worried history will repeat itself again by landing him in another unfulfilling relationship. We need Tony to wake up and see that he loves you, but he has to forgive you in order to do that."

The next time Barbara was on the phone with Tony, she cried and cried. She said she was sorry for not understanding that how she acted affected Tony. She told him she forgave him for everything in their relationship and asked him if he could forgive her? Couldn't he see that she was a good person, and not like the other women he had been with before and that she would never selfishly manipulate him because she was not that kind of person? Tony listened for almost two hours but said very little. Before Barbara hung up she apologized for needing to end all phone communication with him so that she could finally heal.

Two nights later, as Barbara was driving home from work, her phone rang. It was Tony. She pulled over to the side of the road and answered.

"Barbara," he said, "I have to ask you something."

"Ok," she said, "What is it?"

"Do you love me?"

"Yes." She answered quickly.

"Good. Because I love you! I love you. I just woke up and I know that you are the woman I've been waiting for my whole life. We are going to spend our life together and I'm going to make you so happy."

Barbara couldn't believe her ears. "Really? Does this mean you've forgiven me?" She asked.

"Yes," said Tony. "I forgive you and I want to spend my life with you."

Tony and Barbara are now planning the rest of their lives together; where they should live, what vacations to take, and most importantly, where to get married! If they had both held on to self-focused righteousness by blaming the other person for their break-up, or if Tony hadn't broke free of his *Cursed Mind* stuck in the past and realized that Barbara was a different (and loving) woman, they would not be together today and two people who love each other so fiercely would have completely sabotaged their own beautiful relationship. Once the *Cursed Mind* was diminished in both of them, forgiveness was completely effortless.

Now that you know who needs your forgiveness, what do you do? And how will you actually become a forgiving person going forward in life? You cannot force yourself to forgive. You can't say, "I should just forgive this person because it's better for me." That type of effort isn't likely to work. But here is something that might: You must accept that how other people behave, and what they do or don't do is not personal to you. In the previous story, Tony didn't react with anger to Barbara's mistakes and errors because what she was doing was wrong; he reacted in that manner because of his *interpretation* of her actions. He saw dishes in the sink and thought, *"You don't care about me!"* But some other man might see the same dish and think, "I'll clean that later." The truth is that how someone reacts *to you* is not a reflection *of you*. It is a reflection of that person.

This is also true on a larger life scale. If your father abandoned you; your mother ignored you; or your ex-lover humiliated, left, or fooled you, they did so because of their own feelings and beliefs that they held inside themselves. One of my favorite books is *The Four Agreements* by Don Miguel Ruiz, and the second agreement he offers is "Don't take anything personally." In the book, Ruiz points out that you are never responsible for the actions of others; you are only responsible for you. He goes on to say that taking the thoughts, actions, and behavior of others personally is the "maximum expression of selfishness because we make the assumption that everything is about me."

If what was done to you was a horrible atrocity, you have the right to feel sad and victimized, but you must still accept the truth that what was done had nothing to do with you or your value. You did not cause the other person to act badly. Maybe you caught that I used the word "victimized," and that was not a mistake. If you were molested, raped, or abused on any level, you were a victim. There is a big difference in knowing you were preyed upon and had no way to control what happened (victimized) and holding on to a victim identity year after year and allowing it to ruin your other relationships today.

How can you learn not to take things so personally? You can start by accepting the truth that every person on earth has a different life that was shaped by a different upbringing with different beliefs and different experiences. When you connect with another person, you are engaging not only with an individual but also with all those things as well. If someone is carrying around pain from their own life circumstance, it is likely you will eventually feel that pain from them, no matter who you are. What we carry with us each day is what we give to other people. If we carry love, we give love. If we carry pain, we give pain.

There are not many truly evil people in the world, so most hurtful acts are caused by people who have been hurt or wronged themselves. As the saying goes, "Hurt people hurt people." When you begin to see this more clearly, the desire to forgive may grow because you know you are not a determining factor in how someone behaves, and therefore you should never view anything as a personal attack.

Risa, for example, was 50 years old and had never been married. She stumbled from one bad relationship to another her entire life and blamed her father for this. He was a hardworking man who took care of his family but never gave Risa the emotional attention she needed growing up. He never told her she was pretty or even that he loved her. She sought the love she wanted from him from the guys she was dating, but of course, Risa was always attracted to the ones who were not emotionally available —just like her father.

One day she said to me, "Why? Why couldn't my dad just tell me I was pretty? Why couldn't he say he loved me? I wouldn't be in the situation I'm in if he had been the kind of father I needed! I would be married and happy and not chasing guys who aren't interested in a relationship with me."

Risa had the awareness needed to see that her relationship with her dad had caused a pattern for her romantic relationships, but she was not prepared for what I told her she needed to do next: It was time to stop blaming her dad for her poor dating results and forgive him. I asked her if she felt he failed her on purpose or if he was totally unaware of how he had neglected her. Was it possible her dad didn't possess the wisdom of how to love a child or have an example of a loving relationship himself? When I asked her this, she burst into tears, and all the anger she felt poured out of her.

Risa's father was not trying to hurt his daughter's chances for love. He was living his life and being a father the only way he knew how. Once she realized her self-focused mind was only seeing him as her father and not as a human being with faults and his own troubled past, it was clear he wasn't purposefully withholding his emotions because he had a vendetta against her. She realized staying bitter with him was hurting her far more than anything else he did. And although it took a lot of work, she was eventually able to forgive him by not taking his parenting personally.

Risa never humanized her father, and it was a large part of the reason she struggled for years to forgive him. As you've hopefully learned throughout reading this book, the self-absorbed mind only humanizes itself. It sees everyone else as something different and separate, which creates a mentality of "me" versus "them." The Contestant Mind overtly thinks this way with its constant comparing and competing with other people, but all the *Faces* of the *Curse* put you on one side of life and everyone else on another side. It doesn't see the reality — that we are all the same.

I learned to be forgiving when I realized nothing can be personal because nearly everyone on the planet is battling their own *Cursed Mind*; some are just struggling more than others. How can I be upset with a person who has no idea he's being overrun by his worth-searching thoughts, looking to defend or enhance his sense of self? Most people are completely unaware, and this is why they behave and react in the manner they do. I cannot be mad because I was once unaware of my own *Cursed Mind*. I made mistakes and said and did things I can't believe now. I look at people who are *Cursed,* and I see the old unaware me who did not know better and could not do any better.

Eckhart Tolle says this in *A New Earth*: "To forgive is to overlook, or rather to look through. You look through the ego to the sanity that is in every human being at his or her essence." You learn to be forgiving by seeing the *Cursed Mind* in people as they act out of unaware selfishness. Remember, people do not know that their true, loving self has been swallowed up by *Cursed* wants and fears. Attempt to see through to their *Core Self,* who is buried deep inside just like you were. When you see the self-absorbed thinking in others, hopefully you will know that there is nothing for you to forgive because you will instead understand.

Forgiveness Through Understanding

I once had a client who unknowingly fell in love with a married man. He kept his family a secret for months until she discovered the truth. She was devastated to learn of his lies and carried his deceit into her other relationships, worried she would be duped again. She told me repeatedly that she could not get over the fact that her ex could have so selfishly put her through such pain. I encouraged her to forgive him in order to move on, but she found herself getting angry every time she thought of him. For her, forgiveness was not an option. She wanted him to burn for all eternity instead.

When my client finally wanted to end her anger, she had to work on forgiving her ex. It didn't just happen instantly when she said the words out loud. One helpful exercise was speaking about her ex as a child. He was a man who was not loved as a little boy and felt unworthy as he grew older. His parents were not kind to him, and his father never approved of anything he did. Nothing was ever good enough. So, he found worth in winning over women. Each time a woman fell in love or slept with him, he felt a great sense of self-value. His Superior Mind gave him the boost he never got as a child. The good feeling didn't last, of course, so he continued to move on to new women. Each time he slept with someone, his Inferior Mind waned and his Superior Mind triumphed. When he met his wife, she presented the biggest challenge of all for him. In fact, he married her to show himself he could have her. But since he didn't know how to love her because no one ever loved him, he grew tired of his wife over the years and began searching for a way to feel good again through his extramarital relationships.

Once my client understood his internal struggle, the anger she had actually turned to sadness. She began to understand that his behavior was not a representation of her worth or even how he felt about her. It was simply how he felt about himself. He suffered from his own *Curse*. Instead of fixating on how he hurt her, she recognized how empty and painful his own life was. Eventually, she forgave him for hurting her and she was free to love someone else without fear and reservation.

The next time you react with anger at a perceived slight or outright offense, look at the person, see through their *Cursed Mind* to their *Core Self,* and say, "That person is just like me." Instead of viewing that person as being so different from who you are, see how they are like you. Maybe they have been wronged in some way and are acting from the pain; you just happened to get in their way. Or maybe they are so consumed by their conditioned mind and thoughts about their worth, they cannot see past those things to you and your feelings. Can you really be upset with them for not being aware of what is happening inside them? Can you allow your *Core Self* to be more understanding of the situation and in doing so, forgive them?

Forgiving Ourselves

Speaking of you… sometimes the hardest person to forgive is yourself. You make a mistake, behave thoughtlessly, or choose to do something that has massive ramifications. You might beat yourself up worse than anyone else could and use your mistakes as evidence of how bad you are. Often it feels as if you cannot forgive yourself because doing so would be like escaping punishment for your crime.

Refusing to forgive yourself keeps you self-absorbed. *"I should have known better!"* Or, *"I cannot forgive myself for being so wrong"* means you think you should *be* better and *know* better than everyone else. *"I did something unforgivable. I'm so stupid and thoughtless"* means you believe you are inferior and not worthy of love. The truth is, even if what you've done is something you would consider terrible, it is not unforgivable. There are no guidelines or requirements for forgiveness. Since everyone is human and imperfect, everyone qualifies.

A woman who had lost her husband and children in a divorce came to me for advice one day. She had been repeatedly unfaithful in her marriage, and her husband, in anger, turned their children against her. Now she wanted to know how to put the pieces of her life back together and possibly find love again. She was thin, frail, and deeply depressed. It was clear she had remorse for how her relationship had ended, but she had never forgiven herself.

I told her it was time to release herself from her past and her mental prison. It was time to ask for forgiveness, not just from her husband and children but from herself, too. I told her she needed to purge all the awful things she had done from her mind, by either writing them on paper or saying them out loud. Without purging them in one of these ways, they would simply rattle in her head for eternity.

It was not easy, but she did it. It took all the courage she had to say the words and admit how her behavior caused the demise of her family. After she was finished, I told her to say one final thing: I forgive myself.

Much of why we find it hard to forgive is because thus far, we have been living life quite selfishly. As a result, actions coming from that place are naturally hard to forgive. Whether we deceived someone, embarrassed them, invalidated them, berated them, lied, cheated, aggravated, obsessed, judged, failed, or used them, they are all acts deriving from our own selfishness. When we've made mistakes because we caved to selfishness, it's difficult to say, "I forgive myself for that."

But forgiveness of yourself is necessary in order to have a healthy relationship because if you cannot forgive yourself for the foolish or hurtful things you've done, you will always be encumbered by self-absorbed pain. The person you love will feel that suffering from you. And if you can't forgive yourself, you'll never be able to forgive him when he needs it. Bottom line —you only have as much forgiveness for others as you have for yourself.

When you look back at something you did that you struggle to forgive, it's likely you were not functioning as your *Core Self* at the time. It's common to commit offenses when you're under the fog of the self-absorbed *Cursed Mind,* which was focused on getting what it believed was needed to feel good enough or protecting itself from feeling worthless. You might now see clearly how wrong the action you took was, but at the time with the *Cursed Mind* governing you, it would have been impossible to grasp the reality of the situation and make a loving, selfless, or honorable choice. When you are unaware of your *Cursed Mind,* you do not know better, and therefore you cannot do better. Look back at who you were at the time. Do you not see a different person now? Someone who was unaware of her self-absorbed thinking and the choices stemming from that? That is the person you need to forgive, not the aware person you are today. If you aren't able to see the difference yet, it's still okay. This is a lot of heavy and deep information that will take time to absorb. Give yourself that time and consider re-reading this book once you are finished. It's highly likely that every time you do, you'll understand more and more and continue to feel better and better.

If you believe in God, then you know He forgives everything. If you ask for His forgiveness, it will be granted. This may seem too simple of a solution. All you have to do is want to be forgiven and just ask? How could it be that easy?

The truth is, it isn't that easy. If it were, you would have done it already. The catch is that the self-centered part of you and your *Core Self* are at odds, and it feels as if you have to have one last climactic tragedy to even the playing field so that you can say, "There! I've been punished appropriately. Now I can be absolved." But then again, haven't you been punished for years? Hasn't this war been going on inside you so long you don't remember what it's like to feel at peace? It has, you have just gotten so accustomed to it that being at war with yourself seems normal now. You have been punished enough. It's time to be free.

To absolve yourself completely, you may have to purge what you've long been harboring. Take out a paper and pen again and write down the things you have done that you worry cannot be forgiven. List all of them, especially the ones that scare you the most. Then, read them aloud one by one and after each, say the words, "I forgive myself."

I'll help you by giving you a few common scenarios that most women fear are unforgivable:

- I forgive myself for having sex too soon with someone
- I forgive myself for having sex with someone else's boyfriend/husband
- I forgive myself for ruining my relationship with (ex)
- I forgive myself for ending a pregnancy
- I forgive myself for hurting a friend/family member/lover
- I forgive myself for not knowing better (in some past circumstance)
- I forgive myself for not speaking up about an injustice
- I forgive myself for being mean
- I forgive myself for being hateful
- I forgive myself for using people
- I forgive myself for being selfish

If you have trouble with this exercise, take out a picture of yourself when you were young and say these things to that person. It may be easier saying it to yourself when you are staring at the innocence of you. That person is still inside you, of course, and through forgiveness she will fully emerge again. Read your list and look at yourself in the photo as you say the words of forgiveness. For some people, this exercise will be done only once, and they will immediately feel at peace. For others, it will have to be a daily practice for some time.

Forgiveness Cures

Forgiveness not only helps you move forward in your own self-improvement, it is also a gift to the people you love. The next time you think you can't possibly forgive yourself—or anyone else for that matter—think about how your unforgiving nature is affecting your romantic relationship. Are you easygoing, relaxed, happy, and available? Or are you bitter, anxious, angry, and distracted? If you want to be the best partner for someone else, you have to show up for the relationship every day, unfettered by self-absorbed thoughts and pain. With forgiveness, your baseline aura can remain peaceful, which makes being in a relationship with you also peaceful. The good news is that once you start living in the present moment and are more grateful and accepting of life, it becomes easier to forgive because there becomes less to forgive!

Forgiveness is the last component that frees you from the *Cursed Mind* because it's the ultimate expression of love. When you act from love in all situations, the most wonderful transformation occurs: You begin living as your *Core Self!* And living as your *Core Self* means not only acting as your best self but also understanding that regardless of the outcome in your relationships, your core value as a human being can never be affected. When you no longer seek to enhance or protect your sense of worth, when you no longer compare or want to be more, when you embrace who you are right now and not in some other time, you are the truest form of yourself—and nothing on the outside can alter the peace and love inherently within you.

REFLECTION

Reflect for a moment on what you've just learned. Reread this chapter if needed. Put the book down, and for a day see if you can spot instances where you don't forgive. Can you now see the *Curse* in others and in those moments be more understanding of their struggle? Can you forgive the imperfection of life, the imperfection of others, and the imperfection of yourself?

Chapter Thirteen

Be Loving

Congratulations! You have made it to the last chapter of this book! I'm certain it was no easy feat. You probably have a lot of questions swirling around in your head, and you might be on information overload. That's okay! You have all the time in the world to digest this information, and please don't hesitate to re-read chapters and passages because this is not the kind of book that's meant to be read only once. Each time you review it you should see something new because the more you grow from the book, the more its messages should take on a different meaning for you.

And now back to Cures. You have learned to be present, grateful, accepting, and forgiving. It's time to learn to be loving, right? Well, here's some more good news for you. If you are already practicing the four previous cures, you're already being loving! In the beginning of the book we highlighted the definition of love as the benevolent concern for the good of another, and that it's devoid of anything selfish. Therefore, if you are completely present with someone, giving that person the gift of your undivided attention and not retreating into your own head to self-obsess, you are being loving. If you are accepting of who a person is and aren't looking for him to change because it would be better for you and your situation, you are being loving. If you are forgiving in moments of error, when someone doesn't meet your expectation or makes a mistake stemming from their self-absorbed mind, you are being loving. And if a person bears little significance in your life, is merely a passerby on your journey for love, but you appreciate their existence and the encounter you have had with him, you are being loving. All the cures are attributes of love, and when your *Core Self* engages them, you become an embodiment of love.

Being loving is the ultimate transcendental cure for the *Cursed Mind*. Your focus relocates from yourself and your value onto other people, and that shift in mentality will make the most impactful difference in your romantic life. It allows you to better engage with someone, as well as accurately assess who he is and if a meaningful relationship is possible. Instead of reacting to situations with a self-serving or self-protecting response, being loving prompts you to respond with curiosity and a desire for understanding, which can radically change the course of any relationship. Practicing this cure will take your energy from guarded, cold, dramatic or even clingy, and transform it to an energy that is open, peaceful, appealing and inviting. Love is the most wonderful and powerful quality we possess as human beings, and if we learn to be loving in all circumstances, it can be the most compelling attractor of love from other people.

It's Better To Give

Growing up, I was a hopeless romantic. I watched movies like *Casablanca, Gone with the Wind* and *Titanic* over and over, hoping that one day a man would love me the way Rick, Rhett, and Jack loved their leading ladies. There they were —fighting wars, other men, and even sinking ships to honor and protect the woman of their dreams. I didn't realize then, but the female in each storyline, although beautiful and intelligent, was lacking in someway and needed rescuing from something – even if that something was herself. Ilsa, Scarlett, and Rose were damsels in distress, hoping and waiting to be saved by love. I was drawn to them because I could identify with them. I was hoping and waiting, too.

Whenever I was lucky enough to get a boyfriend, I felt more complete, more worthy, more important than when I was alone. I loved the feeling of being chosen by someone. It gave me confidence and a renewed sense of purpose. It didn't matter if the relationship wasn't perfect – if we fought all the time, if he cheated, if I stayed so I wouldn't have to be alone – because at least I had become *more* than what I was before. I had been rescued from the deep feeling of lacking and just like the movies I thought love had saved me. In retrospect, I was as far from love as I could possibly be.

It wasn't until I met my husband at thirty-one years old that I awoke from my self-absorbed thought patterns and learned to really love. Until then*,* I was blindly serving my *Cursed Mind*, which was concentrated on being loved and maintaining that feeling from whomever I was involved with. If I gave affection, gifts, time, or anything resembling love, it was largely driven by the fear of being abandoned or the need for attention or approval. I wasn't consciously aware of this, but I know now that I was giving to get something. My self-absorbed mind spearheaded all of my relationships and prevented me from utilizing the greatest power any person on earth possesses –the power to give love, unencumbered and without the need for reciprocity.

For most of my young life I wasn't at peace with myself, and so I was not free to truly be loving. Being loving means giving of yourself without the need to be compensated, and that is scary for the self-absorbed mind because it always expects something in return. If love is given and it's not received by the other person in a favorable way, or reciprocated appropriately, the mind feels it has been diminished. It thinks it has become less by the other persons' inadequate or adverse reaction. *"I shouldn't have put myself out there! I have been reduced now,"* the self-absorbed mind thinks. If you are at peace with yourself, however, you know that you cannot ever be diminished and that love is to be given without stipulation. If someone doesn't want it or appreciate it, that doesn't matter or make a difference. You have given a gift – how it is received has no bearing on you. It took a long time for me to realize this truth, but once I did my life radically changed for the better and I finally experienced the joy that had been missing since I was a young child. I was able to love without any reservation because I no longer attached my value to other people and their reactions to me. My perspective on myself changed from a victim who needed to be saved, to a whole and complete person with ample love to give. Without making that transformation, I know I wouldn't still be happily married today.

Being at peace with yourself allows you to do the one thing the self-absorbed mind can't do, the one thing that matters most whether you are currently in a relationship or not, and that is be loving. It's common to think that love happens when you say, "I love you" to someone, but that misconception is what typically hinders a date from flourishing into a relationship. Being loving doesn't happen at "I love you." It happens at hello. When you smile and look someone in the eye, showing him you recognize his need to connect just as you have that need that is being loving. When you listen intently on a date and ask thoughtful questions that is being loving. When you graciously say goodbye, whether you plan to see the person again or not, that is being loving. And when you surrender to whatever happens next and spend no time wanting a person to do something – to text you, to ask you out, to buy you dinner – and accept that he will do what feels right for himself, that is being loving. When you reach peace within yourself, you let down your guard and are able to be loving from the moment you meet someone, wholeheartedly, without any fear or wanting. This makes you far more attractive to any potential date because he won't suspect that you are searching for someone else to make you feel good about yourself. There will be no sense of use coming from you that will exhaust or exploit him. He will only see and feel your *Core Self* and your genuine, good-hearted nature. If you want to become the most attractive and engaging version of yourself, all you really need to do is be loving.

When you are able to show love to anyone without certain conditions, dating will not only become easier for you, but it can actually become enjoyable. Your perspective on a first date will change from it being a stressful and taxing affair that may or may not result in your favor, to a pleasant and satisfying experience where you, at the very least, might laugh and learn about someone new. You won't worry about someone breaking your heart because being at peace means you no longer attach your worth or inherent joy to another person and their reaction to you. If someone doesn't follow up for a second date, or decides he's not interested, you might be a little disappointed but you can accept his decision more readily because your worthiness has been taken out of the equation. This makes you nearly impervious to the feeling of rejection, which can only happen when you make your value a factor in your relationships.

When you look at every encounter with someone as a beautiful opportunity to connect with another human being on his own journey for love, and not just as a chance to make yourself more complete and happy, the stress, pressure, and deep disappointment that used to accompany you on dates, begins to fade. Suddenly, you are sitting for an hour with another soul, who is just like you, and embracing the possibility to connect with him. You are able to give him little piece of love so that he walks away from the conversation feeling glad to have met you, and exhilarated from being in the presence of your *Core Self*. You don't assess him through a self-focused lens, which views the behavior of others as a direct reflection of itself. *You see him.* When the time comes for that special person to take the seat across from you, your energy and the atmosphere you've created is prime for real, romantic love. If the person is right for you, the relationship will form effortlessly without you having to do anything more than just be there.

Love Attracts Love

When you wake yourself from the self-absorbed mind and start living everyday as your *Core Self*, the greatest truth of humanity is suddenly so obvious: If you want to receive love, you need to give love. Withholding your heart, protecting it from others, and hoping that someone will prove himself worthy of your affection so that you may finally open yourself to the experience of love, is a doctrine of the *Cursed Mind*. Love cannot occur in that circumstance. In order to receive more love in your life, you must give it first. You will not get what you don't give.

I wish I understood this concept when I was younger as it would not only have changed my early relationships but it would have saved my adolescence from feeling so lonely and isolated. The running thought in my head from the age of sixteen to twenty-six was, *"I hope x person does x thing for me."* I was in a state of perpetually wanting someone else to show me love and make me feel happy. When I attempted to give love by doing something nice, it fell flat and was unappreciated because what I did was rooted in attention seeking, and so it was not what the person needed or wanted at the time. If my boyfriend was distracted, stressed, busy, or simply not showering me with what I thought was sufficient attention, I became depressed or upset. I put a lot of responsibility on the other person not understanding that in a relationship, you get what you give. I wasn't selflessly giving and therefore I never truly got much in return.

If you feel that you don't have any love to give because others have used or taken advantage of you, or you still feel bitter and believe you've been depleted of the power to be loving, I assure you, love is still within you. As Eckhart Tolle says in *The Power of Now*, "Love is a state of being. Your love is not outside; it is deep within you. You can never lose it, and it cannot leave you." The *Cursed Mind* may have fatigued you and made you fearful to love again because it has long worried about being used or returned to painful wanting, and that is very exhausting. But your *Core Self* knows that none of those things will happen again because you are now *aware*. You are aware of the self-absorbed mind and of its many habits, and because of this, you can open yourself up to being loving now without any fear. All you have to do is take the first step. You are risking nothing by being loving.

Cursed?

What happens if you encounter someone who isn't loving? Someone who is *Cursed* and hopes to use or deceive you? Can you love that person yet still shield yourself from their malintent? Yes, absolutely. You can be loving even if a person isn't loving back to you. In the instances where someone is attempting to take advantage of you and your kindness, simply recognize what is happening and why they are acting in a selfish manner, while employing the most powerful boundary tool in your relationship box – the word "No."

"No" is not a dirty word. It does not have to be said in anger or with any negative emotion. You can be loving and stand up for what you think is right for yourself and the other person, by simply declining their request or removing yourself from their presence, if needed. Let your *Core Self* speak freely but lovingly. *"I'm sorry, I'm not going to do that."* Or, *"I am going to have to say, no, but I wish you the best."* And sometimes, no response is the best response. Sometimes remaining quiet, allowing the other person to hear what he said or letting him see what he did is all that is necessary. When you react too quickly or harshly to someone, you can obstruct that view. He notices your reaction and focuses on that instead of his own action. The only way to respond to anyone who is selfish is with the love of your *Core Self* because that's the way you can potentially wake the person to his own self-absorbed mind. As Martin Luther King, Jr. said so eloquently, "Darkness cannot drive out darkness; only light can do that. Hate cannot drive out hate, only love can do that." React with the light of your love when you come face-to-face with the *Curse* in someone else so that you may help drive out their darkness, too. Being loving does not mean doing whatever another person asks of you, it means responding in a loving way to them, whether you oblige their request or decline it, whether you continue a relationship, or part ways. You can be loving in how you handle anyone in any situation, and in doing so; you stay true to the core of who you are.

Love has a wonderful way of protecting you from being harmed and used by someone else. When you are loving to a man who is selfish, instead of attempting to please him so that he will like and accept you,

you shine a light on his intentions to hurt you (and other people as well.) Because you aren't jumping to appease him and are instead presently watching and engaging him, he will feel your intent focus on him. Like a loving mother who spots her child about to stick his hand in the cookie jar, you allow your awareness to say, "I *see* you, and am watching what you are going to do." He will either learn to love by way of your loving nature, or he will feel guilty in his effort to take advantage of you and back away from the relationship.

If you are single and not yet in a relationship, it's crucial that you start being loving today. Love inspires and attracts love. It is the antithesis of wanting; so warm, so inviting, so engaging. It is an irresistible sensation that can draw people to you. This is the secret to relationship success and why so many other attempts to attract or harvest love typically fail. You don't have to be perfect in order to get love. You don't have to become something *more*. You don't have to say or do the right thing, or have the right kind of past. You only need to give real, unstipulated love, and it will come back to you.

When it comes to romantic love, you must be patient. That is a special kind of love that takes time to find. Without being in a state of love first, however, you might pass right by it without notice, or it may pass by you. Waiting to be loving until you think you see your opportunity for a relationship is a mistake, as sometimes it is then too late. It is far better to cast a wide net so that you can catch more opportunity. Even the smallest gesture of love can sprout something bigger and more profound. So give love to *all* people, at all times, regardless of who those people are to you or what they will or will not mean to you. Embrace life and others without wanting or judgment, without using them for your own benefit, comparing yourself to them, or even labeling them in this way or that. Walk through life being loving in thought, word, and deed and you will see how effortless love begins to come back to you.

Here are several ways you can be loving right now, today.

- Give a stranger a compliment.
- Hold the door for someone.
- Let a person cut in front of you on the road.
- Offer a hand to your neighbor.
- Ask, "What can I do to help you?"
- Smile at everyone you pass.
- Listen when someone has a story to share.
- Forgive when someone doesn't meet your expectation.
- Write a friend a message and say, "I'm just thinking about you."
- Celebrate a colleague's achievement.
- Congratulate a friend's success.
- Be kind to the man you know you won't see again.
- Pray for someone else.
- Hug someone who is sad.
- Hug someone who is angry.
- Send a birthday gift.
- Pay for someone's coffee.
- Bring donuts for your officemates.
- Cook dinner for your mom or dad.
- Post a flattering comment about someone else.

Although celebrating a colleague's achievement or promotion doesn't clear an obvious path to a relationship for you, doing something like this is how you become lucky in love. By not being discriminatory with who and when you love, your presence radiates that magical feeling to whoever comes in contact with you. You infect people with the power of love and they, in turn, want to be around you, engage you, and help you. You may not want to date your recently promoted coworker, but he may invite you to his birthday party because he is so fond of you and at that party you meet his younger, and very eligible, brother. Or he may ask you to grab lunch with him and one day he bumps into a single friend and makes an introduction. Being loving to everyone opens doors for you in every direction, even if you can't see that from where you are standing now. Your *Core Self* knows that love can take you to the top of a mountain, without having to carefully plot the way. Trust in love and it will not let you down.

I've saved my favorite story for last.

Years ago, I had a client named Jane who was a very smart, tough, independent woman and who was nearly impossible to coach. She was forty-three years old, and vacillated weekly between feelings of sadness and anger at being single this long in life. She was attracted to all the wrong men, and thus wasted much of her younger years on people who were never going to commit. Many of our sessions were consumed by her venting the various frustrations she had regarding dating and men in general. When I attempted to tell her to be grateful for any date she was going on, or remain open to seeing if feelings could develop for a man she wasn't nuts about at first glance, she would tell me I wasn't helping her; and in fact, I was making her feel worse. We made very little progress for almost fifteen months.

I almost gave up on Jane. I had tried everything to get through to her, but her mind patterns were so strongly rooted they were impervious to my reasoning or suggestions. Finally, I recommended she go on a silent meditation retreat. Perhaps the stillness of total presence would crack her indestructible *Cursed* mind patterns of judgment, lamenting, and taking everything personally. If they didn't, her *Cursed Mind* was going to make the seven-day retreat absolutely miserable. It was risky, but I thought it was my only shot.

When Jane returned from the retreat she told me that it was very emotional for her and she did feel much better than she had in years. The first day she was there, the instructor told all the patrons to meditate on what it felt like to love someone and be loved in return. At that moment, Jane said she thought about her uncle who had just died. He had loved her so much, and she loved him. "It's a little sad that I had to think about an uncle, isn't it?" she said as she retold the story to me.

"Why?" I asked. "You obviously regard that relationship as being full of love. That was the assignment. If there hasn't been a boyfriend who has made you feel unconditionally loved like that and who you felt the same in return, then maybe you've never loved any of the men you've dated."

What I said struck a cord. Jane told me she never realized that romantic love was supposed to feel like comfort and acceptance. She was so used to it feeling like aching and wanting, she realized she had to do something to change that pattern. Jane began meditating each morning on feeling love and giving love back. She thought about the relationships in her life that were unconditionally loving and spent more time with those people. She made a habit of doing something loving for another person at least once a day, even if it was simply letting someone cut in front of her in line for coffee. Two months after she began working on this, she went on a date with a man named Jonathan. He thought Jane was incredible. She felt at ease around him. They began dating and took it slow, as Jane was still working on breaking her old patterns. She wasn't pining to be with Jonathan, but she did like being around him and felt very comfortable. One day, she texted him and she didn't hear back right away like she usually did. After a few hours passed, she became nervous and called me.

"I just realized I love Jonathan!" She exclaimed. "I don't know where he is and why he's not responding, but just the possibility of him ghosting me or this relationship not working out has showed me that I really do love him."

As we were talking on the phone, Jonathan texted back. Everything was fine, of course, because Jonathan was a good man who also really loved Jane.

Jane and Jonathan were married a year ago in a beautiful and intimate ceremony with all their friends and family. They just adopted a rescue dog. Every so often I receive updates from Jane on how married life is going and her emails always end the same:

"Love your toughest client who broke her twenty-five year *Curse*."

Love In A Relationship

The stories we hear and movies we watch make it seem as if love is always effortless – that you are filled with a sense of affection and devotion for your significant other; and that feeling causes you to be selfless and considerate. However, I will tell you what I have learned about love through breaking my own *Curse*: Love is more than a feeling. It's also a choice. There will be many times in life, and in the course of any relationship, where that choice must precede the feeling. If you only give love when you are overcome with emotion instituted by someone else, your love will be conditional and your relationship will not weather any storms. To achieve real, romantic love with another person, and maintain that love for decades, you must make the jump from passively enjoying the feeling of being in love and reacting off that feeling, to *actively* being loving. Without taking ownership of your love, and giving it to your spouse day in and day out (and he doing the same in return), after a few years you will eventually feel like you've fallen out of love with each other.

Choosing to be loving — to give, to appreciate, to accept, and forgive — is key to a long and happy marriage. This means being loving to your significant other even when he is hard to love. If he is tired, grumpy, or stressed and you find yourself in the midst of those feelings, rely on love to guide you. You don't have to be a punching bag for his frustrations, but you have to employ your love for him in order to help him. It does no good to stand up for yourself by attacking him back or shaming him for his behavior when he is not his best self. That kind of retaliation doesn't get through to anybody.

What does work is communicating from a place of love. "I love you but you're so stressed that you're being mean right now. Can you take some deep breaths and remember that I am on your side?" That kind of statement is loving and helpful. If the person is even semi-conscious of his *Cursed Mind*, he will wake up and apologize. If he is completely buried under it, you will at least diffuse the situation. If poor treatment continues by his hand despite your most loving effort, then you have to consider if you are in the right relationship for yourself; but at least you will know that you handled the situation as best you could and feel good about that. You can't force someone be conscious of their *Cursed Mind*, you can only be conscious of your own and in doing so, help your partner to see more clearly by the awareness you create.

Cured

After you've practiced being loving for a time, you will notice how your thinking has begun to shift. Your old self-focused thought patterns will start to fade and lose their grip on you. Reasoning and contemplation from the deepest part of your soul will stand in their place. You'll see this especially in the way you view particular situations that might have made you tense, sad, angry or frustrated in previous years. For instance, when you meet someone new and interesting, you might now think, *"Let me learn about him and see if we would be a good match"* instead of, *"I hope I can get him to like me!"* Or, *"He's never going to be my type."* Your *Cursed Mind* has stopped begging and pleading, *"I hope this works out,"* and now your *Core Self* serenely thinks, *"I'm enjoying what is happening between us right now."* Once you are in a relationship, you'll notice how your thoughts have recalibrated to think more about your partner, instead of ruminating about what you want or feel you aren't getting. When a problem or obstacle arises, you might witness that you don't quickly react with resistance and blame like you used to. *"Why did he do that? He's taken advantage of me. He's being a lazy jerk. I'll tell him off and he won't do that again."* Now, your *Core Self* notices his behavior but remains judgment free. *"I wonder why he did that. I'll have to talk with him. He's normally such a great guy, there must be something really bothering him."* Once your thoughts have transitioned and habituated to think lovingly, all the relationships in your life, not just the one with your partner, will become more symbiotic. You'll notice there is no more drama around you because you aren't interested in winning anymore, even in your disagreements. You will not feel the urge to attack or defend when you don't understand your spouse's behavior because you won't take his behavior personally. All the communication between you and the people you love will become clearer and more productive because you have kept your words and actions rooted in love. When you feel this easiness, this peace between you and other people, at least most of the time, you'll know that you've cured the *Curse*.

The young woman sat down in my office as she had done for many years. But something was noticeably different this time. She wasn't in angst. She wasn't on the brink of tears, or biting her nails. She fell into the chair as if she was going to curl up with a good book for an hour and she was making herself comfortable.

"How are you?" I asked.

"I'm pretty good," she started.

"What's been going on with you?" I asked.

"Not too much. I had a few dates last week and they were nice. We'll see if they go anywhere. One might turn into something but it's too soon to tell," she said nonchalantly.

"You seem relaxed. How have you been feeling lately," I asked her.

She perked up in her chair as if this was the question she came to answer.

" You know, it's funny you ask because I have been feeling better than I have in years. Honestly, I can't remember the last time I felt so good and so...well, peaceful."

"Tell me about it," I urged.

"I haven't found "the one" yet, obviously. I still want to get married and have a family, but I don't feel the way I used to anymore. You remember how I was last year when that one guy disappeared on me. I was a mess, and now I don't even remember why I was so upset. I just don't feel the immense pressure and stress when I go on dates anymore. I don't feel this dark cloud looming overhead, like whatever I do is pointless and my fate as a single woman is sealed. I feel this weird sense of peace for no reason at all, really."

"I bet that's a nice feeling," I said.

"It's incredible, Jess." The tears started forming in the corners of her eyes, but they were not the kind of tears she has shed in that chair before. These were tears of joy.

"I don't know when it happened. You know I've been meditating to stay present and I write in my gratitude journal every night, but over the last month I haven't been anxious or sad. I haven't even been thinking about how much I want a relationship. I've just been enjoying my life as it is, and it is actually pretty good," she nodded.

"And what about your feelings about yourself? Are you feeling more self-assured and confident?" I asked.

"It's funny because I really try not to think about myself so much anymore. I am so focused on living outside my head, but now that you ask, I think I am feeling more confident. I've been talking to more people when I'm out. I am not afraid to ask questions on dates anymore. Maybe my self-esteem is improving," she suggested.

"I'm so happy to hear that. You've done the work and now you're feeling the reward." I said.

"It wasn't an easy journey to get here," the young woman said. "I feel like I had to get pretty low at first. I wasn't sure if I was going to come back from it at the time. But I held on to what you said about allowing light into my wound, and I have arrived here at a place I never thought possible. I think I've found the way to be okay and happy on my own. The very place everyone said I needed to be in order to really find love."

"I could not be more happy or proud of you," I told her. "Your relationships will be easier from here forward. Your patterns are going to change. You'll see how different life is going to be for you now," I said.

"Thank you. It already is different. I have something now that I never thought I could have being single," she said.

"What is that?" I asked, curiously.

A smile spread across her face as she wiped a happy tear. "*Hope.*"

Cursed?

A Letter From the Author

Hello Dear Reader!

Thank you for picking up this book. I do hope you've enjoyed it and found the answers you were seeking. This book was a labor of love for me, taking the better part of nine years to write. I wasn't sure if I would ever complete it, let alone, have it published. What kept me going was you. I believed I could help you in the way that I've helped my personal coaching clients, and if I could just get the information I had into your hands, I was hopeful I could be of service to you. If you have enjoyed the book and seen changes in your life as a result of reading it, I'd love to hear from you. Please feel free to contact me through my website at www.jessmccann.com. Also, a book review is greatly appreciated, as it is the best way to help me spread the word to other people who might also be struggling with their relationships and not yet understand why. Thank you for any kind words, in person or online, that you may pass on.

I have two other books that are not nearly as intense as this that focus on the strategy and tactics of relationship building. They are both fun reads; loaded with tips and techniques to help you navigate the sometimes complicated world of relationships. They are, *"You Lost Him at Hello"* and *"Was It Something I Said?"* I hope you will check them out as well. Thank you again!

Acknowledgements

Thank you Eckhart Tolle for bringing me to awareness through your powerful written works. Without you, I would not have been able to write "Cursed?" I hope many of my readers will feel inspired to read, "The Power of Now," and "A New Earth" after reading this book.

Thank you to my husband for his love and support for the eight years it took to complete this project. It was a long and arduous journey at times, but you never let me quit and gave me any assistance I needed to get the job done. I am grateful for you and your unconditional love. I am also grateful for the awareness you brought to my life, which was instrumental in breaking my own *Curse*.

Thank you to my clients for allowing me to help you, and in turn, provide me with better insight to the Cursed Mind and the cures needed to tackle it. Thank you to all my beta readers; without you this book would have not gotten to a point of publication! Your feedback was crucial. A special thanks to Victoria, Annie, Manisha, and most of all, Laurie who provided me with several insightful suggestions and critiques that made this book what it is today.

Made in the USA
Middletown, DE
17 February 2020